CHANGING DALITS

Changing Dalits

Exploration Across Time

PARAMJIT S. JUDGE

RAWAT PUBLICATIONS

Jaipur • New Delhi • Bangalore • Hyderabad • Guwahati

ISBN 81-316-0361-X

Published by
Prem Rawat for **Rawat Publications**
Satyam Apts, Sector 3, Jawahar Nagar, Jaipur 302 004 (India)
Phone: 0141 265 1748 / 7006 Fax: 0141 265 1748
E-mail: info@rawatbooks.com
Website: www.rawatbooks.com

New Delhi Office
4858/24, Ansari Road, Daryaganj, New Delhi 110 002
Phone: 011 2326 3290

Also at *Bangalore, Hyderabad* and *Guwahati*

Typeset by Rawat Computers, Jaipur
Printed at Chaman Enterprises, New Delhi

Contents

Preface

In the last decade of 20th century, the issue of identity emerged as the main concern for social scientists. Ethnicity reigned supreme. It was no accident of history. Turning to identity and ethnicity was due to two major reasons, one of which was the ethnic cleansing that was taking place in the erstwhile Yugoslavia; and secondly, large-scale immigration to the developed countries from the Third World countries made ethnicity and multiculturalism relevant issues for analysis in the immigrant receiving countries. At the heart of all these issues was the question of identity. Those who concentrated on the identity issue in India had to handle pluralities that were quite dissimilar to the western ethnicities. However, the western concerns of identity in a different context initiated lot of studies in India. Many books on the Punjabi identity, Sikh identity and identity politics in Punjab got published during this period.

Ironically, most of the books on Punjabi/Sikh identity did not devote a single page to the discussion of the Punjabi dalits or Sikh dalits. The dalits constitute about 29 per cent of the total population of Punjab as per the figures of the Census of India, 2001, and this proportion is the highest in India among the states. The Punjabi dalits are also distinct from their counterparts in other states. They have been visible in the social and cultural life of Punjab. Ignoring them implies the absence of understanding of the Punjabi society. Till recently, the intellectuals have also paid little attention to the existence and persistence of castes in Punjabi society. Universities and their social science departments did not conduct sufficient amount of research on the dalits in Punjab. It began modestly in the sociology department of Panjab University, Chandigarh in late 1970s. Most of the social scientists who are currently involved in the study of dalits in Punjab are directly or indirectly connected with that beginning.

This volume covers four decades of the empirical reality of Punjab. The data for the study on the class analysis of the scheduled castes was collected in 1978 whereas the last chapter on dalit assertion in Punjab is based on the fieldwork done in 2004–05. Most of the papers are based on the data collected in the Doaba region of Punjab. Doaba region is now comprised by Hoshiarpur, Jalandhar, Kapurthala and Nawan Shahar districts and may be regarded as the most developed region of Punjab. This development has been a consequence of the international migration of the people of Doaba. In terms of literacy rate too, this region has done much better than rest of Punjab. Most of the movements of the dalits have taken place in this region. In certain ways, this region shows the future to other regions of the state. Here is the paradox. If the dalits of Doaba region have failed to come completely out of caste-based exclusion, then, one may think the fate of dalits belonging to other parts of the state.

In the preparation of this volume the initial impetus came from my publisher Pranit Rawat, who showed keen interest in the project. I am grateful to him for bringing out this volume in time with meticulous care. During the last three decades many friends and colleagues motivated me to take up the research on the dalits. I am grateful to all of them. However, I must mention Satish K. Sharma, S.R. Ahlawat, J.R. Panda, Ronki Ram and Manjit Singh. Satya Pal Gautam and Rajivlochan have always been very kind in helping me to modify my arguments through their critical comments. I always remain indebted to them. Prof. P.N. Pimpley has always been an inspiration. So has been my wife, Gurpreet Bal. I joined the Centre for Social Studies, Surat, in 1988. During my stay there till May 1991, I had the benefit of interacting with some of the finest minds. Some of them also worked on the dalits. I should mention Sudhir Chandra, Ghanshyam Shah, S.P. Punalekar, Gopal Guru and Biswaroop Das. I must also acknowledge my younger colleagues, Harpreet Kaur, Manjit Kaur and Bhupinder Thakur at the Centre for the Study of Social Exclusion and Inclusive Policy, Guru Nanak Dev University, Amritsar, for their help. I am also grateful to my friend, Des Raj Kali for providing me the photograph for the cover page of the book. In the end, I thank all those persons who willingly gave their interviews.

Paramjit S. Judge

Introduction

Understanding the Intersubjective World

In 1976, when I joined as a postgraduate student at Panjab University, Chandigarh, the academic atmosphere of the department gave the impression of the powerful influence of Parsonian functionalism in sociology. Combined with functionalism was the strong emphasis on empirical sociology. That was the time when India was undergoing political turmoil. A year had already passed since Indira Gandhi had imposed emergency and most of the dissenting democratic voices were muted and put behind bars. I found it strange to admit the entire idea of consensus of values in the society in which political and social conflicts were so visible. Since I came from the background of the radical students' politics, sociology as a 'science' of society began to seem utopian and stranger to the reality we were confronting at that time. The awareness of this situation added to my failure to comprehend the practice of sociology. William Cowper has beautifully described such a state of mind in his 'Conversation' thus:

> Our sensibilities are so acute,
> The fear of being silent makes us mute.

It slowly began to dawn on me that functionalism is not the only perspective in sociology. It had an equally powerful and opposite paradigm in the form of Marxism. However, Marxism was interpreted in terms of economic determinism. When we studied the recent trends in sociological theory, including neo-Marxism, issues became clearer and the reasons for the domination of functionalism could also become discernible. Soon I became aware that both the functionalism and Marxism had limitations in general and provided partial explanations to the social reality. Every aspect of human action could not be analysed within the framework of these two paradigms. It brought in the phenomenological/hermeneutical approach and qualitative methods of study to fill the gap. The phenomenological/hermeneutical approach to understand society gained in popularity as the important theoretical system sometimes in the beginning of 1980s in the Indian universities. Its popularity and, to a great extent, its relevance could be traced back to the continuous and inconclusive debate between positivist and interpretative sociologies. Also, there was a growing disillusionment with the explanatory paradigms offered by functionalism and Marxism. Whereas functionalism, as popularised by Parsons and Merton, emphasised consensus of values as the basis of social organisation, Marxism provided an understanding of society as based on conflict.

The popularity of the 'Treatise' by Berger and Luckman (1971) in 1980s, though published in 1966, was an indication of a trend that came out of disillusionment with positivism exemplified by the empirical methods the epistemological basis of which was that knowledge could be got through sense experience. Though the validity of the knowledge derived through the sense experience could not be arbitrarily denied, yet the problem with the social sciences claims persisted due to many reasons. Gautam has shown the limitations of the empirical method with regard to knowledge thus: "It can be shown that there is a close relationship between perception, imagination and conceptual abilities. The empiricist philosophers found it difficult to account for knowledge, for they concentrated exclusively on 'pure' sense-impressions. A sense-impression cannot, by itself, tell me that the object of my sense-perception is a table. To know that I am seeing a table is to subsume the impression under a concept"(1983: 60). Moreover, in social research, the objects of inquiry are characterised by subjectivity and consciousness as a result of which one empirical method cannot be a sufficient basis of explanation. Another reason is that a collection of aggregate data does not become knowledge.

Positivists tend to view society in the mirror image of nature as an objective reality. The view that society could be understood, examined and explained in a manner similar to the natural sciences was dented by some of the issues raised in the context of epistemological basis of the social science methods. However, empirical studies still exist and persist and have shown to be more valuable in the context of policy matters and the understanding of ground reality. The interpretative analysis of social reality as a binary opposition of empirical study may not achieve legitimacy for various practical purposes in which systematic and synthesised knowledge is required. In certain situations interpretative understanding could only follow the collection of information about a social situation. The most important aspect is the concept of verstehen as formulated by Weber. For reaching an understanding of the reasons for action of the social agent/actor, it is important that the researcher should develop an empathy with the actors. Weber is quite clear on this matter when he says that it is impossible for a researcher to understand the motives of an actor whose culture and civilisation are strange to him (Oakes, 1977). In other words, if we want to deal with the motives and intentions underlying the action of the people and offer an interpretation of the same, then it is crucial for the researcher to have the common stock of knowledge with the subjects of his study.

However, Weber never provided any clear account of the object-subject unity, for he delved into the issue of value neutrality confusing the same with objectivity. The phenomenological perspective views a comprehension of lived intersubjectivity as a necessary step for the interpretation and understanding of social reality. Intersubjective world is constructed by the interactive process in the routine life of the actors in which they share common stock of knowledge. Routinisation of life is an important basis of the common stock of knowledge. Routines are not events but elements in ongoing practices in which the actors are involved through actions and interactions by constructing and reconstructing meanings by constantly referring to their common stock of knowledge. Once the intersubjective world is understood as the social reality of the members of the society, certain aspects of identity of the individuals as members of the shared subjective world becomes crucial. Zeitlin explicates the ideas of Schutz lucidly when he writes:

> The social world of everyday life, Schutz tells us, is always an intersubjective one. This is the world I share with my fellowmen,

> with others, who also experience and interpret it. My world is therefore never wholly private; even in my consciousness I find evidence of others, evidence that my unique biographical situation is not wholly product of my own actions (2004: 17).

It becomes clear from the above that subjective world of an individual is not an isolated and unique experience that lacks typicality and social basis. The most fundamental component of society as a subjective reality, according to Berger and Luckman (1971), is socialisation process and they make it clear that an individual "is not born as member of the society"; rather "he becomes a member of the society" (ibid.: 149). The process of becoming member of the society is mediated through socialisation. In other words, becoming is a process through which a person acquires meanings of objects – both concrete and abstract – and relationships. He/she develops the stock of knowledge that is a shared consciousness. Schutz states it clearly and leaves no doubt how the intersubjective social world is comprehended thus:

> In the everyday world in which both the I and the Thou turn up, not as transcendental but as psychological subjects, there corresponds to each stream of the lived experience of the I a stream of subjective experience of the Thou. This, to be sure, refers back to my own stream of lived experience, just as does the body of the other person to my body. During this process, the peculiar reference of my own ego to the other's ego holds, in the sense that my stream of lived experience is for you that of other person, just as my body is another's body for you (1967: 102).

It is in this context of the existence of the intersubjective world as everyday social realty that Gopal Guru's views should be situated. Let us begin by his interesting remark thus: "In view of the complete lack of theoretical intervention from dalit/bahujan scholars, some non-dalit messiahs have offered to represent dalit/bahujans theoretically" (Guru, 2002: 5008). He further comments:

> ...[T]his epistemological enthusiasm of the non-dalits also suffers from... serious malady. This intellectual representation remains epistemologically posterior. That is to say, the discovery of the dalit epistemological standpoint fails to explain who has arrived – whether the object (dalit) or the subject (muknayaks). ... This inability to either recover or throw up an alternative concept happens because

> these scholars choose to theorise dalit experience standing outside the dalit experience (ibid.: 5009).

The implications of the argument of Guru are clear with regard to the theorisation of dalit experience, that is, nobody other than the dalit can/should theorise the dalit experience. Experience and understanding are very closely linked, as the two are mediated through language. Wittgenstein remarked, "The limits of my language are the limits of my world" (1961: 56). Language constitutes the common communicative environment through which actions can be understood and interaction becomes plausible and meaningful. Gautam points out, "The process of formation of an individual's consciousness is mediated through culture which acts as a pre-requisite for its growth. For the individual, culture appears immediately as a web of meanings which have been reified into an objective reality existing independently of him" (1983: 61). For having a specific experience the individual/group must have a distinctive language, that is, an ensemble of meanings. For such a situation to emerge, there is a pre-condition of an existence of exclusive social space. The experience of dalits in India cannot be exclusive as their unique social situation emerged as a result of their position in the caste hierarchy that presupposed the existence of other caste communities in a hierarchical order. If the experience is an outcome of the interaction in asymmetrical context in which more than one hierarchical position is involved, then it cannot be inner experience without shared meanings.

Phenomenology recognises the biographically informed situation in which every individual has something specific and unique about him/her, but without the shared meanings he/she cannot make any sense of the self. Therefore, the dalit and upper caste persons may have different meanings attached to their interaction, but at the same time there is nothing which prohibits the other from an empathetic understanding. Some dalit sociologists argue that certain experiences of the dalits cannot be explicated, described or felt because such experiences are unique to the everyday life of dalits only. I have often heard one such example and producing it verbatim here: "A woman is carrying human excreta on her head in some leaking container on a rainy day." I do not think anybody would deny the inhumanity and degradation involved in the situation unless somebody turns one's eyes away. Forcing the individual to do such a job is a sure sign of inhumanity.

One does not need a dalit to narrate his/her experience. Ideological blinkers need to be removed for seeing the inhumanity of such practices. However, articulating the experience in a proper context still requires language and theory. After all, a dalit cannot tell (if we accept Guru's argument) how a non-dalit experiences the sight of a dalit woman carrying human excreta. His response cannot be anticipated and taken as a priori in the sense that he/she would not bother. Even if it seems natural, there is reification involved in which the ideology of caste has been so powerfully internalised that something inhuman is perceived as natural. If it has actually been the case, then, it implies that the hegemonic power of ideology is to be deconstructed through different forms of praxis. One such form is the legal praxis after independence, with all its shortcomings at the level of implementation. History is full of examples of inhuman treatment to individuals, groups and communities. We may refer to slavery in the age of reason in Europe, and the Nazi holocaust in recent history. Societies and states have been intervening on behalf of the damned at different points of time though the initiatives always came through either the rebellions/protests of the victims of the system or the intellectuals through the emergence of theory. The revolt of and the articulation offered by the damned were simultaneous or consecutive – one preceding the other without any set norms of the order of precedence. It is also not necessary that the two would go together. Experiencing inhuman treatment and not reconciling to it does not imply that revolt or protest would follow. Otherwise, instead of Chokamela and Nam Dev, there would have been only Spartacus.

Having stated my position with regard to the experience and sole monopoly over theorising that experience, I may now turn to the sharing of the experience that I had had by being on the other side of the relationship with regard to caste, dalits, and caste-based discrimination. The narrative is based on the personal experience of my life in the village as belonging to the landowning caste. It is not necessary that my experience of the caste hierarchy is universal in the sense that all those who belong to the landowning castes will have the same experience. The reason for my unique experience does not lie in my isolated existence by my biographically determined situation. In the words of Gautam, "...[I]n society human beings find not only the external conditions to which they respond but also that these very conditions provide grounds for alternative possibilities in and through which each individual forms his purposes and projects" (1983: 61).

The village to which I belong falls in the Hoshiarpur district. In fact, it is not the native village of my family. I belong to a family that migrated from the Montgomery district (now Sahiwal) of western Punjab, which after partition became a part of Pakistan. As a matter of fact, I have now three villages out of which I am intimately familiar with only two that are neighbouring villages. Hoshiarpur district is the only district of Punjab in which the Hindus are in a majority. One may conjecture that as a result of the Hindu majority, the influence of Brahmanism could be stronger here than in other districts. Interestingly, the literacy rate in my district has remained the highest in Punjab. Not only that, even the literacy rate among the scheduled castes (SCs) has been the highest in this district, that is, 77.66 per cent according to 2001 census. Literacy rates among the SCs in Punjab in 1971, 1981 and 1991 were 16.12 per cent, 23.85 per cent and 41.09 per cent respectively. All these years the Hoshiarpur district topped with 29.16 per cent in 1971, 41.57 per cent in 1981 and 63.82 per cent in 1991. The district also witnessed an effective Arya Samaj movement in the first half of the 20th century. Despite its Hindu majority, Brahmanism was not dominantly visible in its social landscape in the form of powerful enforcement of caste-based discriminations. However, learning and knowledge of Sanskrit had strong roots in the district. As a result, in comparison to other parts of Punjab, the Brahmins enjoyed a greater respect. The Jats remained ingrained to the Hindu Sanatan tradition even when the Singh Sabha movement converted most of the Hindu Jats to Sikhism in other parts of Punjab. Srinivas has also mentioned in his *Social Change in India* (1966: 101) that Sanatani Jats had lower status than the Sikh Jats in Hoshiarpur district. It could be true in the first half of 20th century, but there are also instances, mostly present in oral historical accounts of the elderly, of a person being excommunicated on charges of attending some function of the Singh Sabha. Some of the Jat families of my native village, Sahri have continued to stick to the Sanatani practices with tremendous tenacity. However, they have continued to intermarry with Sikhs of their caste. At present, almost three-fifths of the total Jat families are Sikhs. However, there is no tenable difference between the two in terms of their attitudes, prejudices and behaviour towards the dalits.

My earliest memory of dalits is with regard to their names. Till 1975 I had not come across any Jat addressing the dalit respectfully. The names of dalits were without any suffix and were called Fatta, Kaddo, Laloo, Meela, Munshi, Rakha, Shooka, etc. and so on. Among the landowning families who were mainly the Jats, the practice was to address them by their names irrespective of the age difference. It implies that a very young Jat would address an old dalit by his name. There were some Ad-dharmis who would get some respect from the Jats and I always believed that this respect was accorded to them due to their better economic status. One of them was Ram Chand, who was once elected Sarpanch of the village. There were some other well-to-do Ad-dharmi families who had longer names.

There were three localities of the dalits out of which two comprised of Ad-dharmis. These localities were referred to as 'chamarhlis' in the village. The Balmikis lived in the third locality. Since the village was settled on a mound, the dalits had their homes on the southern side of the village towards which the entire village water flowed. At the top were located the houses of the Jats and other non-dalit castes. In the conversations among the upper castes all the dalits were referred as 'Chamars', 'Churhas', 'Julahas' and 'Bazigars'. The two localities of the Chamars/Ad-dharmis were divided along the sub-caste lines. They never got together in the panchayat elections. Both the localities of the Chamars were together in their caste-ridden negative attitude towards the Balmikis. For the powerful Jat landowners it was not difficult to control the dalits in elections. However, both the Chamars and Balmikis were staunch supporters of the Congress party, whereas the Jats were divided in their party commitment ranging between Communist parties, Akali Dal and the Congress party.

All the landowning families, whether Jats or Mehtons were displaced from the Canal Colonies and they mainly belonged to two districts of western Punjab, namely, Faislabad (then Lyallpur) and Sahiwal (then Montgomery). The dalits of the village were used to the Muslim landowners of the village. The arrival of the Jats who were predominantly Sikhs was not welcome by the dalits. In initial stages they thought that they would go back and the Muslims would return. When the Jats were resettled in the village and allotted lands temporarily, the kharif crop had not been harvested. Since the Muslims had left the village, the dalits thought that the crops belonged to them. The allotment of land to Jats was not taken lightly by the dalits. Thus sporadic clashes between the landowners and dalits occurred in the first couple of months. The Jats had the experience of handling dalits in their earlier locations and they used force wherever required with the ruthlessness of a landowner. The beginning of relationship between two communities overlapped with certain set of castes had consequences in the early 1950s when the language census was conducted in Punjab in consistence with the policy of Congress leadership with regard to the linguistic reorganisation of Indian states. With the exception of the Julahas and the family of Attra Ramdasia and his four sons, all the dalits of the village recorded Hindi as their mother tongue. Interestingly, none of them could speak Hindi. Their hostility towards the Jat Sikhs pushed them towards a kind of defiance. The language census also brought out the lingering and hidden conflicts between the Hindus and the Sikhs. All those dalits who had recorded Punjabi as their mother tongue were Sikhs.

All the above events and stories we would hear from our parents and other people. My first memory is related with commensality. The Balmiki woman, Bawi, used to come to our house for sweeping the courtyard and cleaning the area called 'haveli' where milch animals were kept. Her utensils were kept separate and away from the kitchen. She would get food in those utensils, which she would wash afterwards and keep them at the fixed place. She would never be allowed to sweep the kitchen. Obviously, there was limited tolerance towards her entering the kitchen. Her frequent entry could be perceived as transgression of caste rules. Bawi remained present in our lives from 1947 to 2000 when she stopped working. She died after six years. From 1947 to 2006, the village had changed beyond recognition. Her sons had constructed bricked houses. More importantly, she would not sit on the ground while engaging in conversation sharing gossip about the village with my mother. She would sit on another cot. The change from sitting on the floor to the cot was not a result of any change in the attitude of my parents, particularly my mother. It was a result of change in the conditions of the dalits and it did not happen overnight. Many factors contributed towards this change one of which was the economic improvement of the dalits in such a way that they ceased to be dependent on the landowners for their survival.

As a young boy I noticed the dalits always speaking reverently to my father who being a prosperous landowner would invariably help them in need in lieu of their services. In the month of March, many dalit families would face the threat of partial starvation. They would come to our house requesting my father to give them some work. Later, when I became a social activist, I noticed the fact that these dalits had never begged for food or money. They asked for either some work or a loan. However, the landowners would invariably help those families which were working as their *siris* under the *sepidari* system. They would show utter indifference towards rest of them.

As most of the Jats were Sikhs, it was expected from them not to practise untouchability at any level. However, this was not the case. One major factor that created repulsion between the dalits and the upper castes was some tenets of Sikhism. Most of the dalits would smoke cigarette or hookah, whereas the consumption of tobacco was prohibited among the Sikhs. It was one of the major reasons for the repulsion between the two. However, there were Brahmin families and some of Brahmin men were smokers, but there was no repulsion resulting from the tobacco consumption. The place where the dalits were visibly excluded was the gurdwara. On the first day of the month, as per the Bikarami calendar, called *sangrad*, there used to be congregation in the gurdwara. I do not remember the presence of dalits in the gurdwara. As a matter of fact, dalits of my village were not Sikhs excepting three families of Julahas and a few families of Chamars. However, to get *prasad* there used to be a crowd of youngsters, many of them were my class fellows in the school, outside the gurdwara. The code was unwritten in the sense that the dalit rarely tried to enter the gurdwara building though could come into the open area within the precincts of the gurdwara. Similarly, whenever *Akhand Path* would be organised by some family, the *langar* was inseparable part of it. The dalit would never sit along with the Jats in the same queue. Prior to green revolution trickle-down effect, which could be pinpointed to somewhere in the mid-seventies, the dalit kids could be abused by the adult Jats and bashed on account of even minor violation.

As the relations between the Jats and the dalits were significantly dependent on agriculture, the dalit landless men hardly had the resources to stand against the landowners. There could be certain minor exceptions to the rule, but the pattern remained the same. In 1960s the village witnessed the polarisation among the people along the lines of political parties between the supporters of the Congress and the Akali Dal. Most of the dalits used to vote for the Congress, whereas the number of Jats voting for the Akali Dal was much more than those supporting Congress. After the elections the Jats would invariably abuse them for voting for the Congress party. After the formation of the Punjabi suba in 1966 this polarisation became quite visible. The period of 1960s was marked by sugar scarcity in the country. The sugar would be available from the licensed depots in the villages. Consumption of sugar used to be a luxury, which was not possible for the dalits. The ration cards of the dalits would be misused by the Jats to get more sugar. For the Jats it became a habit.

The production of jaggery was very important part of the activity of the landowners. The way the jaggery is prepared is an age-old system that might have been periodically modified with the change in technology. The number of sugar factories was less in Punjab and there were only two such factories near our village – one at Phagwara (Kapurthala district) and the other at Bhogpur (Jalandhar district) – each of which was more than 20 kilometres away. In the absence of tractors, covering the distances on bullock cart used to take lot of time. Preparing jaggery for personal consumption was an indispensable undertaking for the landowners due to scarcity of sugar and high cost of jaggery in the market. Preparation of jaggery is a time-consuming process. It is interesting to mention that except for the green top of sugarcane all other parts are used to prepare the jaggery. The green top was generally used as animal fodder. The sugarcane juice in huge quantity would put in the cauldron and would be heated by using the dry parts of the sugarcane as well as that part from which the juice would be removed with the bullock run crusher. In order to remove impurities from the sugarcane juice to have good quality jaggery, the simple practice was to put liquid sodium bicarbonate in small quantities in the sugarcane juice when it was heated. Every time when the solution would be put, there would be some chemical reaction in the heated juice that brought these impurities on the surface of the juice which was constantly heated but not yet boiling. These would be removed and put in a container. In the evening the scum so collected would fill the container and some person belonging to the Chamar caste would get it from the landowner as a favour. In the school the Jat boys would invariably address some of them as scum-eaters (*mael-khane*). It took a little longer for me to understand the meanings of this word. It was quite humiliating for them.

When we were studying in school, there would invariably be a discussion among the Jats and other non-SCs over the issue of reservation. The discussion would revolve around how the Indian government has made the dalits its sons-in-law. Most of the blame would be put on the Congress party and there was widespread impression that the reservation policy was formulated and implemented by the Congress party in order to increase its vote bank. The case of Lal Chand is a typical one to illustrate how reality was different from the impressions and perceptions of the upper and dominant castes. Lal Chand and I were class fellows from the first standard to matriculation. We were competitors in the sense that from standard VI onwards we would both work hard to top the class. After matriculation he could not pursue his studies further simply because of his economic conditions. Last time when I met him, he was a casual labourer. He was not the only one among the dalits who could not continue studies. Education among the dalit girls was even lower than the boys.

The sexual exploitation of dalit women and girls was an unquestioned feature of the village life. It was so common that it was just taken for granted. There were hardly any protests against it. I can recall only two events that involved dalit women and Jat men. The first occurred sometimes in late 1960s and the issue came before the village panchayat. I witnessed it as a school boy who just happened to be there out of curiosity. The matter had been reported to the Sarpanch of the village by an Ad-dharmi who complained against a Jat that he had misbehaved with his wife. The Sarpanch who was also a Jat, as I speculate it now, might not have bothered about it if a large number of Ad-dharmis had not accompanied the complainant. Solely with the purpose of ending the matter there and then so that the Ad-dharmis would not go to complain to the police, as my father told me later, the Sarpanch called all the men of the village. The matter was resolved after the offender apologised in a manner that also saved his pride. His basic line of defence was that whatever he said was to save his crop, as she was cutting fodder from his field. As a matter of fact, the dependence of the dalits even for animal fodder was a major factor in the sexual exploitation of dalit women. It may also be mentioned that there were incidences of rapes also. One such case occurred sometimes in 1970s. I was studying in college at that time. It involved two Jat boys and a dalit woman. The victim filed a complaint with the police. The police arrested both the boys but they were acquitted for lack of evidence. During the last eight years there have been two cases of rape reported to the police and in both the cases there have been convictions by the court. In one case the dalit family refused to accept the offer of money in lieu of withdrawal of their complaint.

The changes that have occurred over the years are quite obvious. One that immediately draws attention is the construction of *pucca* houses. In 1960s four houses of the Ad-dharmis were *pucca* and the rest were *kutcha*. In 1978 when I first collected data for my research in the village half of the houses had become *pucca*. In 1990s there was not a single *kutcha* house of the dalits. The second change that became evident was the assertion of the dalits in their day-to-day life in the late 1990s. The period between 1984 and 1993 was marked by an uneasy quiet in the caste-class relations due to widespread terrorism in Punjab. An overwhelming number of terrorists/Sikh militants were drawn from the Jat caste. The Jats, being the landowners, fully used the terrorist violence to terrorise the dalits. It only happened if some Jat boy had joined a terrorist outfit. That is exactly what happened in my village. A Jat boy, who had joined the militants continued to dominate in the village even after surrendering to the police. He was the son of the Sarpanch of the village. Interestingly, after the death of the Sarpanch, he has now succeeded his father. At the political level the ownership of means of coercion are important in maintaining and sustaining domination, which some of the Jat families have been able to do. However, these families do not represent the entire Jat caste, because it has individualised the intercaste relationships.

Over a period of time, there have been many incidents of conflicts between the Jats and dalits mostly along the caste/class lines and local political power issues. At the time of elections at all levels the caste dynamics worked in unique ways. The Jat landowners would be quite aware of the fact that the dalit votes were 70 per cent of the total in the village, and they would decide the fate of the candidates. At the levels of Vidhan Sabha and Lok Sabha the matter was invariably determined by the party affiliations. A majority of the dalits in 1950s and 1960s would vote for the Congress party. The Republican Party's influence on many Ad-dharmis votes did/could not change the already existing pattern. In 1970s the influence of Dalit Panthers also reached the village, but it was politically far less effective than expected. Whereas the Ad-dharmis dwindled between the Congress and the Republican Party, the Balmikis remained loyal to the Congress.

The caste dynamism reflected in its entirety during the panchayat elections. As mentioned earlier, there were three localities of the dalits, two of which were comprised of the Ad-dharmis, whereas the other had the Balmikis. The Ad-dharmis were divided along the sub-caste (*gotra*) lines. The *gotra* of one locality was Sandhu, whereas the Khutan was the *gotra* of the other locality. Since there could be three social groups of dalits, besides few Bazigars and Julahas, the situation was conducive to create divisions within dalits. How did the Jats do it? It is quite difficult to comprehend, because the major source of difficulty is the informal nature of the relationships between the families of the Jats and the dalits due to the jajmani system. There could be clandestine distribution of some liquor/money to some of the dalit families. It may also be true that they were already divided.

Despite these divisions, they occasionally got together on many issues. The panchayat elections in 1978 were one such occasion when they got together. The unity that the dalits showed was along caste lines as the Balmikis did not join the Ad-dharmis. The panchayat elections in 1978 were fought with different rules from the previous elections. According to new rules, the members would be elected who would elect the Sarpanch among themselves. One post of the members was reserved for the SCs. At that time the Naujawan Sabha had come to exist in the village. It had numerical preponderance of dalit boys. They decided to put up their own candidate. The person chosen by them as their candidate was an ex-Dalit Panther activist. The Jats fearing the change manipulated the situation in such a way that all the Ad-dharmi candidates turned into each others' contenders as all of them filled their papers on the reserved seat. The papers of the ex-Dalit Panther activists were rejected on flimsy grounds of wrong information. Enraged by the manipulation of the Jats, the Ad-dharmis went to the district headquarters and met the deputy commissioner who took time to meet them though he ordered that all the candidates should be considered in terms of number of votes polled to them. However, when they returned, the trick had been played and only one dalit could be elected and he belonged to the Balmiki caste.

Agriculture wage rate was another issue that created unity among the dalits in 1970s. The issue in the 1970s was not confined to one village. In 1970s most of the villages witnessed the strike of the agricultural labourers who predominantly belonged to the dalit castes. Everywhere the modus operandi of the landowners was same.

I may just mention that every village may not necessarily be dominated by Jat landowners. For example, in the neighbouring villages Sainis and Mehtons also owned land. Since each village was comprised of one landowning caste, the villages were identified by the caste of landowners. Thus, there were Jat villages, Saini villages, Mehton villages, etc. However, even in recent times, the reaction of the landowners to the strike has remained the same. During the strike in my village the landowners got together and made it sure that no dalit entered their fields. The landowners implemented the resolution ruthlessly. Armed with lathis they organised into gangs of six to ten young persons who would watch their fields. It was done round the clock. Wherever they saw any dalit in the fields they would abuse them and ask him to leave the fields. There was one case of beating a dalit. The matter was resolved through the intervention of district administration.

There were two reasons due to which the *nakabandi* imposed by the landowners could never be a complete success. First of all, some dalit families owned land and this land could be used by them. Secondly, the village had lot of wasteland. In Hoshiarpur district there is large number of *choes* (seasonal brooks). In the District Census Handbook of 1961, the Hoshiarpur district is described as a land of *choes* and *chaudharys.* The former mentions the seasonal brooks, whereas the latter mentions Hindu Jats. Over a period of time, these Hindu Jats have converted to Sikhism, but their practices remained hybrid of both Hinduism and Sikhism till Bhinderanwala phenomenon intervened to create singular Khalsa identity – the endeavour in which he failed. As a matter of fact, all such attempts would fail so long as the people are connected with agriculture. Despite irrigation, agriculture is still dependent on monsoon rains and there is always a degree of uncertainty. Moreover, the Sikh belief system does not take into cognisance praying for rains.

The relationship between the Jats and dalits took a dramatic turn after 1984 when the Blue Star Operation, launched by the Union Government of India to flush out Jarnail Singh Bhinderanwala and his militants from the Golden Temple in Amritsar, further intensified previously prevalent the communal divisions in Punjab. For the first time after the language conflict in the 1950s, the Hindu-Sikh divide became visible. Despite the fact that the Ad-dharmis claimed to be different religious community after it was recognised so in the 1931 census, they always considered to be part of Hinduism – a perception that in itself has been the end of Ad-dharma movement's objectives. In fact, the Jat had some lingering doubts before 1984 that owing to their overwhelming number the dalits could attack them if the Hindu-Sikh issue took some violent turn in the state. The Balmikis were believed to have entertained such an idea though these apprehensions of the Jats might have been imaginary and out of fear.

Some months after the Blue Star Operation the situation turned normal as militant activities had subsided and Indira Gandhi seemed to have controlled the Sikhs. On October 31, 1984, Indira Gandhi was assassinated. The news of Indira Gandhi's assassination led to celebrations among the Jats from which the old Congressmen kept themselves quietly at a distance. From then onward began nine years' period of unabated violence in which the dalits of the village remained subdued and quiet in their relationship with the Jat landowners. Since a young boy of the village had joined the militants, the coercive power of the Jats increased. Terrorist violence, however, did not lead to the stifling of agricultural development. It implied that the slow but sure improvement in the conditions of the dalits continued to take place even during these tumultuous times.

When the Sikh militancy was suppressed in 1993, India was already experiencing the pangs of globalisation, liberalisation and privatisation. The responsibility of the Indian state in the social sector was no longer a part of the commitment for socialism. The already powerful private sector began to intrude in the area that was the exclusive concern of social welfare approach of the Indian state. Education and health became part of the private enterprise for the purpose of profit. However, the ground village reality hardly changed in the last years of 20th century. At political level, Punjab saw the quiet, unnoticed and unheeded arrival of the Bahujan Samaj Party. Some years earlier, there used to be slogans and graffiti on walls about the DS-4 (Dalit Shoshit Samaj Sangharash Samiti) and one could occasionally see young Ad-dharmi boys marching on cycles with blue flags. All this emerged as significant in Hoshiarpur only after Kanshi Ram was elected from the Hoshiarpur Lok Sabha constituency. It seemed that the BSP juggernaut would overrun one of the two major parties in Punjab, namely, the Akali Dal and the Congress. Some social anthropologists also visited Hoshiarpur and conducted a serious study on the BSP phenomenon. Kanchan Chandra (2000) predicted the rise of the BSP, but that was not to be. Though she used a misplaced notion of ethnicity in the context of caste, but such a view was not new. My teacher, Prof. Victor D'souza also viewed caste as an ethnic group way back in 1970s and he developed this idea in his book, *Inequality and its Perpetuation*, published in 1981. Prof. D'souza's concerns were different from those of Chandra. She was essentially involved in a debate that might have been taking place in the West.

One of the major reasons for the collapse of Chandra's thesis was that she did not consider the political sociology of caste. Social identities in Punjab cut across along caste, religious and regional lines in such a way that they inhibit each other. The victory of Kanshi Ram should not have been taken as a sign of dalit resurgence in Punjab. It was essentially confined to Ad-dharmis. Two things happened subsequently. The BSP became faction-ridden and secondly, other dalit castes turned against the BSP. Within five years things turned to square one. At present, the BSP does not have nay sign of strength even in the areas dominated by Ad-dharmis. However, what is noticeable in the first decade of the 21st century is the rising assertion of dalits about their identity. They are becoming proud of their caste identity. This is the change which is expected to take longer than even the change in the material conditions.

The caste identities have shown no sign of disappearance. Ironically, since the very first election in 1952, the political leaders continue to believe that they can use castes as vote banks. The dalit leaders now use dalit identity for capturing political power. Ram Vilas Paswan and Mayawati have reoriented their perspective on the change of the caste system in their own ways by asserting their dalit identity. It is not the loss of identity, but the assertion of it that is likely to move to other areas than politics, for identity assertion is not simply limited to the building of vote banks – it is an objective with intention and motive which is taken negatively. Assertion of dalit identity is also a transformation in the consciousness. The transformation of consciousness has taken much longer to change. My first perceptive encounter with this aspect of caste hierarchy was sometimes in 1967 when Mohna, who was a Balmiki, and Jeet, who was a Jat, wrestled and the latter defeated the former. Interestingly, Mohna looked much stronger than Jeet. After the defeat Mohna was ridiculed by Jeet. Mohna's response was quite interesting. He said, "You don't know, even if a Balmiki is stronger than a Jat, he cannot defeat him". Like me, both were young, in their late teens. The second encounter took place in 1978 when I was collecting data for my term paper. An elderly dalit respondent said, "You know, all this is a result of karma of our previous birth". I had not heard much along these lines from the dalits earlier. However, during data collection it was invariably found that lack of education was considered the major reason for the lower position of the dalits. Landlessness was another reason. The 'karma' principle began to recede from the consciousness of the people in 1980s and 1990s. However, hiding one's dalit identity was an important indicator of their low self-esteem. I always understood it as result of the intersubjective reality in which the dalit could make it out what others would think when they would come to know their lower caste status. Om Prakash Valmiki's (1998) autography eloquently depicts this issue in a small narrative towards the end of the story that how after hearing from his wife about their caste, a family suddenly withdrew from active interaction to silence.

In 2008 I overheard conversation between two Balmiki men while sipping tea in a roadside *dhaba*. The younger between the two said, "If God asks me in which community I should be born in my next birth, I will say, I want to be Balmiki again. You know, ours is the best community. We are happy and united". The older nodded in agreement. This transformation in the collective self-perception could not have been anticipated two decades ago. Though one may say that such an expression is also a sign of lack of consciousness, yet by looking into the present circumstances there could be only one reasonable interpretation. That is, the dalit assertion of identity has become the rule rather than an exception.

II

I think that the papers included in this collection being put together, make an organic whole. They have been, with the exception of the first paper, are chronologically ordered. In a way, they are markers of my academic-intellectual journey into the terrain of caste and caste inequality with a special focus on the dalits. Taken individually, these papers may not sum up my position and perspective on the dalits and caste system. Rather, it is quite possible that the reader would see in them a journey of sorts from 1970s to the early years of 21st century to view the changing character of caste and the dalits. The first paper is not directly related to the issue of dalits, but takes stock of a particular situation of religion and communalism in the 1980s prevailing in Punjab. It makes a fresh effort to understand the issue of caste among non-Hindus, particularly in the Sikh community. There are studies referred to in the paper, which show that the caste system continues to exist among the Sikhs. However, the issue of exclusiveness of the caste hierarchy, irrespective of religious communities being investigated, has not been touched in these studies. It can be argued that the caste hierarchy among the Sikhs is distinct from the Hindu caste hierarchy. Since Sikhism is regarded as an egalitarian order, the existence of caste hierarchy should not be confused with the usual caste system constructed by the sociologists. Interestingly, the self-acclaimed upper castes among the Sikhs, such as Jats, Ramgarhias, Ahluwalias, etc., do not occupy the highest position when seen from the spectacles of the Hindu caste hierarchy. The second issue of importance dealt with in this paper is the broader understanding of caste hierarchy as based on the division between the physical and non-physical labour. Owing to these two issues, this paper has been put as the leading one in the collection.

The second paper was published in 1985, but the data were collected in 1978. The purpose of the study was to look into the caste-class relationship in the case of dalits. In his study of dreams, Freud begins his analysis of unconscious by first interpreting his dreams. In a way, I conducted this study in one of my villages. I was quite familiar with the village, but when I began conducting interviews, I understood how wrong my impressions about the dalits of my village were. Being influenced by the Marxist class analysis, I assumed that it would be a straightforward analysis, but it did not happen like that. The dalit respondents, though were economically better off, showed me how caste could be seen independently from economic dimension. After completing the fieldwork I discussed the entire issue with my teacher, Prof. P.N. Pimpley, who reminded me of the contributions of Lukács and Gramsci. Lukács, in his *History and Class Consciousness*, has discussed how the process of reification occurs when the historical products (objects, relations and institutions) are perceived as ahistorical and natural. Gramsci's notion of myth and creation of hegemonic control was another aspect of understanding how consciousness is relevant in making sense of the maintenance of birth-ascribed hierarchies. Obviously, the attempt at understanding caste system remained fundamentally within the paradigm of Marxism. The period of 1970s was the period of popularisation of Gramsci in Indian universities. Marx's *Economic and Philosophical Manuscripts* of 1844 was hailed as a kind of discovery that provided a fresh look into Marx's writings though the main function of the text was to show that Marx was not a mechanical thinker. Those were the times of contestation between the protagonists of functionalism and Marxism. In sociology the former were numerous and anybody giving economic reasons as the explanatory force was branded as Marxist.

Marxist scholarship in India did not take the caste system seriously – a lacuna that also created handicap in the political actions of the communist parties. Punjab was the classical example of the character of the communist parties. All communist parties, including all the Naxalite groups and factions, were predominantly based on the peasant classes both in terms of cadres and struggle. Most of the prominent communists, including the most powerful communist leader in the country from Punjab so far, that is, Harkishan Singh Surjit, belonged to the Jat caste. The Punjabi Jats are mostly Sikhs and most of them still maintain the Khalsa appearance by keeping beard and tying turban. The domination of the Jat peasantry in Punjab sidelined the issue of dalit agricultural labourers. Two most important movements organised by the communists after independence were mainly the peasant-based movements. The tenancy movements in the PEPSU (Patiala and Eastern Punjab States Union) consisted of Jat tenants who were occupancy tenants. After they got the ownership rights they immediately withdrew from the movement. The peasant communist leaders saw no reason to continue with the struggle. The second movement was the Anti-Betterment Levy Struggle, which concerned the landowning peasantry. In the communist imagining of revolution Mao Tse-tung became more important, because he talked about peasantry. In the communist scholarship the most popular theme had been the middle peasant thesis and the revolutionary character of peasantry. Caste and dalit remained at the periphery of the theory and practice of Indian Marxists, whereas it was always possible to integrate Marxism and Indian social reality for them. The class interests of the leading communists prevented them from recognising the revolutionary potential of dalits.

The elimination of the dalits from the discourse of culture and identity in Punjab was a process of decentring them from their own history and traditions. The Marxist scholarship also contributed to this marginalisation. Marginality of dalits witnessed its extreme in the area of religion in which everything was subsumed under two major religions of Punjab, namely, Hinduism and Sikhism. However, times were fast changing. When I resumed my interest in dalit studies in 1980s, the dalits were experiencing economic change – could be the beneficiaries of trickle-down effect of the green revolution. I took up the project on the dalit women and their work participation. The next three papers are a result of the project I undertook in 1985. The data were collected in 1985 and 1986 in five villages of Hoshiarpur district. In a way these papers take stock of the conditions of the dalits in the 1980s and certain changes among them which had started taking place. One paper deals with how the government efforts at bringing economic development among the dalits are falling short of expectations. The next paper was perhaps the first to examine the Punjabi dalit women in a systematic way. The issue of gender and caste has not drawn the attention of social scientists engaged in research on dalits. The issue of gender is regarded as the domain of women social scientists, as if only women can understand the experiences of women. Feminisation of gender studies is an unfortunate process in the country. The present scenario in dalit studies also indicates similar trend. Since this issue has been extensively dealt with in the beginning of this chapter, my position is clear. There could be certain experiences of women that they would not like to share with men, but it is always possible to situate the women's experience in the sociological imagination for interpretation.

Woman as a social category shares one thing common with the dalits, that is, women were not accommodated in the social theory of 19th century and the first half of the 20th century. Therefore, the sociological perspectives generally fail to integrate gender in theoretical conceptualisations. Recently, Adams and Sydie (2002) have brought out a textbook in which they have evaluated various theories and thinkers from the conceptual paradigm of race, class and gender. Most of the classical thinkers do not take cognisance of gender as a sociological category worthy of theorisation. Some attempts were made to treat women as class, which created confusion rather than clarity. The issue of caste and gender may not be synonymous with the issue of race and gender, but I am of the view that all the birth ascribed immutable features are socially constructed into a system of inequality and when two such features overlap the nature and character of marginality and oppression also increases. Even now, the issue remains a riddle to be explicated and solved. By way of stating a conjecture, difference is the basis of strengthening inequalities in such situations.

The next paper among the three focuses on the identification of changes that have occurred among the dalits across generations. Based on the data collected in 1985, it was written in 1990s in order to take stock of the educational and occupational changes that could be traced by comparing the same across generations. The second part of the paper takes stock of the contemporary reality of the 1990s by situating these changes in the context of capitalism in agriculture. In a way, it was my first attempt to argue that the Punjabi dalits are undergoing economic changes. It also became evident that certain castes such as Ad-dharmis/Chamars did better than the Balmikis/Mazabis. This analytical distinction among the dalits remained my primary focus in subsequent papers.

The decade starting in 1990 began with certain changes as the Sikh extremist movement in Punjab began to wane. The movement was virtually brutally suppressed in 1993 and thus began an era of dalit assertion. During the period between 1980 and 1993 the dalits of Punjab remained politically mute in certain respects. One of the reasons was the collapse of democratic process in the state. However, the activities of Dalit Shoshit Samaj Sangharash Samiti (DS-4) could be witnessed in late 1980s in Hoshiarpur district through cycle marches with blue flags, but these remained limited to the Ad-dharmis on the one hand and representational politics, on the other. The Bahujan Samaj Party (BSP) emerged as the major player in 1996 when Lok Sabha elections were held. Kanshi Ram, the founder leader of the BSP, was elected from the Hoshiarpur constituency. It seemed that the BSP would become a dominant player in the state politics in coming years. The next paper "Green Revolution and the Bahujan Samaj Party" was written in order to understand the forces behind its rise. The paper primarily argues that the rise of the BSP should be understood in the light of the rise of the Ad-dharmi/Chamar caste in the state. Instead of focusing on the Ad-dharmis as such, it takes cognisance of the rural landless agricultural labourers whose improvement in economic terms as a result of the green revolution has made them more assertive in their political choices. A political scientist may interpret it in terms of the decline of the Congress party as the natural choice of the dalits in Punjab. I regarded such a viewpoint as a trap, because the BSP had just made some gains and the major issue was whether it developed the Punjabi dalits as permanent constituency as it had done in Uttar Pradesh. Still another reason was that Kanshi Ram remained more oriented towards Uttar Pradesh where the process of consolidation of the party seemed to be in progress. Chandra (2000) collected her data during the phase between 1996 and 2000. Most of her thesis has been proved wrong. She took a strange kind of perspective of ethnic politics to understand the rise of the BSP in the Hoshiarpur district. As such, this paper did not take cognisance of the political process in the state as well as the class formation among the Ad-dharmis. It aimed at arguing a point rather establishing it with the power of tremendous data. The reason was highly personal though professional in nature. I was involved in the study of the Sikh terrorist movement in Punjab.

The collection of data in 28 villages of Punjab along with my other colleagues and co-authors was an enlightening experience. Two other colleagues from the university in the Political Science Department made a wonderful team. The caste of the militants/terrorists was part of our investigation. We found that very few among the dalit Sikhs joined the movement though cases of murder of dalit women on account of alleged "loose character" were noticeable. A Mazabi boy became a terrorist in village Sathiala in Amritsar district. So long as he remained alive the Jat landowners treated his father with utmost respect. However, even now, the conditions of dalits, particularly the dalit women, during the Sikh militancy have not been the subject of research so far.

In 1998, I went to Canada, the USA and England to study the Punjab diaspora after getting funding from the Shastri Indo-Canadian Institute, New Delhi and also NRI Sabha, Punjab. The next paper is a result of that field visit. I made it a point to collect data on the dalits and I was fortunate enough to get the help of some of my old friends in Birmingham in particular. I was able to get the responses of non-dalit as well as dalit respondents on the issue of caste. It should be noted that though under the indentured labour migration to sugar plantations of the British colonies a large number of dalits and tribals migrated, yet the phenomenon of voluntary migration of the dalits from Punjab is as old as the Punjabi emigration. As a result, dalits constitute a substantial proportion of the Punjabi diaspora. Juergensmeyer's (1982) estimate is that 10 per cent of the total Punjabi emigrants were dalits in the first two decades after independence. My visit to England was made possible by the funding provided by the NRI Sabha, Jalandhar. The dalit respondents were quite clear about the paradox they faced in England. They were unable to sever ties from the Punjabi community as it implied abandoning Punjabi identity. At the same time, the overwhelming presence of the Jat Sikhs has enforced the recreation of Punjabi caste society. Their only advantageous position was the absence of caste system in the host society. While writing this paper, I gave a special attention to Punjabi immigrant literature. It was the first paper on the dalit immigrants in the field of diaspora studies.

The next three papers deal with the contemporary reality of Punjab, that is, the first decade of the present century. "Interrogating Changing Status of Dalits of Punjab" was an effort at examining the paradox involved in the way the change in the status of dalits was taking place. Written as contribution to the volume being edited by my colleague, it was a study of the same area which had been studied in 1980s that included my both the villages. Changes among the dalits were examined by taking into consideration education, emigration and empowerment, whereas continuity was mapped by investigation into hierarchical differentiation among the dalit castes, social ecology, temple entry and social discrimination. However, the overall evaluation was that noticeable changes have occurred among certain dalit castes.

Then, the clash took place between Ad-dharmis and Jat Sikhs in Talhan village in Jalandhar district in 2003. I knew this village well, as my nephew was married there. Moreover, the Gurdwara Baba Nihal Singh is widely revered in the region, because it is believed that the divinity of the place helped in emigration to the foreign countries. Its anthropological past and presence of graves within the precinct of the gurdwara had not made it less in its Sikh religious ambience and total dominance. The gurdwara being a Sikh religious place was never an issue of contestation in the past. The earnings from the gurdwara were also expended in the development of the village streets and other religious places. The conflict between the Jats and the Ad-dharmis, which allegedly culminated into a clash, was over the management of gurdwara because of two reasons. The Ad-dharmis always claimed that their contribution in the growth of the gurdwara was nothing less than the Jats. Secondly, they wanted to be partners in the management of the gurdwara. However, it was a clash that did not occur due to the conflict over gurdwara, but took place in a different setting. This clash escalated into the Ad-dharmi backlash in Boota Mandi where a young Ad-dharmi died of police firing. Various writings on the clash at Talhan were terribly misplaced, because most of those who wrote on this clash never visited the village. They contacted some dalit leaders in Jalandhar and wrote on the basis of the views they presented. Clash between the dalits and landowning castes did not begin with the Talhan conflict. Nor will it end there. The analysis of Talhan clash was seen in the light of politics of Boota Mandi. On top of that, the issue was raised by serious political sociologists and commentators whether Gurdwara Baba Nihal Singh was a Sikh religious place or not, because the Sikhism discourages grave worship. Most of these scholars also talk about composite religious tradition of Punjab. Whether it is possible for a gurdwara to accommodate a grave was never examined at the empirical level. I think the event provided an opportunity to examine the plight and oppression of dalits at the hands of the Jats. Paradoxically, in the Talhan clash the Ad-dharmis did have the upper hand as they bashed the Jats. The only way it was possible to justify the Ad-dharmis' demand was the principle of equal participation in the village affairs.

The last paper included in this collection is unpublished. It has not been written in order to fill in certain gaps, but its purpose is to touch those issues that have not been adequately covered in this collection. Most of the issues raised in this paper have been extensively discussed in another work (Judge and Bal, 2009). Its primary purpose is to examine the dalit assertion and its changing form and content. In recent years the dalit assertion has changed its character and it has moved to the politics of difference. The manifestation of this is the identity politics of the Bahujan Samaj Party (BSP).

As I have come to the end of explication of various papers included in this collection, Punjab is under turmoil and faces the threat of the emergence of long-term caste war. On May 24, 2009 a group of Sikhs attacked two saints in a gurdwara in Vienna in Austria. These two saints included Sant Niranjan Das – the head of the Dera Sachkhand situated in village Ballan in Jalandhar district, whereas the other was form the same Dera. In this attack the other Sant Ramanand was killed. Not much was known to the public, but it could be discerned that it was not just an attack, but it turned into a clash as result of which some of the attackers got grievously injured and were in the hospital. Sant Niranjan Das was giving sermons when the attack and then clash took place. Within a few hours of the incidents the people connected with the Dera started the protest and turned violent. The epicentre of the violence was Jalandhar and it emanated from Boota Mandi – the place where violence broke out during the Talhan conflict between the Jats and Chamars. The notable aspect of mobilisation of the Chamars/Ad-dharmis is that all of them are not followers of the Dera Sachkhand, Ballan. The ability of the Ad-dharmis to mobilise so quickly lies in their organisational strength in the form of the Ambedker Sena and other Ambederkite groups. The mobilisation was widespread and it turned against the state. It is widely accepted as a fact that the attackers in the gurdwara at Vienna belonged to the landowning Jats. However, the Chamar/Ad-dharmi activists did not directly confront the Jats but resorted to the destruction of government property that included trains and buses and railway stations and bus stands. Private vehicles were also attacked. Since it would take some time to properly analyse the dynamics of recent conflict in which the level of violence has been unparalleled, I can only pinpoint two aspects of this violence. First, religion and religious spaces have become centres of intergroup contestations and it may continue in future. Secondly, the Ad-dharmis/Chamars have shown the ability to collectively respond to a situation in which their collective interests are threatened. In the words of a dalit leader: "We follow Baba Sahib who said 'educate, organise and agitate'. We are organised and prepared to face such challenges."

Marx was right when he commented that "it is absurd to assume that appearance and reality overlap". (Post)Modern times in India seem strongly influenced by media where quick analysis of the events and phenomena is the order of the day. In the process the reality is invented and constructed and it also has spill over effect on the practice of social sciences. We hardly know who killed the saint and what happened in the gurdwara, but many social scientists have come to this conclusion. It should take a reasonably good time to understand what actually happened. For example, most of the experts who showed their powdered faces in English news channels did not know that there was a by election fixed for the Nurmahal Vidhan Sabha constituency in which the dalits had the major share in votes. To what extent the Akali Dal discouraged the police to take action against the rioters is hardly known. Most of the journalists failed to make finer distinctions among Chamar, Ravidasiya, Ramdasiya and Ad-dharmi.

In the end, it is important to add that there are certain repetitions/overlapping in the papers included here. Some repetition is natural, because these papers have been written at different points of time and every time it was thought essential to inform the readers regarding certain facts that have been unique to either Punjab or the area, which was the field of investigation. Some repetition is with regard to the proportion of the SC population in Punjab. Doaba region of Punjab has been defined at more than one place. Spellings of certain names, such as Mazabi, Ad-dharmi, Churha, etc., also vary in these papers. There has not been any standardisation of these names. The spellings that we have inherited from colonial administrators are mostly unsuitable for the exact pronunciation. There is a mention of hierarchical differentiation among the dalits. The issue of presence of caste hierarchy among the dalits has been dealt with/touched upon in some papers. There could be many other such repetitions. Since these are largely the published papers, I have retained them.

References

Adams, Bert N. and R.A. Sydie. 2002. *Sociological Theory.* New Delhi: Vistaar Publications.

Berger, Peter L. and Thomas Luckman. 1971. *The Social Construction of Reality: A Treatise in the Sociology of Knowledge.* Harmondsworth: Penguin Books.

Chandra, Kanchan. 2000. "The Transformation of Ethnic Politics in India: The Decline of Congress and the Rise of the Bahujan Samaj Party in Hoshiarpur", *The Journal of Asian Studies*, 59 (1), February, pp. 26–61.

D'souza, Victor S. 1981. *Inequality and its Perpetuation: A Theory of Social Stratification.* New Delhi: Manohar.

Gautam, Satya P. 1983. *Reasons for Action: A Praxiological Approach to Philosophy of Social Sciences.* New Delhi: Ajanta.

Guru, Gopal. 2002. "How Egalitarian Are the Social Sciences in India?" *Economic and Political Weekly*, XXXVII (50), December 14, pp. 5003–10.

Judge, Paramjit S. and Gurpreet Bal. 2009. *Mapping Dalits: Contemporary Reality and Future Prospects.* Jaipur: Rawat Publications.

Juergensmeyer, Mark. 1982. *Religion as Social Vision: The Movement against Untouchability in 20th Century Punjab.* Berkeley: University of California Press.

Lukács, Georg. 1971. *History and Class Consciousness.* Cambridge: MIT Press.

Oakes, Guy. 1977. "Introductory Essay", in Guy Oakes (ed. and tr.) in Max Weber, *Critique of Stammler.* New York: Free Press

Sarukkai, Sundar. 2007. "Dalit Experience and Theory", *Economic and Political Weekly,* XLI (40), October 6, pp. 4043–48.

Schutz, Alfred.1967. *The Phenomenology of the Social World.* London: Heinemann Educational Books.

Srinivas, M.N. 1966. *Social Change in Modern India.* Bombay: Orient Longman.

Valmiki, Om Prakash.1998. *Jooth.* Ludhiana: Chetna Parkashan.

Wittgenstein, Ludwig. 1961. *Tractatus Logico-Philosophicus.* London: Routledge & Kegan Paul.

Zeitlin, Irwing M. 2004. *Rethinking Sociology: A Critique of Contemporary Theory.* Jaipur: Rawat Publications.

1

Religion, Caste and Communalism in Punjab

This paper is primarily aimed at examining the relationship between caste stratification among the Sikhs and the emergence of communalism in Punjab. Most of the studies on caste among the non-Hindus indicate that in India the influence of Hinduism is so strong that the caste stratification has continued to exist among them. Owing to the tendency among the sociologists and social anthropologists to define caste in terms of certain general criteria and/or as a system of social stratification, the existence of caste stratification among the non-Hindus is regarded as similar to that of Hindus. Still another major factor contributing to the prevalent misunderstanding in this context is the concept of 'dominant caste' as propounded by M.N. Srinivas.[1] The concept has been applied so indiscriminately that any middle caste could be termed dominant caste provided it has high status combined with domination. Various combinations of indicators could prompt a sociologist to jump to the conclusion that a particular caste has been dominant. However, in the case of non-Hindus, what is being called a dominant caste may, in fact, be an upper caste.

The discussion in this paper has been divided into three parts. In the first part an attempt has been made to understand the concept of caste as a process. It has been argued that certain issues have been missing in the understanding of the caste, particularly in the context of non-Hindu religious communities. In the second part the analysis of caste among the Sikhs is done. This section also underlines the strength and limitations of the Sikh movement with regard to change in the caste system. The third part explores how the nature of caste hierarchies among the Sikhs and Hindus created tensions in the early decades of the 20th century.

Caste, Ideology and Caste Hierarchies

It is appropriate to begin with the conceptual understanding of the caste. I define caste as a binary opposition of manual and non-manual work. It may not be interpreted as the physical and mental labour as two polar opposites, because certain forms of physical efforts, such as swordsmanship and cooking, are not the same as cultivation and tailoring. Louis Dumont is of the view that the purity-pollution is the defining binary opposition of caste.[2] Dumont's definition, to use Levi-Strauss' term, is a statistical model of the observed phenomenon of intercaste interaction and the caste hierarchy. What lies beneath this purity-pollution is the hierarchical separation of the manual labour from that of the non-manual.

Such an argument may seem simple particularly in the light of the prevailing impression that caste as one of the oldest social formations is a complex phenomenon and social structural element. To an extent it is an appropriate argument against any attempt to simplify it. Let me introduce Berreman's (1979) notion of caste. According to him, caste is to be understood as (i) a system of social stratification, (ii) characterised by cultural plurality, and (iii) a process in which the privileges are maintained through the exercise of power. Seen from this perspective, caste becomes not only a system of social stratification, but also a basis of identity. In this regard, the articulation of identity may not simply occur through the exercise of coercive power. It involves the creation of ideological explanation to the caste system that would sustain and justify the use of power.

The second observation is that the caste system in its ideological sense is the structure and process of the privileged castes. Its strength lies in its ability to include or exclude certain groups from the system. The dalits were neither the part of the varna scheme nor of the caste system. It was in the context of the relation between the caste system and the dalits that the purity-pollution criteria were made not only operational but also enforced fiercely. There could be no mercy on dalits as they were the outsiders. One could thus understand the beheading of a meditating dalit by the incarnation of Lord Vishnu as given in the *Ramayana* – the classic Indian epic.

The caste may thus be understood as the opposition between manual and non-manual labour enforced and sustained by powerful ideology and coercive apparatus (Judge, 1998). Historically, certain ruptures in this seemingly perfect system had developed in the form of the emergence of the peasant proprietary class. A Kshatriya or a Brahmin could be a landowner without being the cultivator for which he could employ a tenant belonging to the Shudra castes. In this situation, the binary opposition of manual and non-manual labour could be maintained in a way that the control over means of production remained in the hands of the *pure* castes. We are not sure of what brought about changes in this structure as a result of which the cultivators also became owners of the means of production. In-migration, invasions and the advent of religions with medieval egalitarianism that attracted the lower castes leading to conversions are identified as the forces of change in the caste system. However, there could be changes from within the Hindu society if we keep in mind the efforts of the Bhakti movement to revitalise Hinduism. At this point it may be pertinent to mention Srinivas' distinction of caste and varna. Srinivas is of the view that varna is static and broad hierarchical division, whereas caste is dynamic and constantly changing both in historical and social contexts. To reinforce his argument Srinivas refers to Pannikar's *History of India*. According to Pannikar, at the time of Mauryas, there was only one Kshatriya caste, i.e., Nandas. The other Kshatriya castes have come to exist through a certain process of caste mobility from among the lower castes (cf. Srinivas, 1996: 9).

It may be noted that despite the dynamic character of the caste, the cases of the dalit castes elevating their status are not available. At the same time, the Shudra castes were among the first to rupture the caste hierarchy. As a historical process, the rupture occurred in the medieval period. The foremost among the events was the interaction between Islam as an egalitarian religion and Hinduism as a caste-based religion. Sikhism evolved as a result of the interaction between Islam and Hinduism. Subsequently, we find the formation of these communities that began the process of coexistence. Recent studies on these communities show that caste stratification exists among the Muslims and the Sikhs. These studies seem to suggest that there is no qualitative difference between the caste hierarchies in these communities and that of the Hindu caste hierarchy.

Sikhism and Caste Hierarchy

The emergence of the Sikh movement was an important occurrence in the medieval Punjab. As stated above, it was one of the consequences of the interaction between Islam and Hinduism. Within the larger tradition of Islam the impact of Sufism and the Kabir-bani on the Sikh movement is quite obvious. From the 16th century to 1699 the movement passed through various phases. Historians have traced the important aspects of the Sikh movement in its different shades. The first Guru initiated the process of bringing about changes in the caste system by starting cultivation after the *udasis*.[3] It was a break from the tradition as it challenged the division between manual and non-manual work as the basis of distinction between pure and the polluting castes. The subsequent tradition of langar and pankit was in the spirit of the equality of all castes (Singh, 1985).

The formation of Khalsa by the tenth Guru was based on the principle of caste equality. It is evident from the fact that the Cherished Five (Panj Piaras) belonged to the Shudra castes. They were baptised as a group and in turn they baptised the Guru. This symbolic action paved the way for the formation of the Khalsa Panth setting in motion the practice of caste equality. The formation of the Khalsa ushered in the militant tradition in the Sikh movement which continued even after the death of the tenth Guru right to the formation of the *misals* and finally culminated in the rule of Maharaja Ranjit Singh in the late 18th century.

The post-Guru Gobind Singh phase was characterised by the armed struggle of the Sikhs. The third battle of Panipat in 1761 left a political vacuum in Punjab. At that time the Sikhs were the best equipped to fill it. This led to the formation of confederation of Sikh chiefs who became rulers in their demarcated territories known as *misals*. It is interesting to note that these chiefs belonged to different castes, like Jats, Tarkhans (later on called Ramgarhias), Kalals (now called Ahluwalias) and Sansis (a Dalit caste). Though the majority of the chiefs were Jats, yet the ruler responsible for creating the Jat aristocracy was Maharaja Ranjit Singh who was not a Jat.

The conversion of Jats to the Sikh faith is one of the significant events in the history of Sikhism. As pointed out by Fenech (2000), the conversion took place at the time of the fifth Sikh Guru. Habib (1976) has suggested that one of the reasons for the Jats' conversion to Sikhism could be the lag between their economic position and social status. In the Hindu fold the Jats carried the status of Shudras. Owing to both the introduction of the Persian wheel for irrigation and their hard working nature, the Jats became peasant proprietors. Their social status remained unchanged. The springing up of Sikhism provided them the opportunity to raise their status. It has been observed that the status of the Hindu Jats in Jalandhar and Hoshiarpur districts was lower than that of their Sikh counterparts (cf. Srinivas, 1966: 101). This observation made in the Punjab Census Reports in 1931 tends to substantiate the views of Habib on this issue.

The relation between the Jats and Sikhism has not been as simple as is found in the essay of Irfan Habib. Sikhism also depended on the Jats. In other words, the relation between the two was dialectical. If Sikhism helped the Jats to improve their social status, the Jats in turn contributed to the consolidation and expansion of Sikhism. Each reinforced the other. It is this dialectics of social change that significantly contributed to the emergence of communalism in Punjab. In order to trace the significance of the conversion of Jats to Sikhism, we may focus on the demographic composition of the Sikhs. The best source for this information is the Census of India, 1931. After 1931 no census operation has included the enumeration of castes in the country. The caste composition of the Sikhs according to the Census of 1931 has been shown in Table 1.

Table 1

Proportions of selected castes in the total Sikh population

Agricultural castes	*Percentage*	*Trading/ business castes*	*Percentage*	*Artisan/ menial castes*	*Percentage*
Jats	60.00	Khatri	2.25	Tarkhan	5.87
Labanas	1.50	Arora	3.43	Lohar	1.05
Kamboh	2.08			Sunar	0.79
Saini	1.02			Chhimba	1.14
Mahatam	1.15			Jheer	1.31
				Nai	1.05
				Chamar	4.81
				Churha	2.29

Note: Castes mentioned in italics are the scheduled castes.

Source: Singh (1997: 179).

What the data in Table 1 indicate is the overwhelming presence of the Jats among the Sikhs. With the exception of Khatris and Aroras no other caste carried the upper caste status in the Hindu caste hierarchy. Notably, all these castes have continued to be endogamous groups. Not only that, owing to certain historical reasons, certain sub-castes among the Khatris began to treat themselves as the upper most castes. Within the caste ideology of intermarriages these sub-castes could accept others' daughters, but did not give away in marriage their own daughters to them. Bedi and Sodhi sub-castes are instances of such a trend. It may be noted that as Khatris these two sub-castes acquired such a status within the framework of Sikhism, because some of the Sikh Gurus belonged to these sub-castes.[4] Oberoi (1994) is of the view that this particular situation gave rise to the practice of female infanticide among the Bedis and Sodhis in the 19th century to the extent that the former acquired the dubious distinction of being called *beti-mar*.[5] However, the Khatris and the Aroras among the Sikhs did not constitute a significant proportion and in actual numbers they were only about 1,64,500 which was far less than the Jats who numbered 21,33,000 in 1931.

The Jats created the major difference in the caste structure among the Sikhs due to three reasons. First, as evidence suggests, the Jats converted to Sikhism after they had achieved economic prosperity. From this perspective, the conversion of Jats to Sikhism took place due to status dissonance. Secondly, Jats constituted more than half of the population of the Sikhs, which implies that the they were central to the affairs of the community. Thirdly, though Maharaja Ranjit Singh did not belong to the Jat caste, yet as a shrewd ruler he could understand the position of Jats within the Sikh community and this led him to create a powerful Jat aristocracy. Not only that, he recruited Jats into the army on preferential basis, particularly those who belonged to the central Punjab districts of Amritsar and Lahore.[6] The British continued the same policy with the exception that they did not confine the recruitment to the central Punjab.

At the time of the annexation of Punjab by the British in 1849 the Jats had already acquired the status of an upper caste. The influence of the Sikh egalitarian ideology had worked to lessen the caste rigidity, but the new upper castes took care to maintain the basic structure. In the process the intercaste relations acquired a significantly distinct character from the Hindu caste structure. One such area was that of intercaste marriages. The practice of hypergamy has been quite common among the Sikh Jats. The practice of female infanticide kept the proportion of women low among them. Traditionally, they handled this situation in two ways, namely, polyandry and the purchase of women from outside.[7] It is because of this reason that the Jats willingly agreed to accept the women from lower castes, but showed no inclination to give their daughters to them. Interestingly, the children from such as these unions faced no problems in terms of social stigma. It is however said that polyandry and purchase of women were common among those Jat families who had earlier married outside their caste. There is no evidence to substantiate such a contention. In other words, there would be no change in the social status of the Sikh Jat family due to a hypergamous marriage. Though the Sikh religion could not create an egalitarian community, yet the character of caste structure underwent a change.

The issue whether caste exists among the non-Hindus has continued to engage social scientists. It may be appropriate to take notice of studies that focus on the caste among the Sikhs to understand the present society. In this regard, the historians have treated caste among the Sikhs as *a priori*, something that requires no examination.[8] This perspective of the historians is largely drawn from the sources, such as Census and District Gazetteers, from the British period. Ibbetson's (1993) famous work on Punjab castes, which was first published in 1916, has continued to be a major source to identify the position of various castes in the hierarchy. However, a systematic attempt to investigate this aspect was started by the sociologists and social anthropologists from 1960s onwards. In this context studies by Harjinder Singh (1977), Singh (1977) and D'souza (1985) are worth mentioning. All these studies have two things in common, i.e., they are based on fieldwork conducted in the village (s) in Punjab, and they assume that the castes among both the Sikhs and the Hindus can be put on the same hierarchical scale. In a way, these studies tend to refer to the castes in the Sikh villages, but if examined closely the studies Singh (1977) and Harjinder Singh (1977) are in fact investigating castes among the Sikhs. The first and the widely referred study is that of Singh. We may take it up for closer analysis to make our point clear. While referring to the position of Jats in the caste hierarchy, he (ibid., 70) writes, "... Most of the Sikh values are Jat values and the Jats assert that they occupy the highest position among the Sikh castes... ." This observation provides us not only with the field reality, but also the way the researcher looks at it. Treating the Jats as agriculturists, Singh tends to suggest that it is because of their control over land that they *claim* the highest caste status. He has also informed that some of the ex-ruling families of Punjab belong to the Jat caste. However, Singh overlooks two important points here. First, most of the soldiers in the Khalsa army belonged to this caste for which there is no need of proof and even in the British army the Jats were in large numbers. All Kshatriyas were not rulers. Thus, it is not only the agriculturist but also the warrior status they have in their minds. Second, it may be noted that there is no permanent caste of the priests in the Sikh temples, known as gurdwaras. Most of the persons who perform these duties belong to the middle castes. In the absence of any priestly caste like Brahmins among the Sikhs the caste with the warrior status and control over land would like to claim for itself the highest status in the caste hierarchy within the religious community.

The subsequent analysis of Singh (ibid., 71) based on data creates further confusion. A caste hierarchy has been constructed, which tends to suggest that the Jat be placed at the top, whereas the Brahmin occupies a subordinate position. This construction of hierarchy transforms the Jats into a dominant caste. This happens because Singh does not make a difference in castes between the Sikhs and the Hindus. In the case of the Hindu caste system the Brahmins are at the top, but, as suggested by Srinivas (1987), there could be the dominant caste in a particular region whose caste status may not necessarily be high. To include Jat Sikhs and Brahmins in the same hierarchy of caste amounts to the creation of discourse that caste system cuts across religious boundaries. This, in fact, is not the case. It may apply to the Hindu Jats of Haryana, Uttar Pradesh and Rajasthan, but not to the Sikh Jats. As pointed out earlier, the Sikh movement transformed the fundamental criteria of hierarchy by making manual labour desirable.

Once we accept that there are distinctions in hierarchies of castes, it becomes clear that certain rules of endogamy might have been undergone a change. In this regard, the following incident recorded by Singh (1977: 72) is worth mentioning:

> Once a preacher came to village gurdwara and profoundly advocated the abolition of caste distinctions favouring inter-caste marriages. One of the Mazhbis listening to him got up and requested the speaker to solve the problem of finding husbands for his four

daughters. The speaker asked those wishing to accept the Mazhjbi's daughters in marriage to raise their hands. Practically everybody in the audience, consisting of all castes, raised his hands. Apparently being satisfied with the result, the Mazhbi asked for girls to marry his sons. This time no hand went up.

The issue of intercaste marriage has already been discussed, particularly in the context of receiving and giving daughters in marriage, as well as female infanticide. Thus hypergamy has remained a noticeable trend among the Sikhs.

We may consider the contemporary social science discourse on the Sikhs. For our purpose we have selected two recent publications. Gurharpal Singh (2000) has provided a classification of the Sikhs which is close to four varnas among the Hindus, viz., *Amrit-dharis, Kesh-dharis, Mona Sikhs and Sahaj-dharis.* While accepting the existence of castes among the Sikhs, he considers these unimportant in the understanding of the dynamics of the Sikh community. Gurharpal Singh writes, "Nevertheless the overall impression is still of caste homogeneity rather than division" (ibid., 85). Unfortunately, he has missed a considerable number of sociological studies that have been consistently taking stock of the existence of castes among the Sikhs. Though the four-fold division of Sikhs cutting across the caste and economic stratification among them is interesting and novel, yet it provides an unrealistic picture. Who are Kesh-dharis? Are they the Sikhs who are not Amrit-dharis, but keep unshorn hair? It may be appropriate to mention that there are numerous varieties of the Kesh-dharis. For example, some trim their beard, but keep unshorn hair. Some trim their hair and beard but wear the turban, and so on. In fact, if we empirically examine this aspect, then we would encounter a baffling variety among the Sikhs. Unfortunately, such a division and hierarchy among the Sikhs tend to negate the entire qualitative elements of Sikhism in which belief and ethical principles acquire significant place.[9]

Jodhka (2000) has not presented any novel thesis on the issue, yet he has provided a panoramic view of various studies on the existence of castes among the Sikhs. Jodhka writes, "While recognising that caste divisions existed among the Sikhs, the available literature also indicates that the change experienced in the attitudes towards caste during the last century has been quite significant in the region" (ibid., 386). However, there is no further probe into this issue, because he is primarily concerned with the dalits. In fact, what Jodhka has done is to repeat the existing perspective and studies on the caste stratification among the non-Hindu communities in India in particular and South Asia in general. The notion of dominant caste and its overriding influence in sociological and anthropological writings has created a paradigm of understanding caste and caste system. The logic of this paradigm is to establish the hegemony of the discourse of Hindu social system. In this discourse, the Hindu caste system is presented as a natural social order in which varnas are fixed and castes are mobile and thus could achieve dominance without questioning the system. Since the varnas are fixed, the caste hierarchy in the ideal typical sense remains unchanged. It logically follows that if a Shudra caste becomes economically prosperous and politically dominant, it does not as a corollary become an upper caste; it rather becomes a dominant caste. Such a discourse legitimises the caste system and the hegemony of Brahmins.

In contradistinction to the discourse of the single hierarchical order, it may be argued that there are competing hierarchies. Competing hierarchies emerge when the defining principle of the Hindu caste system, that is, the binary opposition between the manual and non-manual labour is ruptured by an agency. Sikhism brought about fundamental change in the notion of social relations by changing the dominant paradigm of the opposition between manual and non-manual labour. The first Guru of the Sikhs, Guru Nanak Dev, who himself belonged to the Khatri caste, started farming at Kartarpur (now in Pakistan) leading the way to the subsequent emphasis on human equality on the part of the Sikh Gurus in both theory and practice.

It may not be inferred from the above discussion that Sikhism was able to transform the caste structure into an egalitarian moral community of the Sikhs. Sikhism remained far from a casteless society. The recognition given to the manual labour by the first Guru provided the basis for the emergence of hierarchy distinct from the one witnessed among the Hindus. The Sikh community consisted of various Shudra castes that emerged at the top of the caste hierarchy. Among these the notable are Jats, Mehtons, Sainis, Ramgarhias, and Ahluwalias.[10] None of these castes could claim the upper caste status in the Hindu social order because all of them were engaged in those occupations that involved manual labour. After these castes could attain the upper caste status which was based on the recognition to the manual labour of a particular kind, other castes lower in the hierarchy were subjected to the control which generally is aimed at maintaining the privileges. Such a distinct feature of the caste hierarchy among the Sikhs is one of the reasons for the non-attainment of homogeneity among them. To illustrate this point we may take the instance of the fundamental institution of marriage. In addition to the predominant practice of caste endogamy, there are also variations among the castes in the practise of mate selection; for example, the Aroras still practice cross-cousin marriage, whereas the Jats practice *gotra* exogamy.

To conclude, it may be argued that the nature and character of the caste hierarchy among the Sikhs were qualitatively different from those of the Hindus. Not only was difference discernible in terms of the positioning of castes with the common nomenclature in both the religious communities, even the defining principles of the two hierarchies were contradictory. In the backdrop of this contradiction emerged the interests of the privileged castes among the Sikhs to clearly define boundaries in relation to the Hindus. The next section focuses the discussion on this emphasis in difference that led to communalism in Punjab.

Caste and Communalism in Punjab

In the preceding section, it was argued that caste hierarchies in different religious communities should be understood as competing in the sense that the corresponding positions of the castes with the common names might vary according to religion. Thus, a particular caste occupying low ritual and social status in the Hindu caste hierarchy could enjoy an upper caste status in the Sikh caste hierarchy. In such a situation the hierarchies become competing due to the interest of the upper caste in the non-Hindu caste system to create a distance from the Hindu ideology and structure. It is my contention that the emergence of communalism between Hindus and Sikhs in the late 19th and the 20th centuries owed much to the evolution of competing hierarchies among the two religious communities. Though Punjab has witnessed one of the worst communal riots in the history of India at the time of partition of 1947, yet the purpose of this paper is limited to the understanding of the inseparable link between competing hierarchies and the emergence of communalism in Punjab. To explicate this point it may be pertinent to trace distinctions between communalism and communal riots.

Pannikar (1991: 1) is of the view that "Communalism in India draws sustenance from history, from its interpretation and selective appropriation. It seeks to construct an 'imagined' past in order to legitimise its view of the present." He further points out that "Communalism is a state of consciousness. In making of this consciousness culture comes to play in different ways: first, through the construction of a community culture and secondly, by the appropriation of the existing cultural practices. In both these culture is viewed as synonymous with religion" (ibid., 11). Communalism develops through the articulation of difference in a manner that the plausibility of any integration between the religious groups ceases to exist. Communalism by nature is a consciously created ideology to evolve a more or less permanent difference. It is done, as Pannikar rightly points out, by selective interpretation of the past. It is quite probable that in this process of selective interpretation a new tradition is constructed. This new tradition, which has been successfully constructed, shows that there is a clear-cut demarcation between the 'self' and the 'defined other'. In the context of the Sikhs in Punjab the construction of the 'self' and the 'other' began from "we are not Hindus" and culminated into "Sikhs are a separate community/nation".[11] Predictably, the articulation of these two assertions involved a reasonable discussion on the caste system. For our purpose Kahn Singh Nabha's book and the speeches of Jarnail Singh Bhindranwala, the leader of the militant Sikhs, have been selected to discuss how an attempt to draw a line between the Sikhs and the Hindus led to the construction of a new tradition. However, it may not be inferred that the Sikhs, particularly the leaders of the Singh Sabha movement, were responsible for the emergence of communalism in Punjab. If we look at the second half of the 19th century Punjab, we would find that all the three major religious communities, viz., Muslims, Hindus and Sikhs, had been experiencing religious revivalism (Puri and Judge, 2000). Interestingly, the Arya Samaj movement was the first of its kind to make an attempt to remove untouchability in an organised manner. However, it stretched itself too far when it began the *Shudhi* movement in order to reconvert and raise the status of those Dalits who had become either Muslims or Sikhs (Sharma, 1985). This effort of the Arya Samaj to bring back the converted dalits to the Hindu fold was one of the significant events that contributed to the emergence of communalism in Punjab. Since the issue of caste remained at the forefront of religious revivalism among the Hindus, the Sikhs made it central in the religious discourse.

To put the issue in proper perspective, it is worthwhile to delineate certain features of the Sikhs and the Singh Sabha movement. First, as the Singh Sabha movement progressed, the proportion of the Jats started rising to the extent that among the Akalis 70 per cent were Jats (Fenech, 2000). Thus, the preponderance of the Jats in both the total population of the Sikhs and the Akali movement is not simply an outcome of the arithmetic rule that a particular caste must proportionately be represented in a movement. As pointed out by Oberoi (1994), the emphasis on the Khalsa identity during the Singh Sabha period began with the rise in power of the Tat (true) Khalsa. The Tat Khalsa leaders were drawn from the middle class Sikhs, like teachers and ex-soldiers, who mainly belonged to the Jat caste. Secondly, the Tat Khalsa tried to establish distinct identity of the Sikhs, not from the Muslims but from the Hindus. Interestingly, the construction of the Sikh history took place through the creation of a sacrificing and a struggling community in relation to the Muslim rulers who were presented as cruel and oppressive. The purpose of this construction was to create demarcation between Sikhism and Hinduism. According to Fenech (2000), the purpose of the creation of tradition of martyrdom in Sikhism was to move it away from Hinduism. The reason was that the danger of the loss of Sikh identity and its submergence into Hinduism loomed large. The best way to save Sikhism was not only to purge it from all Sanatan influences but also to construct a new tradition. In the construction of new tradition the Jats acquired more prominent place than the Khatri and Arora Sikhs. For Jats Sikhism was the basis of their upper caste status, whereas for the Khatri and the Arora Sikhs the issue of caste was less important as they already had upper caste status.[12] In the backdrop of these features we now focus on the well-known work of Kahn Singh of Nabha published in 1898.

We Are Not Hindus (Hum Hindu Nahin Hain)

The timing of the publication of this work coincides with the rise of Tat Khalsa in the Singh Sabha movement. Kahn Singh Nabha, who has been widely recognised as a fine scholar of Sikhism owing to his *Mahan Kosh* published in 1930, was a Dhillon Jat by caste. *Hum Hindu Nahin Hain* is a polemical work and its basic purpose is to clearly state that the

Sikhs must not be confused with the Hindus, as they are a distinct religious community. Nabha is very clear to the limited purpose of his work. He (1973: 1) states it clearly thus: "After reading this book the readers must be able to understand that the Sikhism is a distinct religion from Hindu and other religions. However, it should not happen that you begin to oppose Hindus or abuse Hinduism."[13] As a typical polemical work, it covers fifteen areas with sweeping observations by relying heavily on Sikh religious hymns. What draws attention of a sociologist is that he gives second preference to the issue of caste and varna. It is this issue that forms the basis of what he thinks is the real distinction between the Sikhs and the Hindus.

In the section on varna and caste, addressing the Hindus too implies that the book was meant for both the Sikhs and the Hindus. Nabha seems to be telling the Hindus that their religious texts give pre-eminent position to the Brahmins. Here he quotes from *Manusmriti*. Normatively, the position of the Brahmins signifies injustice to the people of the God. The second criticism he labels against the caste system is the ascriptive character of the caste status. Caste is determined by birth. Nabha concedes that there are status groups among the Sikhs, namely, *gyani, granthi, sipahi, zamindar, vipari,* and *langri.*[14] However, these positions are not determined by birth and may change. For example, a scholar may clean the shoes of the devotees. The third and the most important issue, according to Nabha, is the practice of untouchability among the Hindus. The Guru has merged the four varnas and castes and created Sikh religion.

After establishing clear-cut differences between the two religious communities in terms of the social structure, Nabha moves on to the direct attack on Brahmins in particular and Hindus in general. He refers to the story of the martyrdom of the ninth Guru – a story known to every Sikh. It revolves around the forcible conversion of the Hindus to Islam by the Mughal emperor and the visit of Kashmiri Brahmins to the Guru at Anandpur Sahib. Nabha refers to this story to argue that the Hindu is so ungrateful that he manipulates the innocent Sikhs to cut their hair. In a way what the Mughal emperor had done to the Hindus, the same is being done by them to the Sikhs (Nabha, 1973: 43–73).

The above discussion of Nabha's work indicates that though he was primarily concerned with showing that Sikhs are not Hindus, yet his discourse on caste among the Sikhs is unconvincing. For instance, he did not take endogamy to illustrate the difference. One may make a conjecture that he might be painfully aware of the practice of caste endogamy among the Sikhs, particularly the Jats. There is no doubt that through its efforts the Singh Sabha movement sought to undermine the caste distinctions by encouraging the people to drop their sub-caste or gotra suffixes from the names. As an alternative to the ascriptive surname that disclosed the caste of the person the Singh Sabha leaders used village names as suffixes – a practice that still continues today.[15] One may not expect a great deal from a polemical work, but the choice of caste makes it an important text, because there was always a way open for Kahn Singh to defend his arguments if any critic had pointed out the existence of castes among the Sikhs. He could argue that the presence of castes is due to Brahminic influence and also the attempt of the thankless Hindus to cut the hair of the Sikhs and remove their *kachh* and *karha*.[16] Kahn Singh was a pioneer in raising the social issues as the basis for creating a new tradition for the Sikhs. In the subsequent period the ideas of Kahn Singh continued to weigh heavily on any discourse on the relations between the Hindus and Sikhs. In the due process of time, the Sikh leaders reached their ideological end when Jarnail Singh Bhindranwala started his discourse on the basis of Anandpur Sahib Resolution that Sikhs are a distinct community and concluded by claiming that Sikhs are a separate nation.

Sikhs Are a Separate Community/Nation

The period between the publication of Kahn Singh's work and Bhindranwala's speeches is characterised by certain contradictions in the construction of the 'self' and the 'other' by the Sikh leaders. In 1947 India achieved independence and Punjab experienced partition accompanied by the occurrence of the worst communal riots in the history of the country. The migration of population across borders led to the virtual disappearance of Muslims in the Indian Punjab.[17] Thus, in the construction of the 'other' only the Hindus were left. The combination of various events, particularly the language conflict, tended to reinforce boundaries between the two communities with their distinct traditions. Article 25 of the Indian Constitution became the major reason for the articulation of the construction of the 'Hindus' as the 'other'. The Akalis interpreted this Article as if the Sikhs have been defined as part of Hinduism. They demanded that Sikhism should be constitutionally regarded as a separate religion from Hinduism.

Interestingly, they never demanded that in view of the absence of castes among the Sikhs, the reservation policy for the Mazabis, Ramdasias, Sansis and many other Sikhs who were included among the scheduled castes, should be discontinued.

To an extent, the Akalis mobilised the issues in the light of their electoral prospects rather than taking serious view of deviations from the ideal construct of the Sikh community. Bhindranwala burst on the scene in 1978 when 13 persons were killed in a clash between the Nirankaris and his followers.[18] Within a few years he became the dominant figure in the political and religious affairs of the Sikhs. He was able to attract a large number of Sikh youth. During his stay at Golden Temple, Amritsar, he gave numerous speeches in which his frequent discourses focused on the Sikhs as a separate religion and a nation. It may be interesting to note that like Kahn Singh of Nabha he belonged to Jat caste. However, he was not a scholar like Kahn Singh, but a preacher whose religious calling was to preach Sikhism and encourage people to become Amrit-dhari Sikhs (orthodox Khalsa Sikhs with all the five Ks).[19] It is worthwhile to state what Bhindranwala said about the Sikhs as a separate community/nation.

He gave the following arguments to establish the separate identity of the Sikhs:

(a) A person is a Sikh at the time of his birth. It is only when people cut their hair or get circumcised that they become Hindu or Muslim.
(b) All castes are present among the Sikhs. This makes the Sikhs a separate religion.
(c) There is no space for a Muslim in the eighteen chapters of *Gita* and no space for Hindus in the *Koran.* In the Guru Granth Sahib everybody has been given the space. Kabir (Julaha), Ravidas (Chamar), Deviji (Kumhar), Sainji (Nai), Nam Dev (Chhimba), and Dhanna (Jat) are all given space in the holy book of the Sikhs.
(d) A Hindu cannot pay respect in a mosque. A Muslim cannot do the same in the temple. Anybody can come and pray in the Golden Temple.
(e) Nowhere in the world in any religion will you find *langar* (free meals). It is only found among the Sikhs.
(f) A Hindu woman cannot keep *bodi* and put on the sacred thread. A Muslim woman (the question of circumcision does not arise)

cannot read *namaz* in the mosque. If she does it, then she will have to put on veil. You can circumcise a man, but you cannot circumcise a woman. Thus, the Muslims are half Muslim and half Hindu. It is only the Sikh religion where no distinctions exist in the religious practices.

(g) When the leaders of India who were fighting for independence, Tricolour was made as the National Flag. These three colours represented the three religious communities. White was for Hindus, green was for Muslims and the saffron for the Sikhs. At that time the saffron colour was given the third and the lowest place. But, the question was who would fight for independence and sacrifice their lives. These leaders went to Baba Kharak Singh who said that each community should sacrifice according to its position in the hierarchy of colours in the national flag. On hearing this the national leaders, Nehru, Gandhi and Patel put the saffron colour at the top of the hierarchy.[20]

(h) The Sikhs have been sacrificing their lives for the protection of Hindus since the martyrdom of the ninth Guru, but they have been ungrateful.

At the time of Bhindranwala the notion of equality has undergone a change. Though he mentions in another speech that the tenth Guru demolished caste system which is evident from the caste background of the *Panj Piaras* (the five cherished ones) who belonged to the Shudra castes, yet the existence of castes seems to be a natural social reality for him. As is indicated by (b), the presence of all castes makes a religious community self-sufficient. However, there is no discrimination against the lower castes and the women in entering the gurdwaras and practising religion according to the tradition. Hence, social equality is a characteristic feature of Sikhism. Interestingly, the more significant in the speeches of Bhindranwala is his construction of the 'other'. The absence of Muslims has made no difference to his discourse. It seems that the way the Sikh tradition was constructed during the Singh Sabha movement continues to be articulated in the same mode. With all disrespect to history Bhindranwala is further contributing to the construction of the Sikh tradition by making the Hindus as 'the ungrateful other'. In this regard, he comes close to Kahn Singh of Nabha who also articulated the view that the Sikh sacrificed their lives to protect Hinduism, but they proved to be ungrateful. For Kahn Singh the fear was assimilation of the Sikhs in the Hindu composite tradition, whereas for Bhindranwala no such fear exists. The issue for him is more of political than religious in nature. He is demanding for the change in the Article 25 of the Constitution where the Sikhs have been identified with the Hindus. The process that was started by the competing caste hierarchies was completed through the construction of a separate religious tradition. Once the construction of the tradition became a reality, the plausibility structure of merging of Hinduism and Sikhism vanished. At this stage the upper castes among the Sikhs could emulate the super structural components of Hindu caste system to create a structure of discrimination rather than of purity-pollution.

Conclusion

There may be some contention over the question of competing caste hierarchies. It may still be regarded that the Jats are not the upper caste among the Sikhs, but a dominant caste. Anticipating such a view we may just think of some other castes among the Sikhs who are neither backward classes nor scheduled castes according to government classification. In this context, Ramgarhias who were carpenters and masons by occupation were an artisan caste. It is their conversion to Sikhism that made them an upper caste. Interestingly, the non-Sikh carpenters are included in the category of backward classes. The Ramgarhias as an upper caste are interested in keeping the Sikh orthodoxy alive though they are not a dominant caste. To conclude the discussion it may be stated that the caste hierarchies among the Hindus and the Sikhs were qualitatively distinct despite the existence of castes among the latter. These distinct caste hierarchies became the basis of emergence of communalism in Punjab in the twentieth century.

Notes

This paper originally published in *Sociological Bulletin*, Volume 51, Number 2, September, 2002 under the same title. The author is grateful to the Indian Sociological Society for giving permission to reproduce it here.

1. Srinivas (1987: 4) defines dominant caste thus: "A caste may be said to be 'dominant' when it preponderates numerically over the other castes, and when it also wields preponderant economic and political power. A large

and powerful caste group can more easily be dominant if its position in the local caste hierarchy is not too low."

2. Louis Dumont's (1998: 54) basic argument may be traced from his comment thus: "It is clear that the impurity of the Untouchables is conceptually inseparable from the purity of the Brahman. They must have been established together, or in any case have mutually reinforced each other, and we must get used to thinking of them together."

3. This fact is part of the knowledge of Sikh tradition. Most of the books on the life and works of Guru Nanak Dev have included this fact. See A.C. Banerjee, *Guru Nanak To Guru Gobind Singh,* Rajesh Publications, New Delhi, 1978.

4. This again is a well-known fact. To elaborate the matter, it may be informed that so far as the sub-castes of the Sikh gurus were concerned the first Guru was Bedi, the second Trehan, the third Bhalla and the rest were Sodhis.

5. Harjot Oberoi (1994: 227–228) comments: "Among the Sikhs the practice of female infanticide was most widely practiced among the Bedis, the descendants of Sikh gurus. Many of the Bedis occupied prominent positions within the guru lineage, but they ended up paying dearly for their high social and ritual standing. Due to their extraordinary high status they found it difficult to find biradaris of higher status from which to draw husbands for their daughters ... To solve this problem they borrowed a solution which had long been used by the Rajput landed aristocracy in various parts of India: They killed female offspring at birth, thereby avoiding the humiliation of finding a match within low-ranking castes ..."

6. There are certain facts that have not been recorded. An interview with Jagbir Singh Bal who belongs to the nineteenth century Sardar (aristocracy) family brought the fact that Maharaja Ranjit Singh used to recruit soldiers preferably from these districts. To find out, each candidate was asked to count up to twenty-five. The person who would say *yaran* (eleven) instead of *giaran* and *panjhi* (twenty-five) instead of *pachi* was recruited. These pronunciations were confined to these districts.

7. The practice of polyandry has been well depicted in the famous Punjabi play *Ik Ramayan Hor* (One More Ramayan) written by Ajmer Aulakh.

8. See Harjot Oberoi, op. cit. and Louis E. Fenech, op. cit. These two have recently made significant contributions, but the manner in which they have mentioned castes suggests that they assume the existence of caste system among the Sikhs as natural. Other historians have done the same, but these two have been mentioned as the representatives of the general understanding of the historians on Sikhism.

9. Incidentally, a woman scholar pointed out after reading this division of Sikh identity that religion seemed to be the exclusive domain of men where the women are decentered entities.
10. It may be mentioned that Khatri and Arora Sikhs have not been included here, because they already had high caste status in the Hindu caste hierarchy.
11. Kahn Singh of Nabha wrote the book *Hum Hindu Nahin Hain* (We are not Hindus) in 1899. At that time, the Singh Sabha movement had changed its character and had become synonymous with the Tat Khalsa ideology. In 1970s the Akalis initiated the struggle for the Sikhs to be recognised as a distinct religious community in the Indian Constitution. Soon after the militant leader appropriated the slogan of the Akalis to change it into "the Sikhs as a separate nation".
12. For Khatri and Arora Sikhs the political factors like communal representation in the elected bodies in the twentieth century might have become important to emphasise the distinct identity of the Sikhs.
13. Kahn Singh Nabha's *Hum Hindu Nahin Hain,* which has been published by Singh Sabha Shatabadi Committee, Amritsar, in 1973, seems to be the reprint of the revised edition of the book published by Kahn Singh Nabha himself in 1899.
14. All these positions are achieved and correspond closely to the occupations. Thus, these means Pandit or knowledgeable, priest, soldiers, landowner, businessman and cook respectively. See Kahn Singh, ibid., p. 53.
15. For example, Prakash Singh Badal, the present Chief Minister of Punjab, and Jagdev Singh Talwandi, the President of SGPC (Shiromani Gurdwara Parbhandhak Committee) and most of the Akali leaders, use their village names as suffixes.
16. At the time of formation of Khalsa the tenth guru told them to keep 5 Ks, namely *Kes (*unshorn hair), *Kanga (*comb), *Karha* (iron bangle), *Kachh* (long loincloth), and *Kirpan* (sword).
17. The only Muslim population, which was not touched by the communal riots, was that of Malerkotla princely state.
18. For many experts this incident is regarded as the beginning of the Punjab problem. What followed this attack was a series of terrorist action that led to the assassination of the chief of the Nirankari sect. When the editor-in-chief of the *Hind Samachar* group of newspapers, Lala Jagat Narain was killed in 1982, Bhindranwala was arrested and released after few days. Fearing such arrests he moved to the Golden Temple complex at Amritsar. From this place he directed his terrorist operations till June 1984 when the army attacked the Temple in which he died along with his close followers. During his stay at Amritsar he gave speeches which were recorded. There are fourteen audio cassettes of his speeches. These are available in the shops

run by Damdami Taksal – a religious seminary, which was headed by him before his death. The views of Bhindranwala presented here are based on the transcription of these cassettes that has been done by the author himself.

19. In his various speeches as and when he talks about himself, he always mentions these as his duties.
20. Cassettes 6 and 9.

References

Berreman, Gerald D. 1979. *Caste and Other Inequities: Essays on Inequality.* Meerut: Folklore Institute.

D'souza, V.S. 1985. *Economic Development, Social Structure and Population Growth.* New Delhi: Sage.

Dumont, Louis. 1998. *Homo Hierarchicus: The Caste System and its Implications.* New Delhi: Oxford University Press.

Fenech, Louis E. 2000. *Martyrdom in Sikh Tradition: Playing the Game of Love.* New Delhi: Oxford University Press.

Habib, Irfan. 1976. 'Jats of Punjab and Sind' in Harbans Singh and N.G. Barrier (eds.), *Punjab Past and Present: Essays in Honour of Dr. Ganda Singh* (92–103). Patiala: Punjabi University.

Ibbetson, Denzil. 1993. *Punjab Castes.* New Delhi: Low Price Publications. (First Published in 1916)

Jodhka, Surinder S. 2000. "Prejudice' without 'Pollution'? Scheduled Castes in Contemporary Punjab', *Journal of Indian Political Economy,* XII (3–4): 381–403.

Judge, Paramjit S. 1998. 'Limits of Discourse: Examining Social Structure of Punjab, in Gopal Singh (ed.), *South Asia: Democracy, Discontent and Societal Conflicts* (372–391). Delhi: Anamika Publishers.

Nabha, Kahn Singh. 1973. *Hum Hindu Nahin.* Amritsar: Singh Sabha Shatabadi Committee.

Oberoi, Harjot. 1994. *The Construction of Religious Boundaries: Identity and Diversity in the Sikh Tradition.* New Delhi: Oxford University Press.

Pannikar, K.N. 1991. 'Introduction,' in K.N. Pannikar (ed.), *Communalism in India: History, Politics and Culture* (1–17). New Delhi: Manohar.

Puri, Harish K. and Paramjit S. Judge (eds.). 2000. *Social and Political Movements: A Reader on Punjab.* Jaipur: Rawat Publications.

Sharma, Satish K. 1985. *Social Movements and Social Change: A Study of Arya Samaj and Untouchables in Punjab.* New Delhi: B.R. Publishers.

Singh, Gurharpal. 2000. *Ethnic Conflict in India: A Case Study of Punjab.* Houndsmills: Macmillan.

Singh, Harbans (ed.). 1996. *The Encyclopaedia of Sikhism.* Patiala: Punjabi University.

Singh, Harjinder. 1977. 'Caste Ranking in Two Sikh Villages,' in Harjinder Singh (ed.), *Caste among Non-Hindus in India* (84–90). New Delhi: National Publishing House.

Singh, Indera Paul. 1977. 'Caste in a Sikh village,' in Harjinder Singh (ed.), *Caste among Non-Hindus in India* (84–90). New Delhi: National Publishing House.

Singh, Jagjit. 1985. *Perspectives on Sikh Studies.* New Delhi: Guru Nanak Foundation.

Singh, Joginder. 1997. *Sikh Resurgence.* New Delhi: National Book Organisation.

Srinivas, M.N. 1966. *Social Change in Modern India.* Bombay: Allied Publishers.

——. 1987. *The Dominant Caste and Other Essays.* New Delhi: Oxford University Press.

2

Class Analysis of Scheduled Castes

The primary concern of the present paper is to study the class situation of the scheduled castes[1] in the village Ajram, district Hoshiarpur, Punjab. Studies on scheduled castes (SCs) in sociology have mainly been confined to caste analysis with a total exclusion of the class approach to this area. Here, in this paper, an attempt has been made to adopt an alternative approach to the study of underprivileged section of the society. In my view class approach to study the scheduled castes in India would help us understand better the complex dialectical relationship hitherto existing between the scheduled castes and the higher castes.

Perspectives on Class

Some eminent sociologists have tried to categorise various definitions of 'class' on the basis of different criteria. Singh (1977) raises an important issue on the nature of class as to whether it is a universal or particularistic concept. He further argues, whether "class should be attributional or interactional." However, it is the author's contention that such categorisations are fallacious and confusing. Taking up of these criteria shall not lead to any conclusion. To avoid the confusion, I have taken the basic theoretical contradictions which exist in contemporary sociological literature; so also in the definitions of class, i.e., whether the society is viewed as based either on consensus of values or conflict over resources. Thus, various definitions of class have been categorised into two, namely, consensus and conflict, perspectives.

Consensus Perspective

The protagonists of the consensus model are primarily concerned with the maintenance of the existing order. Equilibrium is established in the society on the basis of the consensus of values. All the parts of the system are integrated. Max Weber (1974), in his reaction to the Marxist theory, tried his best to justify the capitalist system. Modern functionalist theorists like Parsons, Davis and Moore, Tumin and Warner, etc. also follow this strand of thought. A brief discussion will help us understand the class position of Harijans in a better way.

Weber has taken three dimensions of inequality in society. These are class, status and party. On these dimensions, Anderson (1974: 117) writes, "One's class situation to Weber, is the typical probability of one's procuring goods, gaining a position in life, and finding satisfactions – a probability which derives from one's relative control over goods and skills and their income producing uses within a given economic order."

According to Weber, "Status of the social variety rests upon a typically effective claim to positive or negative privileges with respect to social prestige derived from the 'mode of living' or the 'style of life' and family hereditary prestige or of an occupation. A social stratum, then, is a plurality of individuals who enjoy the same level of prestige" (Anderson, 1974: 119). Weber also takes cognizance of inequality created through power, which according to him is realising one's will even against the resistance of others (Weber, 1974). In this way, Weber gives three types of classes, i.e., economic class, prestige class and power class. The major concern of Weber was to indicate that a man who is higher in the economic class might be lower in the prestige class. But he failed in his contention, because of the fact that both status and power do not exist independently from the economic class. Anderson (1974: 120) points out, "It is necessary for Weber to affirm that property classes represent the most dominant underpinnings of political parties, together with the influences of acquisition class, where the latter are not in complete harmony with property classes. In other words, the most important seat of power is class, i.e., economic power".

Warner defines class as "two or more orders or people who are believed to, and are accordingly ranked by the members of the community in socially superior and inferior positions" (Reissman, 1970: 223). The individuals are ranked upon the criteria of income, source of income, education, occupation, residence and associates. On the basis of these, Warner has identified six classes in Yankee city from upper-upper class to lower-lower class. But one is surprised as to why Warner called these categories as classes. It appears that Warner's views of stratification deviate not only from the broader theories of both Marx and Weber, but also from the theories of functionalists. Reissman opines that from the wide perspective of industrial societies, we have been brought to a very narrow community level by Warner's formulation. He further adds, "instead of the percept that classes exist in a status of tension, which ignites changes, Warner has advanced the view of status groups living together in relative harmony" (ibid., 224).

Among the living exponents of functional theorists, Parsons, while defining class argues, "We may suggest the usefulness of divorcing the concept of social class from the historic relation to both kinship and property, as such, to define class status, for the unit of social structure, as position on the hierarchical dimension of the differentiation of the societal system, and to consider social class an aggregate of such units, individual and/or collective, that in their own estimation and those of others in the society occupy positions of approximately equal status in this respect" (c.f. Anderson, 1974: 123).

Parsons' conception of class could not escape criticism. Anderson (ibid., 124) raises a methodological issue and argues, "What sort of social science methodological make-believe is it that can find space in learned journals to dispense with kinship, property and the class structure of capitalist society itself in an analysis of stratification and inequality and put in their place such meaty substance as 'position on the hierarchical dimension of differentiation of the societal system ... . 'For those who have not yet understood the meaning of the Marxist phrase 'bourgeois social science,' the foregoing suffices as an illustration".

Conflict Perspective

Conflict theories conceptualise society as made up of different groups having unequal control over scarce resources and in perpetual conflict with each other for greater command over these resources. We begin by discussing Marx's theory of class and class conflict. In Marx's class model, the class position is broadly determined by a person's property placement and relationship to the means of production. Marx (1971: 885) states that "the owners merely of labour-power, owners of capital and land whose respective sources of income are wages, profit and ground-rent, in other words, wage-labourers, capitalists and landowners constitute then three big classes of modern society based upon the capitalist mode of production". But, in the Marxist analysis, the definition of class does not stop here. The conflict is the essential element in Marx's definition of class. The conflict between the haves and have-nots is based on antagonistic interests, which can only be resolved through the overthrow of the existing order.

After Marx, the conflict theories of class can be divided into two strands, namely, the neo-Marxist and the functionalist. In the first strand of thought, the major thinkers are Lenin, Mao Tse-tung, Frantz Fanon, etc. In their analyses these thinkers have endorsed the Marxist definition of class. But, the political power has been stressed more by them. The reason is that the Marxist tradition of class analysis has approached peasantry in terms of power relationships (Shanin, 1976). In the context of colonial countries, Fanon (1967) is of the view that the political system becomes the base and the revolutionary potential of a class depends upon it. Thus, in the colonial countries, there are two basic classes, namely, masters or colonialists and natives or colonised. But still, in all the neo-Marxists theories the conflict remains the pivot of the class analysis. Moreover, the class conflict and the resolution of conflict through organised struggle are inseparable parts of their class analysis.

In the second strand of conflict theorists are included more or less functional conflict theorists. Such as Dahrendorf and Lenksi. Dahrendorf (1959) considers Marx's definition of class as very narrow. According to him, society is not as simple as Marx has visualised. For him, authority is the basis of 'class'. Authority, by definition implies domination and subjection, that is, those who have authority and those who do not have authority. At the same time, he visualises society divided into different imperatively co-ordinated associations. According to Dahrendorf, by social class, "We mean such organized or unorganized collectivities of individuals as share manifest or latent interests arising from and related to the authority structure of imperatively co-ordinated associations. It follows from the definitions of latent and manifest interests that social classes are always conflict groups" (ibid., 238).

But Bryant (1976: 274–277) points out that for Dahrendorf, conflict cannot be resolved; it can only be suppressed, or ignored or regulated. He equates liberalism with an open diversity of interests and a commitment to the regulation of conflict. However, he writes, "Dahrendorf claims priority for conflict theory on the grounds that functionalists discuss class in terms of prestige and income as conflict theorists discuss it in terms of power and power logically precedes distributive inequalities, but integration theorists could reply that they are much more concerned with the part played by common values and norms in making social life possible than they are with social stratification". Like a typical liberal bourgeois, Dahrendorf considers society as Janus-headed exhibiting consent as well as coercion.

Lenski's (1966: 75) synthetic approach is not very different from Dahrendorf's theory. For Lenski class is an aggregation of persons in a society who stand in a similar position with respect to some form of power and privilege. He further suggests that given the definition a single individual may well be a member of half a dozen power classes. For him, the member of every power class shares certain common interests and persuasion of interests constitutes a potential basis for hostility towards other class. Lenski ends this theory of class by agreeing with the 'end of ideology' theorists that with the higher development of technology, the inequalities decline.

Like Dahrendorf, Lenski also visualises society divided into different power classes. The power and authority in both the cases are separated from their existential basis. Now, a crucial issue arises that why power, separated from the ownership of means of production, cannot be the criterion of definition of 'class'. In both the cases, there is a Weberian attempt to show the irregularity in the position of an individual in different imperatively coordinated associations or power classes. It has been pointed out earlier in the discussions on Weber that he failed to separate the status and power dimensions from the class. Similarly, the attempt on the part of both Dahrendorf and Lenski to do the same thing is not convincing.

For Marx power does not operate independent of substructure; otherwise, the Marxist analysis of class becomes meaningless. Though in the Marxist analysis political power comes in the superstructure determined by substructure, yet to go further we find that political power at one point of time becomes an autonomous force and also affects the substructure. In the Marxist theory of revolution, it is found that to change the relations of production, the proletariat organises itself as a political organisation and captures the political system. The careful understanding of Marxist position indicates that power is the manifestation of both economic and political situations which are inseparable. Marx qualifies it when he talks of 'ruling class'. Taking into consideration various viewpoints, it is our contention that in this paper the term 'class' should be understood in terms of economic and political power. The conflict is to be understood as an essential element in the definition of class. Finally, contrary to the thesis of regulation of conflict as given by Dahrendorf, our commitment is to the resolution of conflict between classes.

Social Profile of the Village

Hoshiarpur is a backward district of Punjab and has a total population of 1,052,153 persons. According to the 1971 census, the percentage of the scheduled castes in Hoshiarpur district was 28.75, which is higher than that of either Punjab (24.7%) or India as a whole (14.67%). Arjam is a big village occupying 2,319 acres of land. In the district of Hoshiarpur, those villages whose areas are between 2,001 to 5,000 acres number 66 (4.03%). Arjam is at a distance of 15 Km from Hoshiarpur. It has a pucca road which links it with both the Hoshiarpur-Jullundur and the Hoshiarpur-Phagwara main roads. It is 5 km from the nearest railway station, Sham Chaurasi. Bus facility is also available to the village. A government operated bus comes to the village in the evening from Hoshiarpur and goes back in the next morning. The village can also boast of having electricity. It has a medical sub-centre under the Family Planning Programme. Drinking water is supplied through the village wells and handpumps. The total number of wells in the village is seven. Besides there are two schools both being co-educational. The total number of literate persons in the village is 589 (416 males and 173 females), the literacy being 33.40 per cent of the total village population. The village has a lower percentage of literacy than that of the whole district Hoshiarpur, i.e., 40.89 per cent. The Punjab state has only 33.67 per cent literates which is little higher than the village.

Apart from a post office, two cooperative banks, namely, Patti Rehmat Khan Bank and the Ajram Jadid Bank, also function in the village. There are eight petty shops. There are two Gurdwaras in the village one for higher caste Sikhs and backward classes, and the other is for Chamars/Ad-dharmis.

At present, the village has a total population of 2,259 persons. Nearly 61 per cent of the village population consists of the scheduled castes. The village has three distinct caste groups: the upper castes predominantly represented by Jats, the backward classes (intermediate castes) and the scheduled castes. In terms of the number of households and population, the scheduled castes have the largest number (61.26%), followed by upper castes (29.04%). The backward classes are numerically the smallest in the village (8.70%). There are 95 households of Jats, two of Brahmins, five of Mehtons (Rajput Sikhs), two each of Sainis and Banias and one of Suniara. There are fourteen households of Tarkhans (carpenter caste), seven of Kumhars, three of Jheers, five of Bhanjras (barber caste) and one of Bhatras. In the case of scheduled castes, 117 households belong to Chamars/Ad-dharmis, 55 to Churhas, five to Julahas and four to Bazigars. The caste composition of Ajram and number of households are given in Table 1.

Distribution of Harijan Population

The four Harijan castes having 201 households in the village have a population of 1,390. The distribution of Harijan population and number of households according to the castes is given in Table 2.

Table 1

Number of castes and their respective households

Castes	*Households*
• Upper Castes	
Jat	95
Brahmin	2
Mehton	5
Saini	2
Bania	2
Suniara	1

cont'd...

cont'd...

• Backward Classes	
Tarkhan	14
Kumhar	7
Jheer	3
Bhanjra	5
Bhatra	1
• Scheduled Castes	
Julaha	5
Chamar	147
Churha/Balmiki	55
Bazigar	4
Total	348

Table 2

Number of scheduled castes and their households and population

Scheduled Castes	*No. of Households*	*Population*
Julaha	5	31
Chamar	147	981
Churha/Balmiki	55	357
Bazigar	4	21
Total	211	1390

Land Use and Landholdings

According to the village Patwari, Ajram has 2,280 acres of land under cultivation. Most of the land in the village belongs to the Jat families. The Mehtons rank second in the landholdings. The backward classes, especially the Tarkhans and the Kumhars, have land between three to twelve acres. Most of the scheduled castes are landless. Among them only 21 families own half to six acres of land. It is of significance to note that all the land owned by the scheduled castes is not of good quality. It is called 'Rakkar' (cultivable waste) in the regional language and is not fertile at all.

Table 3
Land use

Type of Land	*Land (in acres)*
Irrigated	56
Unirrigated	2,117
Cultivable waste	53
Area not available for cultivation	93
Total	2,319

Source: Census of India 1971, District Census Handbook, District Hoshiarpur (Village and Town Directory), Part X-A and B.

Table 4
Population, households and landholdings of different caste groups

Caste Groups	*Households*	*Population*	*Landholdings (in acres)*
Higher castes	107	659	2177.5
Backward classes (intermediate castes)	30	210	36.0
Scheduled castes	211	1,390	66.5
Total	348	2,259	2,280

Political Conditions

Here, the primary concern is with the panchayat elections and the caste status of office bearers of village panchayat and decision-making process in the village. The caste of the office bearers of village panchayat in 1972 is described in Table 5.

Table 5
Office bearers of village panchayat elected in 1972 according to caste, level of education and landholdings

Caste	*Designation*	*Education*	*Landholding (in acres)*
Jat	Sarpanch	Matriculation	50
Jat	Panch	Intermediate	30
Jat	Panch	Matric	10
Jat	Panch	Primary	8.5
Jat	Panch	Primary	35
Jat (female)	Panch	Illiterate	13*
Chamar	Panch	Illiterate	3

*Husband's landholdings.

The Sarpanch as well as five members of the panchayat belonged to the Jat caste. There was only one scheduled caste member. The caste status of office bearers according to the 1978 panchayat elections, which underwent some change, is given in Table 6.

Table 6

Office bearers of village panchayat elected in 1978 according to caste, level of education and landholdings

Caste	*Designation*	*Education*	*Landholding (in acres)*
Jat	Sarpanch	Matric*	50
Jat	Panch	Illiterate*	6.5
Jat	Panch	Matric*	10
Jat (female)	Panch	Illiterate	30**
Tarkhan (female)	Panch	Illiterate	4**
Chamar	Panch	Illiterate*	No land
Chamar	Panch	Illiterate	3
Chamar	Panch	Primary	3

* Re-elected.
**Husband's landholdings.

Besides the Sarpanch who belongs to the Jat caste, there are three other member in the village panchayat from amongst Jats. Among the remaining members one is from Tarkhan caste while three are Chamars.

In the history of the village panchayat the village had a scheduled caste Sarpanch only once. But, the Jats have been dominating the decision-making process in the village since 1947. The Harijan Sarpanch was undoubtedly helpless against the power of landowners. He could never settle any dispute among the Jats. Sometimes he was beaten by the Jats. The overall profile of the village was characterised by two interrelated dimensions, namely, the economic and political domination of the Jat Sikhs and numerical preponderance of the scheduled castes.

Profile of the Respondents

The respondents constituted the village elite in terms of participation in the political process though at the same time efforts were made to give the Harijans more coverage than that of the upper castes. In all 20 persons of the village were interviewed and all of them were involved in the village level politics. It is worthwhile to examine their socio-economic profile.

Occupation

All the Jat respondents were owner-cultivators. But leaving two respondents, seven of them were engaged in some other occupations than agriculture. Two were in military service, two were drivers (one was truck-driver, the other was taxi-driver), one was and is still a teacher, one was and is still a Registered Medical Practitioner and the last one was a clerk in Khadi Bhandar. The fathers of all the Jat respondents were the owner-cultivators. In the case of three respondents, their fathers had also served in the army.

The occupational status of Harijan respondents is given below: Out of eleven respondents eight were agricultural labourers. Some of them did other jobs than wage labour. Majority of them (6) were also the weavers. Four of them were also owner-cultivators. One was a sharecropper. One was petty shopkeeper. Similarly, their father's occupations were weaving (7) and sharecropping (4). The data reveal that one Harijan has to do more than one job because of his economic conditions. Even some of them who are owner-cultivators are also agricultural workers, which shows there lower positions in the economic hierarchy.

Ownership of Wealth

All the Jat respondents owned land. One Jat respondent owned 50 acres of land. Three of them had 20 to 24 acres. Two had twelve and thirteen acres of land, one owned ten acres of land and the two others owned 8.5 acres and six acres of land. All of them had tubewells. All had irrigated land. But, in some cases, the half of the land was irrigated. In the case of seven Jat respondents everyone had two tubewells. Two had tractors. Every Jat respondent had a pucca house. The number of rooms varied from three to eight.

In the case of Harijan respondents, six of them did not have any land. In case of three respondents each one of them owned three acres of land. One had four acres of land. One had bought eight acres of land by taking loan from the government, but that land was outside the village. Of the five landowner Harijans, three had non-irrigated land and two had irrigated land having their own tubewells. But it is significant to note that the land belonging to the Harijan respondents is invariably semi-fertile. Table 7 indicates the size of landholdings of both the Jat and the Harijan respondents. Though only one of the Harijan respondents had kutcha house, yet as compared to the Jats the Harijan respondents had one to three rooms semi-pucca or pucca houses.

Table 7

Landholdings of the respondents

Landholding (in acres)	*Jats*	*Scheduled Castes*
No land	0	6
1–5	0	4
6–10	3	1
11–20	2	0
21–30	3	0
31–50	1	0

Educational Status

It is interesting to note that out of nine Jat respondents only one was illiterate. Out of eight educated respondents, one had got primary education. Out of the remaining five were matriculates, one was intermediate and one was O.T. (an examination to pass to be a Punjabi teacher). Out of eleven Harijan respondents six were illiterates, one was just literate, two had primary education, and the remaining two of them had education up to middle class.

Table 8

Educational status of the respondents

Educational Status	*Jats*	*Scheduled Castes*	*Total*
Illiterate	1	6	7
Literate	0	1	1
Primary	1	2	3
Middle	0	2	2
Matric	5	0	5
Above	2	0	2
Total	9	11	20

So far as the educational status of the fathers of the respondents is concerned, it was found that among the Jat respondents six had literate/educated fathers and the other three had illiterate fathers. None of the fathers of the Harijan respondents were literates. In the case of the educational status of the children of the Jat respondents, it was found that in most of the cases their sons had college education. Out of nine, seven respondents' sons were either studying or had studied. In one respondent's case, his sons had left their studies after having passed the middle standard examination.

In the case of the Harijan respondents, there were only three respondents whose sons had got college education. In the case of the other eight respondents it was found that their sons' education was up to either 8th or 10th class. But it is significant to note that all of them had some of their sons either illiterates or school dropouts.

So far as the reasons for dropping out of the schools are concerned the responses were quite interesting. The Jat respondents informed that their sons were not good in studies. One of the reasons for this was that they had to help their parents in the fields. But, the Harijan respondents said that their sons could not study because of their low economic condition. They could not afford it. The difference in the reasons given by both the Jat and Harijan respondents is significant and reveals how one action could be a result of altogether different factors. The factors betray the inherent structural asymmetries in which caste-class overlap each other.

Indebtedness

Our data reveal that all the Jat respondents were under debt. One respondent's debt was Rs 310, whereas others' debts exceeded Rs 1,000. In the case of two Jats the amounts of debt were Rs 40,000 and Rs 60,000. The sources of money were co-operative societies of the village, Land Mortgage Bank, Hoshiarpur, and Punjab and Sindh Bank, Hoshiarpur. The rates of interest were 10–12 per cent per year. The reasons for debt were related to the economic interests. Some of them had taken crop loans; one took loan to buy a tractor, etc. The other reasons like, to purchase the fertilizers, to level the land, etc., were given by the Jat respondents.

In the case of scheduled caste respondents, three of them were not under debt though in the past they had been under debt. In the case of three respondents, the amount of debt varied between Rs 2,000 to

10,000. The amount of debt in case of four respondents was up to Rs 1,000. For the rest (one) it was below Rs 500. Sources of debt were co-operative societies of the village, Forestry Department, Indian Overseas Bank and the moneylenders. The rates of interest were 10 per cent to 12 per cent in the case of co-operative societies and the banks. But, in the case of moneylenders it was 5 per cent per month (60% per year). The reasons given by them were entirely different from the Jats. Basically, it was survival problem, then to marry their sons or daughters and also in some cases for the development of land.

Selling of Land

Out of nine Jat respondents, seven had sold their land at some point of time. Only two of them had never sold land. Three sold land from 10 to 15 acres costing Rs 50,000 to 1,10,000 and other four had sold one to five acres of land costing Rs 10,000 to 20,000. The reasons given by the respondents were: the land was unmanageable, or it was surplus. In some cases, the purpose was to buy the agricultural equipments, and in one case, a truck. In most of the cases the land was bought again.

In the case of scheduled caste respondents who owned land, none of them have ever sold it. The reason was very simple. The quality of land was not good. Thus, the value of land would be very low. They could not find any person who would buy that land.

Interaction: Formal and Informal

Though there was much interaction both at the formal and informal levels among the different castes, yet all the respondents indicated that they had more interaction with their own caste people. But some of the scheduled castes respondents said that while they visited the Jats but they in turn did not visit them. So, in terms of purity and pollution, the distance between the higher and lower castes is not so wide as is found in various parts of the country.

Criterion of Prestige

Out of the twenty respondents (both Jats and Harijans), ten (six scheduled castes and four Jats) considered landownership as the basis of prestige. Two regarded power as the basis of prestige and rest of them viewed moral character as a very important factor. But interestingly, while majority (9) of the Harijans either gave primary or secondary importance to wealth and power, most of the Jats either gave primary or secondary importance to the moral character. Two Jat respondents did not consider wealth or landownership as the basis of the prestige at all.

Political Characteristics

Out of twenty respondents, six were members of the village panchayat. Besides the Sarpanch, two other members also belonged to the Jat caste. The rest belonged to the Chamar caste. One Jat respondent's wife was earlier a member of panchayat. The other 12 respondents were either ex-panchayat members or had contested the elections but lost. Two of them had been Sarpanch of the village, of which one belonged to the Jat caste while the other was Chamar. One Jat respondent was ex-panch of the village panchayat. Four of the Harijan respondents had also been panchayat members. Three respondents had lost in the elections. One of the Jat respondents had never contested any election, but he had played a major role in the previous two elections.

The political affiliations of the Jat respondents were as follows: five of them were affiliated to the Akali Dal, two were supporters and voters of the Congress, and one each was affiliated to CPI and CPI (M). Among the Harijan respondents it was found that six were pro-Janata Party. One of them had been a member of the Republican Party of India, but at the time of data collection he was not affiliated to any political party. It is interesting to note that out that all the six respondents who voted for the Janata Party in the recent elections had been voting for the Congress in the previous elections. One was affiliated to Akali Dal and the rest supported the Congress. Most of the Harijan respondents answered to this query in terms of voting.

On being asked, "How did the Sarpanch and the Panchs get the votes?", both the Jat and the Harijan respondents said that money was given by the contestants to the voters. Eight out of nine Jat respondents said that some Jats had given inducements in the form of either money or food grains. In some cases liquor had been provided by the contestants. But interestingly none of them had said that they themselves had given money to the voters. Seven out of eleven scheduled caste respondents told that the Jats had given money to the Harijan voters. Some of the Jat respondents (4) and most of the Harijan (7) respondents reported that the Sarpanch had cheated them. He got false votes polled in favour of him. Interestingly, it was found that among the Jat respondents, those who were affiliated to political parties other than the Akali Dal raised strong objections against the Sarpanch.

To the query "Who should be the Sarpanch?" the responses were very notable. Out of nine Jat respondents four gave primary importance to the economic conditions of the Sarpanch and two gave secondary importance to the economic conditions, the rest of the respondents did not regard money as important at all. Five attached primary importance to the educational status of the Sarpanch and only one attached secondary importance to the education. Rest of the respondents did not consider education important. None of the respondents considered caste.

On the other hand, out of 11 scheduled caste respondents, six gave primary importance to wealth, while one gave secondary importance to it. Rest of the respondents did not regard money very important. So far as the education and honesty are concerned, only four attached utmost importance to them. It was only one Harijan respondent who was of the opinion that the Sarpanch of the village should be from that caste whose number was the highest in the village. In an indirect manner, he was advocating for a Chamar Sarpanch. Though it seems that the Jat and the Harijan respondents agree on this issue, yet there is a substantial difference in their statements. While Jat respondents considered that the Sarpanch should be economically sound, the Harijans responded in an entirely different way. They said that a poor man could not be the Sarpanch of the village. So far as the qualifications for a panch were concerned, it was found that majority of the respondents did not attach any importance to them. But some of them viewed that same qualifications are necessary for a panch, which were there for a Sarpanch.

To the query "Who have the political power and why?" the responses were predictable. Eight out of nine Jat respondents informed that Jats had the political power. One of the respondents said that Harijans had the political power. The reasons given by them were the following: six out of the eight respondents said that they had land and economic power; one of them identified more representation of the Jats in the panchayat as a source of power; one other respondent indicated that the Jats were more intelligent than Harijans; only one Jat respondent said that the Jats were not united while the Harijan were.

All the scheduled caste respondents were of the opinion that Jats had the political power in the village. Some of them also used the expression 'Zamindars' for Jats. All the Harijan respondents indicated landownership as the main source of their political power. They told that even when the Harijan Sarpanch had been elected, the Harijans did not have the power though he was able settle disputes even among the Jats. Some of them stated candidly that he had been a puppet in the hands of Jats. They used to provide him liquor and sometimes he was beaten by Jats. Thus, in Ajram, the Harijans never had any power in the decision-making process. Jats had the real power.

The data also reveal that the politics and economics are integrated with each other in the village. The Harijans cannot capture power merely by getting their more members elected in the panchayat. It will become clearer when we discuss the conflict between these two major classes in the village.

Manifestations of Conflict

It is our contention that the unequal distribution of economic and political power has the highest probability of the emergence of conflict between Jats (landowners) and the Harijans (landless wage earners). And this conflict manifests itself when the pressure on the powerless increases. The landowners use every method, like manipulation, force, etc., to keep themselves in power. Though only three issues have been taken to study the conflict between the powerful and the powerless, but during the investigation it was found that the Jats and Harijans had been in perpetual conflict since 1947. Some of the Harijans reported that during 1950s, the major issue of conflict between the two groups was the Punjabi-Hindi conflict. In the history of the village, many such issues of conflict have emerged at different points of time. But, here, we are taking only two incidents, one of which is political, whereas the other is economic. But we shall see how the political and economic powers are integrated with each other in both the cases. The third incident took place in a nearby village. But it aroused the feelings of Harijans of the whole region and they protested against it. It is of relevance to point out here that our contention is to see the conflict as an essential element in the asymmetrical relations when there are classes. The Harijans did not organise themselves along certain ideological lines to transform the existing structure. These conflicts were spontaneous and could not be sustained by them for a long time. Let us examine the incidents one by one, and how the respondents villagers to it.

Conflict over Wages

The first event occurred three years ago.[2] It was a dispute over wages between the Jats and the Harijans. At that time daily wages of a worker was Rs 5 in the village. The Harijans asked the Jats to increase their wages from Rs 5 to Rs 6. But, the latter did not agree. The Harijans' demand was genuine, because in all the nearby villages the wages of agricultural labour were Rs 6 per day. They decided to stop working in the fields of the Jats. Subsequently, they started working on the fields of the Jats in other villages.

The Jats immediately reacted to the strike. They prohibited the Harijans from entering their fields. The Harijans reported to the police. The police urged the panchayat and some important members among Harijans to decide. Since in the panchayat Jats were powerful, they imposed their decision that wages would be increased from Rs 5 to Rs 5.25 per day. It could happen because one of the Harijan leaders accepted the proposal, as he was widely known as a 'chamcha' of the Jats. The police considered it a fair decision and the wages were increased to Rs 5.25 per day. In a way the decision was in favour of the Jats.

When the respondents were asked to comment on the incident, they responded in the following way: Out of nine Jat respondents three considered that the decision was in favour of the Harijans two regarded it a right decision which implied that it was in favour of the Jats, and three were of the opinion that it was against the interests of Harijans. One of the respondents considered it against Harijans at that time, but at the same time he pointed out that their wages at that time were more than enough.

Eight of the Harijan respondents considered that decision was against the interests of the Harijans. Six of them regarded it an atrocity on Harijans. Two others pointed out that even 25 paise were never paid by the Jats. Only one of them was of the opinion that the decision was in favour of Harijans. One other respondent considered it a compromise.

The data thus reveal that the economic and political power of the Jats leads to their domination in the decision-making process. At the same time, it is significant to note that in spite of factional conflicts among the Jats, they unite when there is a threat to their common economic interests from the outside caste groups.

Conflict for Power

This incident is a recent one. It took place in the 1978 panchayat elections. The present Sarpanch was the main instrument behind this conflict. It is important to indicate that this time various rules had changed. Under the new rules, there would be one Harijan member in the panchayat if any one of them was not elected in the elections. But this rule was interpreted to the Harijans in an entirely different way when the nominations were filed. The Harijans came to know that there would be only one Harijan in the panchayat as told by the Presiding Officer. They reacted very strongly and decided that none of the Harijans would vote. All of them went to Hoshiarpur on the day of elections. They met some political leaders, the Deputy Commissioner and Block Development Officer (BDO). All of them advised them not to boycott the elections to which they agreed. They returned to the village. The BDO also reached the village. The remaining votes were polled in the presence of the BDO. More time was also given. But during their absence from the village the polling had continued. Some of the Jat respondents got false votes polled in favour of them. With the result, only three Harijans were elected out of total eight panchayat members. Consequently, a Jat became the Sarpanch of the village.

Out of nine Jat respondents five considered this incident to be in favour of Harijans. Some of them stated that it did not affect the results. Five Jat respondents said that diplomacy was not used by them. But, the other four Jat respondents said that the present Sarpanch cheated the Harijans. They also said that the incident affected the results, otherwise, more Harijans would have been elected.

Out of 11 Harijan respondents nine considered it an example of the atrocity of the Jats on the Harijans. Some of the Harijans pointed out that the Jats had always behaved like that. They said that the result of the elections was in favour of the Jats. There was only one Harijan respondent who thought that the Harijans benefited from it. One of the respondents showed ignorance of the incident.

Thus analysing the above data, we are confronted with the basic question, i.e., "If by mere representation in the panchayat the Harijan cannot have power, then why there was conflict between the Jats and the Harijans in elections". It is a typical example of the role of 'myth' created by the ruling elite. The ruling class does not rule merely through the economic and political control, but it also rules over the consciousness of men. Here, the myth of democracy is created by the ruling class. The Harijans are under the illusion that by more representation in the panchayat, they will have power. Gramsci (1973: 133), in his 'Prison Notes' comments on the myths created by the ruling class in the following way thus:

> "The Modern Prince, the Prince myth, cannot be a real person, a concrete individual, it can only be an organism a complex element of society, in which a collective will ... beings to take concrete form. Such an organism has already been provided by historical development and it is the political party, the first cell in which germs of a collective will come together and tend to become universal and total ... In men's conscience, the Prince takes the place of the divinity or the categorical imperative and becomes the basis for a modern laicism and for a complete laicization of all aspects of life and of all customary relationship."

After the creation of myth, the ruling elites require minimum force to control the underprivileged section of society. In spite of the fact that they are powerless without the economic power, they think that they will get power merely by being elected in the panchayat.

The Murder of a Harijan Woman

This incident occurred in a nearby village. The Harijan woman was killed by some of the Nihangs of a Gurdwara. It will be of relevance to explain how the Nihangs are related to the Jats. In fact, the Nihangs and the Jats are not two different categories. They are one and the same thing. The only difference lies in their activities. While the Jats are landowners, the Nihangs are religious fighters in the Gurdwaras of Punjab. In terms of caste, the Nihangs are Jats and they are also landowners.[3]

The murder of a Harijan woman aroused the feelings of the Harijans and they made an organised protest. Some political parties also tried to exploit the situation to win over the Harijans, while some parties kept quiet. It was found during our investigation that the Jats prevented the Harijans from going to that place. Because of continuous protest by Harijans, the government had to take some action. They arrested some Nihangs of the Gurdwara. At present, there is no overt conflict.

The respondents were asked to narrate the whole incident in their own words and to give their views on it. Out of nine Jat respondents, six regarded the incident a political stunt. It was an unsuccessful effort on the part of the Congress and Nirankaris to make scandal out of nothing. The conditions under which she was murdered were such that any woman could be murdered. Five of the Jat respondents informed that the woman had illicit relations with some 'sewadars' in that Gurdwara. According to them, the question of lower or higher castes did not arise.

It is significant to note that five of them were Akalis and the sixth was a CPI supporter. The other three Jat respondents regarded it as an atrocity of the Nihangs on the Harijans. They were of the opinion that because of her lower caste she was killed. If she were of a higher caste, she could not have been murdered under any conditions. Interestingly, two of the Jat respondents were politically affiliated to the Congress, while the one was CPI (M) supporter.

Out of 11 Harijan respondents 10 considered it an example of atrocities on Harijans. It was only one respondent who was of the opinion that the Akali Dal did not play any negative role. It is interesting to note that he was associated with the Akali Dal, but the other nine respondents regarded that the Akali Dal had played pro-Nihang role in that situation. One of the respondents showed his ignorance of the incident. It is thus clear that in the conflict situation between the Jats and the Harijans, their total perception of the situation depends on their political affiliation and the role played by that political party in that situation.

Conclusion

The analysis of the data on the economic structure of village suggests that the scheduled castes are economically lower placed. The ownership of land and wealth is almost negligible among them. It may be stated that the scheduled castes, who are low in the caste hierarchy, are basically low in the economic hierarchy. This has also been pointed out by Bardhan (1974: 45), when he writes:

> Ours is an extremely unequal society. Not merely is our social structure characterized by some of the most invidious forms of inequalities of income, wealth, status and power, we have also developed over centuries a uniquely elaborate system of legitimizing

them. So deeply ingrained is this system in our social mores and ritual sanctions and so wide-ranging are its everyday manifestations that we are sometimes even regarded as a peculiarly hierarchical breed of people. Yet what may pass for preordained ritual ranking in our society is quite often a form of stratification based ultimately on differential access to economic resources. Social distance caused by wealth and poverty often takes the form of distinctions built around notions of purity and pollution.

The political conditions of the village suggest that the Harijans are a politically deprived class. It is the landowner Jats who have political power even though the Harijans constitute a numerical majority. Since mere representation in the panchayat cannot provide the real political power until they do not have economic power, it is the lower economic status of the scheduled castes, which deprived them of the political power. But, there are some more points, which have emerged in our study. These are as follows:

(i) In spite of the presence of factions among the Jats, they unite when there is a threat to their common economic interests from the outside caste groups.
(ii) In the conflict situation between the Harijans and the Jats, their perception of the situation depends on their association with political party and the role played by that party in that situation.

During the investigation, many Harijan respondents pointed out that if a Jat was poor, he would not be a Harijan, he would consider himself as one of the Jats and if the Harijan was rich, he would still be a Harijan. In a way the important place of one's caste belonging was stressed by the Harijan respondents.

Here, I intend to state that society is much more complex. It is not that the caste system has no autonomy of its own. Fanon has explained the relationship between blacks and the whites in the colonial countries. He writes that the white man is also an oppressed at the same time, while the black man is also an oppressed at the same time. The substructural (political) relationship between the oppressor and the oppressed determines the superstructural relationship between white and black. In this situation blackness becomes stigma attached to the black man (Fanon, 1967). As it has been already pointed out that Gramsci (1973) in his discussion on 'myth' has explained the same thing, i.e., to get the hegemonic control over the masses, the ruling class consciously creates myths. Lukács also discusses the same thing when he talks of reifications. Swingewood (1977) writes that for Lukács, "Reification means the society satisfied its needs through commodity exchange, capitalist development thus brings with it a deepening structure of reification which fatefully dominates social consciousness. Like Simmel, Lukács sees this process as total stamping its 'imprint upon the whole consciousness of man' so that his various qualities and abilities ceases to be his expression, but that of another, things which he can own or 'dispose of' like the various objects of the external world."

Our contention is to point out that the caste system in terms of purity and pollution is a myth created by the upper castes to control the underprivileged sections of Hindu society. The philosophy of karma is a classic example of the 'myths'. Thus, the problem of the scheduled castes is embodied in the social system itself. The only possible way for them, if we follow Fanon, is to annihilate these stigmas in an organised violent struggle. But, unlike Fanon's blacks in the colonial countries, the Harijans in India are a large minority. There are approximately half of the total population which are below poverty line, whereas the scheduled castes constitute only 14 per cent of the Indian population. Taking Marx's 'law of quantity and quality' into consideration, only Harijans cannot transform the system. They will have to make alliances with the other economically deprived castes. This paradox will take time to resolve. Till then, what is needed is long struggle both at the level of consciousness, and political practice.

Notes

This paper was earlier published in P.N. Pimpley and Satish K. Sharma (eds.) *Struggle for Status*, B.R. Publishers, 1985. Apart from a few slight changes on the part of the publishers, one of the modifications made in this version is that its referencing system has been changed for the sake of uniformity.

1. In this paper the words 'Harijans' and 'scheduled castes' have been used interchangeably. At the time of writing this article, the expression 'Harijan' was quite popular. It was later on rejected on account of its association with Gandhi by the dalit leaders.
2. It occurred in 1975. Since this paper was written in 1978 the expression 'three years ago' was suffice fro the limited purpose as a project report.

3. For the sake of argument I have made Jat and Nihang coterminous, but it is not in reality. Among the Nihangs, one of the organisations is called Rangretas, which is comprised by the Mazabis.

References

Anderson, Charles H. 1974. *The Political Economy of Social Class.* New Jersey: Englewood Cliffs, Prentice Hall.

Bardhan, Pranab K. 1974. *Some Aspects of inequality in Population in India's Development, 1947–2000.* New Delhi: Vikas Publishers.

Bryant, C.C.A. 1976. *Sociology in Action*, London: George Alien and Unwin Ltd.

Dahrendorf, R. 1959. *Class and Class Conflict in Industrial Society.* London: Routledge and Kegan Paul.

Fanon, Frantz. 1967. *The Wretched of the Earth.* Harmondsworth: Penguin Books.

Gramsci, Antonio. 1973. *Selections from Prison Notebooks.* New York: International Publishers.

Lenski, G.E. 1966. *Power and Privilege: A Theory of Social Stratification.* New York: McGraw Hill Inc.

Marx, Karl. 1971. *Capital: A Critique of Political Economy* (Vol. III). Moscow: Progress Publishers.

Reissman, L. 1970. "Social Stratification" in Neil J. Smelser (ed.), *Sociology: An Introduction.* New Delhi: Wiley Eastern Pvt. Ltd.

Shanin, T. (ed.). 1976. *Peasants and Peasant Societies.* Harmondsworth: Penguin Books.

Singh, Yogendra. 1977. *Social Stratification and Social Change in India.* Delhi: Manohar Publishers.

Swingewood, A. 1977. *Marx and Modern Social Theory.* London: The Macmillan Press, Ltd.

Weber, Max. 1974. "Class, Status and Party", in Joseph Lopreats and Lionel S. Levis (eds.), *Social Stratification: A Reader.* New York: Harper and Row.

3

Scheduled Castes and Development from Above

The present paper is mainly aimed at highlighting the effectiveness of governmental efforts to improve the economic conditions of the scheduled castes living below the poverty line. The objective of this paper is to evaluate the Special Component Plan (SCP) for the scheduled castes drafted by the Government of Punjab for the Sixth Five-Year Plan.

The Government of India, in accordance with the 20-Point Economic Programme, has stressed the economic uplift of the depressed sections like the scheduled castes, the scheduled tribes, women and children. The SCP is one of the major steps towards that goal. The SCP has been accorded a significant place in the Sixth Plan. The Government of Punjab has also made efforts to implement this plan. The objectives of the SCP are as follows:

- To enable at least 50 per cent of the scheduled castes in the country to cross the poverty line by the end of the Sixth Plan period.
- To remove the lag in the educational levels of the scheduled castes.

- To improve the working and living conditions of the scheduled castes.
- To promote occupational mobility among the scheduled castes.
- To give special attention in the development efforts to the most vulnerable groups among the scheduled castes, namely, sweepers and scavengers, nomadic, semi-nomadic communities, bonded labourers, and women and children.

The SCP has identified some core sections for economic development of the scheduled castes, viz., animal husbandry, land development and agricultural production, leather, weaving, other cottage and village industries, including sericulture, fisheries and small-scale and tiny sector industries (Government of Punjab, 1984–85).

As compared with the all-India target of putting 50 per cent of the scheduled castes above the poverty line during the Sixth Plan period, the Government of Punjab has set the goal to help all the scheduled castes to cross the poverty line. The Punjab government has made efforts to formulate various schemes in this direction under various development programmes like IRDP (Integrated Rural Development Programme), RLEGP (Rural Landless Employment Guarantee Scheme), NREP (National Rural Employment Programme) among others. The SCP has been implemented by involving various governmental departments.

According to the claims made by the Government of Punjab, 58,064 families during 1981–82 and 84,452 during 1982–83 have been helped to cross the poverty line. The anticipated achievements for 1983–84 and 1984–85 are 95,431 and 99,107 families respectively.

In the light of above, it becomes essential to examine whether all the scheduled castes have been able to cross the poverty line. Since the data had been collected towards the end of 1985 and in the beginning of 1986 when the Sixth Plan period was completed, it was expected that the claims made by the Punjab government would have been fulfilled. During the fieldwork, it was found that the IRDP was the only programme implemented quite seriously irrespective of the extent of its positive implementation. Therefore, data presented in the following discussion will be confined to the IRDP and its evaluation.

The study was carried out in five villages in Hoshiarpur district. In all, 400 interviews were conducted. The selection of the respondents was made on the proportionate-random sampling basis. An interview schedule was administered for the purpose of data collection. Hoshiarpur district has a high concentration scheduled castes. According to the 1981 census, the scheduled castes constitute 30.84 per cent of the total population of the district. This proportion of the scheduled castes is higher than the state average of 26.9 per cent.

The first query was made whether the respondents' families were having yellow cards or not. The yellow cards are meant for those households who have been living below the poverty line and are supposed to get benefits from the various developmental programmes introduced by the government. To this query 60.50 per cent of the respondents replied in the affirmative. The reasons for not issuing yellow cards to the remaining 39.50 per cent were many. Table 1 below shows the reasons for not having the cards according to caste of the respondents. It was only in the case of 12.25 per cent of the respondents' families whose income exceeds the limit, otherwise all other reasons pointed toward some kind of malpractice among the concerned officials, particularly the Gram Sewaks.

Table 1

Caste and reasons for not getting yellow card

Caste	*Did not bribe Gram Sewak*	*Negligence of officials time*	*Reasons not informed in*	*Income exceeds the loan*	*Not applicable*	*Total*
Chamar/ Ramdasya	15 (4.35) (88.24)	42 (12.17) (76.36)	31 (8.99) (83.78)	45 (13.04) (91.84)	212 (61.45) (87.60)	345 (100)
Bhanjra	–	–	–	1 (100) (2.04)	–	1 (100)
Julaha	–	–	–	1 (100) (2.04)	–	1 (100)
Bazigar	–	3 (27.27) (5.46)	–	1 (9.09) (2.04)	7 (63.64) (2.89)	11 (100)
Balmiki	2 (4.76) (11.76)	10 (23.81) (18.18)	6 (14.29) (16.22)	1 (2.38) (2.04)	23 (54.76) (9.50)	42 (100)
Total	17 (4.25) (100)	55 (13.75) (100)	37 (9.25) (100)	49 (12.25) (100)	242 (60.50) (100)	400 (100)

Figures in parentheses indicate percentages.

Table 2

Loan obtained and source of knowledge about the provision of loan

Total loan obtained	*Villagers*	*Source of knowledge*					*Total*
		Friends and acquai-n tances	*Sarpanch or other panchayat members*	*Govt. agencies*	*Bank official*	*Not applicable*	
Yes	19(16.25) (100)	11(9.57) (100)	25(21.74) (100)	46(40.00) (100)	14(12.17) (100)	–	115 (100)
No	–	–	–	–	–	127(100) (44.56)	127 (100)
Not applicable	–	–	–	–	–	158 (100) (55.44)	158 (100)
Total	19 (4.75) (100)	11 (2.75) (100)	25 (23.75) (100)	46 (11.50) (100)	14 (3.50) (100)	285 (71.25) (100)	400 (100)

Figures in parentheses indicate percentages.

It was further found that only 28.75 per cent of the respondents' families obtained loans (see Table 2). Interestingly, a considerable number of the respondents got information regarding these provisions from the informal sources like villagers, friends etc. Of course, in majority of the cases, the government agencies concerned and banks contacted them and gave them information. But more than one-half of the families (i.e., 60 out of 115) who got loans were not helped by anybody. But, in the rest of the cases, the village Sarpanch or Gram Sewak or bank official helped them to get loans. Furthermore, the time taken to get a loan was not very long. It may be understood that most of the official concerned were to complete the target in the given financial year. When the time is running out, they become more eager to give loans than the beneficiaries themselves. But, even then, there were certain cases where it took a relatively long time to get the loan (see Table 3).

Table 3

Time taken to get the loan and the person who helped in getting the loan

	Who helped in getting the loan					
Time taken (in days)	*No body*	*Sarpanch*	*Gram Sewak*	*Bank officers*	*Not applicable*	*Total*
Upto 15	26 (70.27) (43.33)	1 (2.70) (25.0)	8 (21.62) (19.51)	2 (5.41) (20.00)	–	37 (100) (9.25)
16–30	19 (44.19) (31.67)	2 (4.65) (50.00)	19 (44.18) (46.34)	3 (6.98) (30.00)	–	43 (100) (10.75)
31–60	7 (33.33) (11.67)	10 (47.62)	4 (19.05) (24.39)	(40.00)	–	21 (100) (5.25)
61–90	8 (57.14) (13.3 3)	1 (7.14) (25.00)	4 (28.57) (9.76)	1 (7.15) (10.00)	–	14 (100) (3.50)
Not applicable	–	–	–	–	285 (71.25) (100)	285 (100) (71.25)
Total	60 (15.00) (100)	4 (1.00) (100)	41 (10.25) (100)	10 (2.50) (100)	285 (71.25) (100)	400 (100)

Note: Mean number of days spent in getting the loan: 25.25.

Figures in parentheses indicate percentages.

When the respondents were asked to evaluate the time taken to get the loan, 61 of those who obtained loans said that the loans were provided quickly whereas 54 were of the view that there was delay in their getting loans. The responsibility was attributed to the procedure and the attitudes of the officials (see Table 4). Of those respondents who found faults with official procedure 37.5 per cent belonged to Sahari and 27.08 per cent to Bajwara.

One of the important aspects concerning these loan provisions is to know whether the beneficiaries spent the loan amount on what it was meant for. Table 5 reveals the purpose/utilization of loan according to the family income of the respondents. It was found that in the case of only two respondents the loan was utilised not for purpose it was taken but for house construction. But, at the same time, it can be observed that a majority of the respondents who got loans lived above the poverty line. It points towards the fact that the benefits are not properly reaching the very poor families among the scheduled castes. Out of those respondents whose annual family income was up to Rs 3600, 73.08 per cent did not get these benefits.

Table 4

Village and reasons for delay in getting the loan

Village	*Reasons*				*Total*
	Officials procedure	*Indifferent behaviour of official*	*No delay*	*Not applicable*	
Badowal	5 (29.41) (10.42)	–	3 (17.65) (4.92)	9 (52.94) (3.16)	17 (100)
Bajwara	13 (8.07) (27.08)	2 (1.24) (33.33)	15 (9.32) (24.59)	131 (81.37) (45.96)	161 (100)
Mehtiana	2 (3.85) (4.17)	–	1 (19.23) (16.39)	4 (76.92) (14.04)	5 (100)
Phuglana	10 (11.77) (20.83)	3 (3.53) (50.00)	5 (5.88) (8.20)	67 (78.82) (23.51)	85 (100)
Sahri	1 (21.18) (37.5)	(1.18) (16.67)	2 (32.94) (45.90)	3 (44.70) (13.33)	8 (100)
Total	48 (12.00) (100)	6 (1.50) (100)	61 (15.25) (100)	28 (71.25) (100)	400 (100)

Figures in parentheses indicate percentages.

In order to further probe the proper utilisation of benefits accrued to the scheduled castes, a query was made whether other families had properly used the loans. Fewer (4.50 %) respondents indicated that the loans were misutilised by the beneficiaries. But corruption among officials was pointed out by many (10 %). The officials who often took bribes included veterinary doctors, bankmen and Gram Sewaks. Though the discussion on the negative consequences of the IRDP will be undertaken after the description of data, it is relevant to point out that quickness in beneficiaries' getting the loan might be due to the greed of some officers who would be making money out of these benefits for the poor.

Other information gathered about the effectiveness of the IRDP was about the increase in income of those who got the loan. It is important to know how the respondents perceived the role of the IRDP in raising the living standards of the poor. It is relevant to indicate that the income of the respondents before and after getting the loan was not taken into account because in all cases they failed to provide information either intentionally or unintentionally.

Table 5

Family income and utilisation of loan

Total income (Rs)	*Buffalo*	*Shop*	*Weaving machine*	*Handicraft material*	*Shoe making material*	*Jute spinning machine*	*House Construction*	*Not applicable*	*Total*
Up to 3600	13 (30.23)	5 (25)	11 (31.43)	–	1 (16.67)	5 (71.44)	–	95 (33.33)	130
3601–6400	20 (46.52)	8 (40)	15 (42.86)	–	4 (66.67)	1 (14.28)	2 (100)	97 (34.03)	147
6401–10,000	8 (18.60)	5 (25)	8 (22.86)	–	–	1 (14.28)	–	52 (18.25)	74
10,000–45,000	2 (4.65)	2 (10)	1 (2.85)	2 (100)	1 (16)	–	–	41 (14.39)	49
Total	43 (100)	20 (100)	36 (100)	2 (100)	6 (100)	7 (100)	2 (100)	285 (100)	

Note: Figure in parentheses are columnwise percentage.

Table 6
Total amount of loan and increase in income

Loan amount (Rs)	*Income increased*	*Marginally increased*	*No effect*	*Not applicable*	*Total*
Up to 3,000	31 (64.58)	21 (72.41)	27 (71.05)	–	79 (19.75)
3001–6000	17 (35.42)	8 (27.59)	11 (28.95)	–	36 (9)
Not applicable	–	–	–	285 (100)	285 (71,25)
Total	48 (100)	29 (100)	38 (100)	285 (100)	400 (100)

Note: Figure in parentheses are columnwise percentage.

Table 6 presents data on the amount of loan taken and the increase in income, if any. The data reveal that of all those respondents who took a loan up to Rs 3,000, 34.18 per cent pointed out that there was no effect, whereas 39.24 per cent and 26.58 per cent respectively said that their income increased significantly or marginally. But, in the case of those respondents who took loans amounting between Rs 3,001 and Rs 6,000, the increase in income was significant. It may, however, be pointed out that most of the respondents took loans only once which in the case of loan for milch animals is not economically viable (see Table 7). In fact, according to the IRDP, the beneficiary is supposed to buy the second animal after a particular period of time about which none of the respondents was conscious of.

Table 7
Number of times got the loan

Number of times	*Number*	*Percentage*
Once	92	23.00
Twice	23	5.75
Not applicable	285	71.25
Total	400	100

To the query whether these provisions were helpful, 66.75 per cent said that these generated income. But 29.50 per cent of the total who said that these provisions were not helpful gave reasons like:

(a) provisions are not reaching the poor (15.50% of the total);
(b) purchased assets are not sufficient to generate income (0.75%);

(c) no market for the finished products (0.75%);
(d) it is a political stunt or eye-wash (4.75%); and
(e) corruption in the governmental machinery (1.00%).

Thus, the implementation of the IRDP is weak. It will become further clear from the following discussion based on the field observation:

(a) A considerable number of scheduled castes living below the poverty line did not possess yellow cards. The fault lies in the way the yellow cards are issued according to the political interest of the village Sarpanch. In all the cases, the officials, responsible for identifying the potential beneficiaries, would go to the village Sarpanch who, motivated by his local political interests, would see to it that only his supporters get the yellow cards. Since the Sarpanch in most of the cases is a landlord also, he would favour his own class. Thus, a general consequence is that the most deserving families do not get the yellow cards.
(b) Even if poor families manage to get the yellow cards which also happens in good number of cases, then they face problems in actually getting the benefits. The families which get loans to buy milch animals face various problems. First, they have to wait for a cattle fair from where they are supposed to buy milch animals. The cattle fair may not necessarily be held at a nearby place which implies additional costs for the transportation of animals. Second, to get the animal declared fit, they often have to bribe the veterinary doctor up to Rs 50 per animal. Those who get loans to start their own work, the problems are different. They are not given the loan amount in cash but are told to buy materials from a particular shop. The shopkeepers provide them with inferior raw material at high prices. After finishing the product, they face marketing problems. In the absence of government help, they have to sell their products at lower prices.
(c) There is no follow-up action, i.e., the officials concerned do not bother whether the purpose of giving the loan has been achieved. In the absence of such practical orientations the entire purpose is defeated. It can be seen that in spite of the provisions for the second buffalo or other milch animals, most of the beneficiaries get one animal only.

(d) There is a tendency to misutilise the loans or the subsidy amount. Loans are often used to meet marriage expenses, in clearing debt with landlords or the house construction. The landlord, when the indebted person fails to return the debt, tells him to apply for a loan from a government agency. The landlord also helps him in obtaining the loan and then corners all the money. Then, it is the responsibility of the loanee to return the loan. This practice becomes possible because of the corruption among various officials. The loan in such cases is generally taken by showing milch animal which the beneficiary already possesses. This is done in connivance with the loan issuing authorities.

During the field investigation three interesting cases were found:

(i) In one of the villages studied, a scheduled caste person contacted the researcher in order to seek help. He told him that he had bought a goat by obtaining a loan. After some time the goat died and in spite of his appeals to the authority concerned, he had not been compensated. When he was asked who, according to him, was the real culprit, he named a particular bank manager. To probe the issue further, the researcher took him to that bank official where, to his embarrassment, he confessed that he obtained the loan for goats which he already possessed. But, the story does not end there. Later, the researcher discovered that the subsidy amount was divided among different persons involved in this deal including the beneficiary.

(ii) The second case is based on the information provided by some people of yet another village studied. This related to a bank manager who in order to achieve the target set by the government, devised a peculiar method. Instead of disbursing loans to the beneficiaries, he would take the entire amount and deposit it in another bank where he had already opened his account. After that he would pay the monthly instalment to his own bank quite regularly. Since a lot of officials were involved in the identification of such beneficiaries, the subsidy amount was divided among them. This is a case where the bank manager could demonstrate absolute success not only in achieving the targets to disburse loans but also in the repayment of loans. Perhaps, such officers have helped the Punjab government to claim that the poverty has been eradicated in the state by the end of the Sixth Plan.

(iii) The third case pertains to the way a beneficiary exploited the rules governing the IRDP. He took a loan for a buffalo which he never purchased. By manipulating the officials through bribes he showed the buffalo owned by his neighbour as his own. After that, somebody else's buffalo died and he claimed the compensation by informing officials that the buffalo purchased by him had died. He managed to get the certificate from the veterinary doctor by bribing him and got the compensation.

On the basis of the above discussions and the three cases, the following conclusions can be drawn:

(a) There is a gross bungling in the distribution of yellow cards. A few scheduled castes who are really poor have got yellow cards; otherwise influential people have managed to get yellow cards.
(b) There does not seem to be any systematic attempt to identify a beneficiary by the officials. They seem to pick up the persons at random.
(c) The government agencies, including banks, are more concerned in achieving the targets than giving attention to the utilisation of loans in a proper manner.
(d) The people who have taken loans fail to generate sufficient income.
(e) The provision of subsidy has brought corruption among the officials as well as among beneficiaries.

A recent survey conducted by Goyal (1986) in Hoshiarpur and seven other districts of Punjab points out the same results in the IRDP. In most of the cases, according to this survey, the already better off were able to get benefits from the IRDP. The views of other scholars like Aiyar (1985), Bandyopadhyay (1984), Jain et al (1985), Parthasarathy (1985) also support the above contention.

Bandyopadhyay (1984: 50) goes to the root of the problem when he comments: "The most difficult aspect of the Programme (IRDP) in its implementation at the grass-root has been the identification of the beneficiaries. It may look paradoxical, but it is a fact that when the question of choice of a few among the many comes up, it becomes extremely difficult to pick-up the right category of beneficiaries…" .

On the basis of field evidence, Jain et al (1985) concluded that the benefits were not reaching the poor. Similarly, Parthasarathy (1985: 2127) identifies three deficiencies in the implementation of the IRDP. These relate to:

(1) infrastructural support required for forward and backward linkages;
(2) weak and un-coordinated delivery and marketing system and
(3) inability of the selected household to undertake the risk and managerial functions particularly when it happens to be the poorest of the poor and is hopelessly involved in debt.

While commenting on the mixed results of the IRDP, Aiyar (1985) calls this programme a 'qualified failure'.

Jain et al (1985: 197) blame the bureaucracy for poor implementation of the IRDP when they comment: "The foremost reason for this unfortunate state of affairs is that the people themselves have no place in rural development, every available inch is occupied by the bureaucracy ..." But, the faith they seem to have put on the panchayats seems to be misplaced. The panchayats are not synonymous with the people, particularly the poorest of the poor. As it was obvious in the present study, the panchayats have the same tendency not to allow the benefits to reach the poor.

Table 8

Reasons for various governmental efforts to remove poverty not being effective

Reasons	*Number*	*Percentage*
Not reaching the poor	62	15.50
Purchased assets are not sufficient to generate income	3	.75
No market for finished products	3	.75
Political stunt or eye wash	19	4.75
Corruption in government	4	1.00
Do not know	42	10.50
Not applicable	267	66.75
Total	400	100.00

In the light of the above discussion, the issue of paramount importance is: what is to be done to remove these lacunae to help the poorest of the poor? One aspect of this issue was to know the expectations which the scheduled castes had from the government. Table 9 indicates the expectations from the government to improve the lot of the scheduled castes. It is clear from the table that more employment opportunities, reform in the loan disbursing system, removal of corruption and provision of technical training were some of the steps which the respondents wanted the government to undertake. But even these measures may not help the scheduled castes. In fact, there are two ways of looking into the matter. First, the need of the hour is to bring administrative and organisational changes for rural development (De, 1985). Second, the involvement of the people in rural development as it happened in the case of Sidhwan Bet block of Ludhiana district where the efforts of one person by involving the people of that area resulted in a radical change in the people's economic conditions (De, 1986).

Table 9

Expectations from the government to improve the lot of the Harijans

Expectations	*Number*	*Percentage*	*Total*
Provide more employment opportunities	153	38.25	40 (100)
Provide technical training	079	19.75	40 (100)
Reform the loan disbursing system	118	29.50	40 (100)
Open low- price shops	005	1.25	40 (100)
Increase daily wages	005	1.25	40 (100)
Provide house-bound self-employment for women	43	10.75	40 (100)
Provide land for cultivation	019	4.75	400 (100)
Remove corruption in the government	080	20.00	40 (100)
Provide pension for old widows	033	8.25	40 (100)
Provide proper health care system	003	.75	40 (100)

Note

This article was earlier published in Pimpley, P.N., Singh, K.P. and Mahajan, A. (eds.), *Social Development: Processes and Consequences*, Rawat, Jaipur, 1989. References have been changed for the sake of uniformity.

References

Aiyar, Swaminathan S. 1985. "Reforming IRDP: Unsuccessful Attack on Poverty", *Indian Express*, August 19.

Bandyopadhayay, D. 1984. "An Evaluation of Policies and Programmes for the Alleviation of Rural Poverty in India", *Qualify of Work Life*, Vol. I, No. 1–2, January–April.

De, Nitish. 1985. "Poverty Programmes: I – Administrative innovations. II – Organisation Innovations", *The Economic Times*, November 1–2, 1985.

——.1986. "Some Lessons from People's Development in Sidhwan Bet Block, Ludhiana, Punjab" Chandigarh: Punjab State Institute of Public Administration (mimeo).

Goyal, T.C.1986. "IRDP Implementation in Punjab", Chandigarh, Punjab State Institute of Public Administration (mimeo).

Jain, L.C. et. al. 1985. *Grass Without Roots: Rural Development under Government Auspices*. New Delhi: Sage Publications.

Parthasarathy, G. 1985. "Reorientation of Rural Development Programmes: A Note on Basic Issues", *Economic and Political Weekly*, Vol. XX, No 48, November 30.

4

Scheduled Castes Women's Work Participation in Rural Punjab

In patriarchal societies, the status of women continues to be subordinate to men. The factors responsible for their lower position have been a matter of debate. Factors like biological limitation of women to the revivification of the earlier expedient, division of labour at home etc. have been put forward time and again. The analytical framework for the study of women's position in society involves class and gender variables. However, in the Indian context, the caste factor has also been taken into account as a person's caste has a considerable bearing on his/her status in the community. In recent years, owing to the feminist movement all over the world, significant contributions have been made on the women's position vis-à-vis their work participation. Some of the issues dealt with in these studies have been listed below:[1]

1. It is only in the case of females that work is dichotomised into domestic work and gainful employment. Domestic work is not regarded as a part of productive labour, whereas its various components, such as cooking, cleaning etc., become parts of productive labour in other setting. Therefore, the work which women do to earn income is recognised as 'work'. In order to be designated as gainfully employed, women have to do more work

than men. It is understandable in the light of the fact that most men do not assist their wives in the household chores, whereas the working women have to do the domestic work.

2. Participation of women in work has been declining over the years in India whereas in the developed and developing countries like China and Vietnam, it is on the increase. Following major causes are attributed to explain the phenomenon of declining rate of female participation in workforce in India: (i) There have been changes in the definition of 'worker' in two censuses, i.e., 1961 and 1971. (ii) The pauperisation process affected the work participation of both men and women. At the time of implementation of land reform laws, the tenancy reforms led to certain unintended consequences. Instead of giving the ownership rights to tenants, particularly the non-occupancy tenants, landowners evicted them from land by using various questionable methods such as taking back the land for self-cultivation, filing law suits against tenants who had not paid the rent, etc. These evicted tenants joined the ranks of agricultural labourers and in the process displaced women workers from the agricultural sector. (iii) If men of the households are having high status occupation, the participation of their wives in lower status occupations is conspicuous by its absence.
3. There are regional variations in the proportion of women's work participation in India. According to 1981 census data, the tribal areas have registered high rate of female work participation. All those states having higher female work participation rates are agriculturally backward.
4. According to the 1981 census, 79.4 per cent of the women workers are in agriculture, mainly doing wage labour. The caste background of these women reveals that a majority of them belongs to the scheduled castes and the scheduled tribes. Women are paid fewer wages than men. The average income of female workers is two-thirds of the average income of male workers.
5. The effect of technological changes on women's work participation is yet another issue which has been widely discussed. The technological changes have occurred only in men's work, whereas women's work has remained more or less manual. Moreover, after mechanisation, the production of certain goods passes into the hands of men, controlled earlier by women.

6. The working women face a set of problems from which the male world is free. It has been observed that the working women have to face the prejudices of men at workplaces. The sexual exploitation of women workers by their male employers, particularly in the unorganised sector, is a common occurrence.

The issues delineated above indicate not only the lower position of women in general, but also its consequences for their work situation. So far as the scheduled caste women are concerned, we could only discern that among the women labourers they constitute a majority along with the scheduled tribe women. The preponderance of the scheduled caste women in the low level of occupational category needs to be explained not only in terms of the class and gender variables, but also in terms of the caste factor.

The scheduled castes, named by Mahatma Gandhi as Harijans, belong to the lowest rung of the Indian stratification system. As untouchables in the caste hierarchy, they have been the most oppressed section of the Indian society. The disabilities imposed upon them by the privileged castes of the society covered the whole gamut of economic, social, political and cultural conditions. They could not opt for occupations that were exclusively meant for upper castes. The abolition of untouchability and the preferential treatment in jobs have been some of the measures undertaken by the government for them after independence. However, the conditions of most of the scheduled castes in general remained more or less unchanged. This can be understood in the light of the perspective provided by Berreman (1979) that the basis of the intercaste relations in terms of power hierarchy has not changed. Furthermore, as agricultural labourers, they constitute 48.22 per cent of the total scheduled caste workers' population in India.[2]

According to the 1981 census, the scheduled castes constitute 15.75 per cent of the total population of India, excluding Assam. Though present in all states, they are more preponderant in Punjab, Uttar Pradesh, Tamil Nadu and Orissa. In Punjab they form 26.9 per cent of the total population which is the highest for a state in the country. Placed in this context are the scheduled caste women workers who are mainly the agricultural labourers in the rural areas. These women are underprivileged not only on the basis of gender and class but also along caste lines.

This study was conducted by setting the following objectives in the light of the issues discussed above:

(a) The identification of different levels of work in which the scheduled caste women participate in rural areas.
(b) Effect of technology change on their work.
(c) Comparison of the nature and features of scheduled caste women's employment with those of their husbands.
(d) Whether there is sexual exploitation of scheduled caste women in general and agricultural labourers in particular.

Before the discussion on the methods used in the present study, it is pertinent to clarify two aspects of scheduled caste women's work. Firstly, since most of the scheduled caste women are agricultural labourers, an attempt has been made to provide detailed descriptions of agricultural labourers. Secondly, keeping in mind the issue regarding women's work, the term 'gainful employment' has been used to describe any kind of mental or physical labour expended to earn income for any number of days in a year. We have not taken into consideration the census definition of 'worker' according to which a particular person qualifies to be a main worker if he/she is engaged in gainful employment for 183 days (or six months) or more during a year. Hence, in this paper, both the main and marginal workers are not discussed separately.

This paper is divided into three parts. The first part deals with the methods used in conducting the study, the second gives a description of some social and demographic characteristics of the respondents and the third deals with various features of women's work participation.

Methods Used

This study was conducted in the Hoshiarpur district of Punjab which has, over the time, undergone certain changes in cropping pattern and intensity. Wheat and potatoes form the major crops in most parts of the district. It has a sizeable scheduled caste population, i.e., 30.84 per cent of the total population of the district according to the 1981 census which is the second highest in the state. We covered five villages by using a simple random method. We selected these villages from the list prepared only to include those villages whose scheduled caste population was above the district average.

It was decided to have a sample size of 400 households of the scheduled castes. To draw this desired sample of 400 from these five villages the method of proportionate stratified multistage random sampling was used.

To begin with, a house-to-house survey was conducted to know the exact number of scheduled caste households, the villages were arranged in a descending order. Since the scheduled castes are comprised of various castes, it was important that every caste should be represented in the sample.

The total number of scheduled caste households was treated as population. In order to get the desired sample of 400, following steps were undertaken:

(a) The proportion of households of each village from the total population.

(b) Then, to determine how many households should be taken, the following calculation was done: taking each proportion of the stratified characteristics, in the population and multiplying it by the sample size.

(c) Since there were different castes among the scheduled castes in each village, it was essential to determine how many households were to be selected from each caste. In order to draw sample size the same method was adopted for each village. Table 1 indicates the size of sample drawn according to village and caste.

(d) After going through this procedure we came to know the exact number of households to be taken from each caste from five villages. For drawing the desired number of households from each category, simple random method was used.

For the purpose of data collection an interview schedule was prepared and administered.

Table 1

Castewise size of sample selected in each village

Castes	*Bajwara*	*Phuglana*	*Sahri*	*Mehtiana*	*Badowal*	*Total*
Ad-dharmi	126	74	83	47	17	347
Balmiki	24	11	2	5	–	42
Bazigar	11	–	–	–	–	11
Total	161	85	85	52	17	400

Social Background of the Respondents

The main purpose of presenting the social characteristics of the respondents is to provide an idea about the living conditions of the respondents and their households. A majority, i.e., 347 respondents belong to the Ad-dharmi caste, 42 to the Balmiki and 11 to Bazigar caste. The mean age of the respondents is 37.74 years. Most of the respondents (88.5%) are illiterate. None has gone to college. In all the five villages the scheduled caste houses were segregated from those of the upper caste houses. The houses of the scheduled castes were located in the form of clusters on one side of the village. Even among the scheduled caste houses, separate localities of Ad-dharmi, Balmiki and Bazigar houses could be observed. In terms of landownership among the households interviewed, 94 per cent are landless and 4.50 per cent operate marginal holdings. However, 55.5 per cent of the households own milch animals, mainly buffaloes. The above information places the scheduled caste households in a situation where it is expected that most of them depend upon the daily wages for survival. It would be worthwhile to discuss different features of employment of the respondents and their husbands.

Women's Work Participation

We would now focus on the gainful employment of the scheduled caste women to understand their productivity. However, an attempt will also be made to look into the total contribution, direct or indirect, of women including the domestic work within the household.

Nature and Features of Scheduled Caste Women's Employment

Table 2 shows the gainful employment of the respondents and husbands. It is evident from the data that a majority of the respondents (41.75%) and husbands (53.50%) are casually employed. There are also some cases of multiple employments (5.75% respondents, 11% husbands). This implies that there are some households which have to engage themselves in different occupations not necessarily for additional income but often for making both ends meet. The proportions of the self-employed (11% respondents, 16.75% husbands) indicate that very few have a clear picture of their employment conditions. An exact scenario would emerge only after the discussion of each type of gainful employment separately.

Table 2
Gainful employment of the respondents and their husbands

Employment	*Respondents*		*Husbands*	
	Number	*%*	*Number*	*%*
Permanent employment	44	11.00	67	16.75
Casual employment	22	5.50	43	10.75
Multiple employment	167	41.75	214	53.50
No employment	24	6.00	44	11.00
Not applicable	143	35.75	32	8.00
Total	400	100.00	400	100.00

Note: Casual employment includes agricultural labourers and casual workers. Multiple employment implies that the nature of a person's employment is of more than one type, for instance, in addition to agricultural labour, a person may be either permanently employed or self-employed.

Self -Employment

It is clear from the Tables 3 and 4 that only a few respondents (16.12%) and husbands (16.67%) are occupying relatively higher occupational positions among the self-employed. Most of them are doing low status and less remunerative jobs. In case of respondents, it was found that they were assisting their husbands in these self-employment activities.

Table 3
Nature of self-employment of the respondents

Self-employment	*Number*	*Percentage*
Teaching (tuition)	1	1.61
Shopkeeping	3	4.84
Own cultivation + sharecropping	6	9.67
Midwife	2	3.23
Weaving	39	62.90
Toy making	2	3.23
Tailoring	3	4.84
Jute spinning	4	6.45
Vending	2	3.23
Total	62	3.23

Note: The category 'not applicable' has been expunged.

It is particularly evident from the daily hours of work of the respondents. It is also important to mention that in the case of self-employment the scheduled castes have to work for longer periods.

Table 4

Nature of self-employment of the respondents' husbands

Self Employment	*Number*	*Percentage*
Teaching (tuition)	1	0.93
Shopkeeping	11	10.18
Own cultivation	6	5.56
Carpenter	1	0.93
Blacksmith	2	1.85
Weaving	47	43.52
Jute spinning	6	5.56
Toy making	2	1.85
Tailoring	4	3.70
Share cropping	4	3.70
Tinning	1	0.93
Vending	2	1.85
Shoe-mending	12	11.11
Horse cart driving or rickshaw pulling	7	6.48
Laundering	2	1.85
Total	108	100.00

Table 5 provides that 77.78 per cent of the households spend more than ten hours on work.

Table 5

Hours of participation (daily) in work as self employed (respondents and husbands)

Hours	*Respondents*		*Husbands*	
	Number	*Percentage*	*Number*	*Percentage*
7	46	74.19	1	0.93
8	10	16.13	14	12.96
9	6	9.68	9	8.33
10 and above	0	0.00	84	77.78
Total	62	100.00	108	100.00

Note: The category 'not applicable' has been expunged.

Permanent Employment

Permanent employment includes those government or non-government jobs in which the security of job is provided by law. Besides, those occupations which are governed by traditions under the 'jajmani' system have also been included. Seen from the durability of an employment, these jobs under the jajmani system are permanent and are characterised by generational continuity. The nature of permanent employment indicates that 28 respondents and 48 husbands are permanently employed. Most of the respondents (25) are permanently employed under the jajmani system, whereas a majority of the husbands (42) have government employment. The castewise nature of permanent employment of the respondents indicates that all the Balmiki respondents (26), who are permanently employed, are sweeper – a traditional occupation of this caste – of which one is a government employee and rest are doing the work under the jajmani system. Two Ad-dharmi respondents are teachers. If we look at the nature of the permanent employment of the husbands (see Table 6), we find that high status occupations are confined to the Ad-dharmi caste. In the case of government employment the mean monthly income of the government employees ranges between Rs 700 and Rs 1,500. A Balmiki woman, who works under the jajmani system as a sweeper/scavenger at the house of a landowner, gets 10–12 kilograms of wheat or maize per animal after every six months. In addition to foodgrains, she is given four *chapatis* every day.

Casual Employment

The term 'casual employment' refers to daily wage work which may not be available throughout the year. In fact, casual employment includes a large number of categories of workers ranging from agricultural labourers to skilled workers like masons, carpenters, etc. In the present study we have made two categories of casual workers, viz., agricultural labourers and other casual workers. It was found that those respondents who were casual workers were agricultural labourers. Among the husbands only 20.50 per cent were in the category of other casual workers, whereas 55 per cent of the total were agricultural labourers. In view of the fact that none of the respondents was involved in other casual employment, the analysis of husbands' other casual employment has not been made here. The succeeding discussion focuses on various features of agricultural labour in respect of both the respondents and their husbands.

Table 6

Caste and nature of husband's permanent employment

Caste	Nature of Employment											
	Teacher	*Panchayat secretary*	*Clerk*	*Conductor/ driver*	*Police/ army man*	*Mechanic/ operator*	*Peon*	*Post-man*	*Watch-man*	*Ward boy*	*Sweeper*	*Total*
Ad-dharmi	6	2	10	3	8	3	5	–	3	–	1	41
Bazigar	–	–	–	1	–	–	–	–	–	–	–	1
Balmiki	–	–	–	–	–	–	–	1	–	1	4	6
Total	6	2	10	4	8	3	5	1	3	1	5	48

(a) Work operation: Work operation refers to the nature of work which the women respondents and their husbands do as agricultural labourers. It is obvious from Table 7 that every agricultural labourer performs multiple operations. Sowing, weeding, harvesting and peeling (for maize only) are common operations among both the respondents and the husbands. Threshing was not being performed by any respondent.

Table 7

Respondents' and their husbands' nature of work operation as agricultural labourers

Work operation	*Respondents*		*Husbands*	
	Number	*Percentage*	*Number*	*Percentage*
Sowing, weeding and harvesting	175	91.62	206	93.64
Harvesting	13	6.81	3	1.36
Sowing, weeding, harvesting and peeling	3	1.57	3	1.36
Sowing, weeding, harvesting and threshing	–	–	–	–
Total	62	100.00	108	100.00

Note: The category 'not applicable' has been expunged.

Threshing being the hardest of all operations involving danger seems to be considered an operation which women could not do. Scholars like Omvedt (1980) and Singh (1980) have also pointed out that there is difference in the nature of work women do from that of men. Furthermore, it is in the case of threshing that mechanisation in Punjab can be perceived to be total. This is an indication of displacement of women by machines.

This view can be reinforced by comparing the traditional method of threshing with the present one. In the traditional method winnowing was a major work operation. After the introduction of mechanical threshers, winnowing has ceased to be an operation as such. Though most of the agricultural labourers, both men and women, are involved in harvesting, yet the future of labour employment does not seem to be promising. It is only because of the perpetual need for dry fodder for cattle that most of the farmers have not been using harvesting machines. If some new machines are manufactured whereby it would be possible to get dry fodder also, the labour input will be drastically reduced. The rise in the price of dry fodder (Rs 100 per quintal) in 1985 was a result of a large scale use of harvesting machines by big farmers in the previous wheat harvesting season due to danger of heavy rainfall around that period. Similar can be the case with the operations of weeding, sowing and harvesting of potatoes.

(b) Working hours and daily wages: Daily working hours of respondents and their husbands have been shown in Table 8. It is clear that a majority among them work for more than eight hours. Before we explain why they have to work for such a long time, it is essential to understand the mode of payment of daily wages of agricultural labourers – both women and men. There seem to be two reasons for long working hours, First, the landowners may be forcing them to work for long hours by keeping the wages same. Second, the mode of payment may be such that the agricultural labourers are motivated to work for longer hours. The first reason points towards the coercive exploitation of labour, whereas the second reason indicates incentive for work involving latent exploitation.[3]

Table 8

Hours of agricultural labour of respondents and husbands

Hours	*Respondents*		*Husbands*	
	Number	*Percentage*	*Number*	*Percentage*
8	82	42.93	74	33.64
9	11	5.76	10	4.54
10 and above	98	51.31	136	61.82
Total	191	100.00	220	100.00

Note: The category 'not applicable' has been expunged.

Table 9

Respondents' and husbands' mode of payment as agricultural labourers

Mode of payment	*Respondents*		*Husbands*	
	Number	*Percentage*	*Number*	*Percentage*
Cash	43	22.51	14	6.36
Cash and kind	148	77.49	206	93.64
Total	191	100.00.	220	100.00

Note: The category 'not applicable' has been expunged.

Data in Table 9 show the mode of payment to both the respondents and their husbands. Among the agricultural labourers, only 22.51 per cent of the respondents and 6.36 per cent of the husbands are getting cash wages. The rest, i.e., 77.49 per cent of the respondents and 93.64 per cent of the husbands are getting wages in both cash and kind. Why do these modes of payment exist? A general view is that one of the indicators of capitalist development in agriculture is that the mode of payment should be in cash. Rudra (1970) considers wage payment in cash per acre of farm size as an important variable in the identification of capitalism in agriculture. But, the payment in kind is still going on. The explanation lies in the different mode of payment for different operations of crops. In the case of all operations relating to the potato crop the payment is always made in cash, but in case of wheat harvesting and threshing, the payment is generally made in kind. On the basis of the above explanation, Table 9 can be interpreted in a meaningful manner, i.e., the respondents and husbands who are getting wages in cash have been involved as labourers in various operations of potato crop, whereas those who are getting payment in both cash and kind have been involved in various operations of both potato and wheat crops and for that matter in the case of maize crop.

The reason for the agricultural labourers' getting the payment in kind, particularly in the case of wheat, requires to be understood in the light of felt needs of the labourers and economic considerations of the farmer. Wheat is a staple food in Punjab and the labourer is interested in receiving wheat in lieu of cash wages instead of buying it from the open market at high prices. The farmers also seem to be willing to pay their wages in kind due to three reasons. Firstly, after the Green Revolution phenomenon the cropping intensity has increased in Punjab. On an average, a farmer takes three to four crops a year. To have so many numbers of crops, the harvesting period has to be reduced to clear the fields for the next crop and the farmer thinks that payment in kind gets the work of wheat harvesting done. Secondly, most of the farmers do not have sufficient cash to pay to the labourers at the harvest time. Thirdly, as we shall see soon, the payment in kind is also linked with contract terms. This generally motivates the labourers to work for extra hours every day. This helps the farmers to harvest the wheat crop quickly as the unpredictable weather during this period always weighs heavily on farmers' mind.

After the discussion on modes of payment to agricultural labourers, it is important to see their actual wages in both kind and cash. It may be mentioned that besides the information provided by the respondents and their husbands, we also contacted the landowners in these villages. It was observed that during the wheat harvesting, there was a contract between a landowner and a particular number of agricultural labourers who invariably belonged to one or more families. According to this contract, of all the bundles of wheat harvested every twenty-first bundle would belong to the labourers, i.e., if the labourers manage to harvest hundred and five bundles, then five would belong to the labourers. The method of counting is also very important here. When twenty bundles are counted, the next bundle is given to the labourers. After that the counting starts from one to twenty. In view of the fact that the agricultural labourers work on family basis, they are highly motivated to earn more in kind. That is the reason the working hours increase during the harvesting season.

So far as the daily wages in cash are concerned, the mean of the respondents and husbands is Rs 10.05 and Rs 13.78 respectively[4] (see Table 10 and 11). According to a Government of Punjab (1985) publication, the statutory minimum wage for agricultural labourers was Rs 14 in 1985. This implies that agricultural workers were getting fewer wages than the minimum wages fixed by the government in the study area.[5] However, in the case of most of the male agricultural labourers, the wages either approximated or were more than the minimum wages but none of the women labourers was getting even the minimum wages. As mentioned in the beginning, various other studies have also revealed that women workers are paid less than the men workers. When the landowners were asked to describe this aspect, they said that they preferred women workers to men workers in the case of various operations involved in potato crop on two counts. Firstly, women worked as efficiently as men and two, women worked for lower wages. Thus, instead of employing two men, they could employ three women, by spending the same amount on wages. Labour cost remained the same while labour input increased. This arrangement suited the farmers' interest.

(c) Working days: Tables 10 and 11 provide the total number of days of agricultural work in a year of the respondents and husbands respectively according to their daily wages. The mean value for

women's number of days of work is 87.08 whereas for husbands it is 104.08. Contrary to expectations, there does not seem to be any interdependent relationship between the wages and days of work. However, men remain employed in agriculture for more number of days than women. But, in light of census definition of 'worker', all the wage earning respondents and husbands are marginal workers. According to the landowners interviewed, it is only during the potato season that most men and women are able to get work in the real sense. Their information about the number of working days in a year was that each worker got around 20 days of work for sowing, 10–15 days for weeding, and 25–30 days for harvesting.

Table 10

Daily wages and total number of days of agricultural work in a year of the respondents

Daily wages (Rs)	*No. of days work in a year*			*Total*
	41–85	*86–120*	*121–155*	
8	2 (00.25)	5 (62.5)	1 (12.50)	8 (100) (4.19)
9	9 (42.86)	1 (57.14)	–	21 (100) (10.99)
10	51 (44.35)	62 (53.91)	2 (1.74)	115 (100) (60.21)
11	12 (52.17)	1 (43.48)	1 (4.35)	23 (100) (12.04)
12	10 (41.67)	1 (50.00)	2 (8.33)	24 (100) (12.57)
Total	84 (43.98)	101 (52.88)	6 (3.14)	191 (100)

Mean value of number of days of work a year = 87.08

Mean wages = 10.05

Note: The category 'not applicable' has been expunged.

Added to the above are 20–25 days of more work during harvesting of wheat. In all, their working days do not exceed 100 days anywhere. Some of the men and women workers also go to other villages for agricultural labour. It was found that 56 respondents (29.32%) have been going to other villages for work. It was also found that the work outside the villages never exceeded 60 days or two months. Most of these commuting respondents were getting higher wages outside than what they had been receiving in their own village. However, even outside, they did not receive more than Rs 12 as daily wages.

Table 11

Daily wages and number of days of work in a year of agricultural labourers of husbands

Daily wages (Rs)	*No. of days work in a year*			*Total*
	71–115	*116–160*	*161–205*	
10	(85.71)	–	(14.29)	(100) (3.18)
12	5 (90.62)	(9.38)	–	6 (00) (29.09)
13–17	10 (67.11)	4 (32.89)	–	14 (100) (67.73)
Total	16 (74.55)	5 (25.00)	(0.45)	220 (100)

Mean value of number of days of work a year = 104.08

Mean wages (Rs) = 13.78

Note: The category 'not applicable' has been expunged.

One may wonder that keeping in view the profit orientation of the capitalist farmers how these few respondents manage to get higher wages. These two situations though apparently contradictory, yet in essence they are not. It has already been noted that the villages covered under the present study have numerical preponderance of the scheduled caste population. Since most of the scheduled castes are agricultural labourers, the labour becomes surplus when the peak periods in various crop operations start following a downward trend. This also means that the landowners of these villages do not employ labour from other villages. At the same time, some contiguous villages to these villages do not have a very high proportion of the scheduled caste population.

Interestingly, most of the labourers would go to other villages for work when they come to know that there would be no work in their own village. One of the reasons could be that it is always expedient to work in one's own village due to the problem of commutation. It was found that most of the women who went to work in other villages were provided with free transportation facilities (i.e., the concerned farmer from the other village would come to their village with tractor and trailer). The respondents explained this arrangement thus: There seems to be prevalence of the traditional feudal linkages between the scheduled caste families and the landowning families in which the former are dependent on the latter. They are either continuing the same linkage through the jajmani relations, for it is there in the case of Balmiki households or having some sort of sense of loyalty after their services under jajmani system have become redundant. But these traditional ties still continue to occupy a major place in the context of economic relations. Even the landowner would prefer to employ members of a particular scheduled caste family.

However, the above explanation could be partial if seen in the light of the fact that the landowners do not only dominate economically but also socially and politically. A poor scheduled caste family is invariably dependent on a landowner for frequent borrowing during the lean season. During the peak season such family does not have any option other than working in the landowner's fields. Moreover, the overall domination of landowners, including their coercive ability, must be dissuading them to work outside. As a corollary to the above argument, it can be stated that many of the scheduled castes might have preferred their own village landowners because of anticipated needs and threat. These anticipated needs may be a result of false consciousness, but these are real needs so far as the whole social milieu of the villages are concerned.

Since most of the scheduled caste agricultural labourers remain unemployed for about 200 days in a year, one may raise a question: What do they do during these days? The women workers except those belonging to the Balmiki caste stay at home but look after the cattle, which become an important source of income. Men workers sometimes manage to get casual work largely in the city, i.e., Hoshiarpur. But this is true only for the villages like Bajwara, Sahri and Badowal, which are near to the city.

(d) Past work status: There are two aspects of the work status of women agricultural labourers when referred to the past. First, the number of years they have been in work and the age at which they started working. Second, the working conditions in terms of wages, the number of days of work in a year and increase or decrease in the work availability over the last fifteen years or so.

Table 12 shows the years of working according to the age of the respondents. The mean value of the years of working is 18.71 years and the mean age of working respondents is 38.12 years. This indicates that most of women started working at the age of 19 years. However, out of those working respondents who belong to the age group 30–35 years,

21.13 per cent have been working for the last 19 to 26 years. Thus, there are cases where the respondents might have started working at the age of 12.

Table 12

Age and years of working of the working respondents

Age (Year)	*Years of Working*					*Total*
	3–10	*11–18*	*19–26*	*27 & above*	*Do not know*	
20–29	38(74.51)	8(15.69)	–	–	5(9.80)	51(100) (19.84)
30–35	27(38.03)	26(36.62)	15(21.13)	–	3(4.22)	71(100) (27.63)
36–40	4(9.52)	11(26.19)	22(52.38)	3(7.14)	2(4.76)	42(100) (16.34)
41–48	3(6.67)	–	37(82.22)	5(11.11)	–	45(100) (17.51)
49–55	–	–	13(35.14)	24(64.86)	–	37(100) (14.00)
56–65	–	–	1(9.09)	10(90.91)	–	11(100) (4.28)
Total	72(28.02)	45(17.51)	88(34.24)	42(16.34)	10(3.89)	257(100)

Mean years of working = 18.71

Figures in parentheses indicate percentages.

Note: The category 'not applicable' has been expunged.

Table 13

Past working conditions in the five villages

Period	*Nature of work*	*No. of days of work*	*Cash (Rs)*		*Wages fixed by the State Govt.*	*Kind (Male + Female)*	*Meal*
			Male	*Female*			
1982	Agricultural Labour	105	10	8	14	Only in case of wheat and maize (one bundle after 25–30 bundles) or 80–100 kg of grain after harvesting one acre.	Only one tea in case of potatoes
1979	"	105	8	6.50	8.70		
1975	"	60	5.50	3.50	6.70		
1972	"	60	3.00	2.00	5.50		

Source: Economic and Statistical Organization, Punjab, 1985.

Table 13 indicates the past work conditions since 1972. This information was collected through the interviews with the respondents, husbands and landowners. The data collected were compared with the minimum wages fixed by the Punjab government for these years. There is an increase in the number of days of work from 1975 to 1982. If these working days are compared with present average number of working days, it can be stated that there is a decrease. However, money wages show an upward trend. As compared with the minimum wages women labourers have been getting still less than their male counterparts.

To the query whether agricultural work has increased over the years, all the respondents who are agricultural labourers said that it had, in fact, decreased. When they were asked to state the reasons for decrease in the agricultural work, the response was that either further mechanisation (42.41%) of agriculture or migrant labour from Bihar or UP (14.66%) or both (42.93) were responsible for this decline. According to an ILO survey, the improved technology has led to the rise in real wages of the agricultural labourers, but there is a decline in the number of days of work in a year (*The Indian Express*, 1980: 5.). The above observation does not exactly explain the actual situation. It should be noted that the Green Revolution phenomenon has led to the rise in cropping intensity. If before Green Revolution the number of days of work was higher, then number of crops taken in a year rarely exceeded two, which means that it was only in certain operations of two crops that the labour was required. In the area studied these two major crops were wheat and maize. After the Green Revolution some labour intensive crops like potatoes were introduced in a big way. Thus, it was expected that with the additional crops the number of days would not decline as the cropping intensity would balance the decrease in number of days of work in the case of two crops. As we have argued earlier, the mechanisation in certain areas like wheat harvesting can radically affect the working days, which has not occurred to the extent it was expected. Moreover, our data indicate a marginal increase in the number of days between 1975 and 1979. Placed in this context is the incidence of migrant labour from outside the state, which has affected the working days of the local labourers because the migrant labourers are paid fewer wages than the local labourers.[6] In the light of the fact that the migrant labour has been absorbed in Punjab agriculture, the agricultural work has increased, but the working days in various agricultural operations have decreased. This aspect is again linked with the cropping intensity, the logic of which involves extensive labour to complete particularly harvesting and threshing within the shortest period possible.

Employment, Work and Household Dimension

The traditional divide between husband and wife is based on the sexual division of labour reinforced by patriarchy according to which the husband is supposed to be breadwinner and the wife is supposed to do the domestic work including child care. However, it is difficult to establish that women have always been isolated from the production process. In the agrarian society women were not completely isolated from various productive activities, particularly in the case of middle and lower classes and castes. Even taking food for her husband to the fields was an activity which contributed to the production process.

It can be observed that most of the controversies regarding women's work are a result of the changes which occur in certain institutional practices and the way these changes are cognised and interpreted. The separation of domestic work from the gainful work seems to be a result of two factors, viz., the awakening of women, and the definition of worker and subsequent presentation of the data accordingly by the Census of India which excluded all those women who were confined to domestic work. The former contributed by bringing the whole issue of women's work to the fore, while the latter caused the separation of domestic work from the income generating work.

Thus, there is a need to analyse women's work in totality. Furthermore, the specific problems concerning the working women should be considered in a perspective. In a way, we would do well to see who looks after the children, who does the domestic work when the women go out for a work, and what kind of work the working and non-working women do in a day.

Of all the working respondents (excluding those whose gainful employment does not take them out of the house) 24.43 per cent stated that nobody was looking after the children. In the case of about 20 per cent of the respondents, the eldest child in their family, who had not yet reached the working age, was taking care of his or her younger brothers and sisters. This indicated that there was a considerable neglect of children. But, in the case of domestic work, the working respondents were doing the domestic work themselves. It is worthwhile to point out that most of these respondents who replied that nobody was looking after the children and they were doing the domestic work, were working as agricultural labourers and/or sweepers under the jajmani system. Finally, 64.60 per cent of the working respondents informed that in addition to them some other members of the family were doing the domestic work.

As mentioned earlier, one of the most important aspects of women's work is the division between domestic work and gainful work. It was, therefore, important to see the daily routine of women respondents. The data covered two situations of women. One was to see the daily routine of only the working respondents during those periods when they went for work. The other was to know the daily routine of all the respondents. The data were collected during the winter season. This may not hold good for other seasons (see Tables 14 and 15).

Table 14

*Daily routine of the working respondents**

	Routine	*No.*	*%*
1.	**Before going to work**		
(a)	Time when get up 4 am to 5 am	133	53.41
	6 am to 7 am	116	46.59
	Total	249	100.00
(b)	Nature of work done domestic work	117	46.98
	Domestic work plus make dung cakes and/or feed the cattle	132	53.02
	Total	249	100.00
2.	**After coming from work**		
(a)	Nature of work done domestic work	58	23.29
	Domestic work plus bring fuel and fodder	191	76.71
	Total	249	100.00
(b)	Time when go to sleep		
	8 pm	30	12.05
	9 pm	137	55.02
	10 pm	82	32.93
	Total	249	100.00

*Daily routine of some women who are gainfully employed has not been considered here. These are: teachers (3), shopkeepers (3), and midwives (2).

Note: The category 'not applicable' has been expunged.

It is evident from Table 14 that most of the working respondents do three kinds of work, namely, domestic work, gainful work and semi-gainful work.[7] Table 15 indicates that among all the respondents, most (72.75%) are doing two kinds of work, namely, domestic work and semi-gainful work. By semi-gainful work we mean work like collection of fuelwood, making dung cakes, bringing fodder for the cattle and feeding the cattle, in which the economic significance of the work is much more clearly exhibited. It becomes all the more clear when we know that selling the milk becomes an important source of income when the agricultural labour is not available to them. However, it should not mean that milk is sold only when the agricultural labour is not available, but its importance reflects more clearly when the wage work is not available.

Table 15

Daily routine of the respondents

	Routine	*No.*	*%*
1.	**Time when get up**		
	5 am	89	22.25
	6 am	248	62.00
	7 am	63	15.75
	Total	400	100.00
2.	**Work done during day time**		
	Domestic work	109	27.25
	Domestic work plus collect fodder and fuel and make dung cakes and/or feed the cattle	291	72.75
	Total	400	100.00
3.	**Time when go to sleep**		
	8 pm	113	28.25
	9 pm	157	39.25
	10 pm	130	32.50
	Total	400	100.00

The second dimension of women's work in totality as it reflects in their daily routine is the two-fold work done by the working respondents and 13 to 16 hours of perpetual occupation in various activities throughout the day of all the respondents. Sharma (1985) has correctly depicted the life of rural women thus: "Village women of all castes spend hours of the day, rising as early as 5 am and retiring as late as ten in the night, is an endless round of household chores. None of this, of course, is included in the official statistics, and 88 per cent of Indian women are gratuitously granted the title of non worker".

Relations at Work

One of the important dimensions of women's work is the behaviour of their employers towards them. In the present circumstances in which a woman is treated as an object of sex, the probability of exploitation or humiliation of women seems to be very high. Furthermore, the women workers who are working for survival are the most vulnerable in this context. There are two dimensions of the behaviour of the employers who are mainly the landowners – one, the way they address to the women in the work situation, and two, the sexual exploitation of the women. These two dimensions are also linked with the type of work the scheduled caste women do. In this context, we can identify three types of work the women do which overlap with each other in most the cases, viz., the agricultural labour, work of scavenging under the jajmani system, and the collection of fuelwood and fodder from the fields of the landowners. Of these three types of work, which have direct consequences on the nature of relationship between the landowners and the scheduled caste women, the scavenging is only carried out by the Balmiki women. The other two jobs are done by the women belonging to all the three castes, i.e., Ad-dharmi, Bazigar and Balmiki. The collection of fuelwood and fodder for cattle is also undertaken by many non-employed scheduled caste women.

The first dimension of behaviour of landowners, which may be characterised as interpersonal behaviour, includes former two types of work situations.

When these women were asked this question, 53 per cent of them stated that the landowners used abusive language frequently in the work situations. The rest 47 per cent viewed their behaviour as acceptable. But, the picture was radically different. Though most of the women workers made distinctions between the good and the bad landowners, we found that these women were not very well treated by the landowners in general. We could find only one case in Phuglana village, where a woman worker got a beating from the landowner as a consequence of her answering back. However, in the case of wheat harvesting and other work situations where the entire family works together, the landowners keep themselves in limits. Abusing is particularly noticeable in various operations of potato cultivation where women are almost exclusively employed.

The second dimension concerning sexual exploitation of women presented great difficulties in collecting information. There were hardly any cases of reporting of rapes. However, certain observations need to be made which are not based on the women's responses but on basis of information of provided by certain activists belonging to Bajwara and Sahri villages. The nature of sexual exploitation of the scheduled caste women in general which is very common has an element of being taken for granted. To certain queries we could get the response like 'this happens'. The sexual exploitation of women belonging to the service castes seems to be a decades old phenomenon. However, the worst sufferers are the Balmiki women.

Conclusions

The scheduled castes in rural areas are largely the agricultural labourers. However, there are castewise variations among the scheduled caste women in terms of their gainful employment. The women belonging to the Ad-dharmi castes are also involved in relatively high status occupations. Women are still working under the jajmani system despite the penetration of capital in Punjab agriculture.

The wage structure of women agricultural labourers indicates that they have been paid less than the men labourers. In a most of the cases the working days of women agricultural labourers do not exceed 100 days. The working days in a year have registered a marginal increase since 1972. This has been a consequence of certain complex changes which have taken place in the Punjab agriculture. On the one hand, the mechanisation process has reduced the number of days to complete a particular operation, and on the other hand, the cropping intensity has resulted in the increase in work availability.

There is a convincing evidence to suggest that the mechanisation has replaced the women by men. One important agricultural operation, viz., winnowing, has disappeared and women are not employed to work on threshers. Thus, technology change has negative consequences for women's work. The sexual exploitation of the scheduled caste women in general and agricultural labourers and scavengers in particular is one of the distressing reality, and it is a taken for granted reality. The conditions of the scheduled caste women are inseparably linked with their caste are largely landless and politically ineffective. They have to depend heavily on the landowning classes for survival. In the lean seasons they depend upon landowners for short-term loans which they repay by working in their fields. The very existential reality of the scheduled castes has an inbuilt structure of exploitation. A very few among them have been able to move high in economic hierarchy. But for a majority of them most of things have remained unchanged.

Notes

This article was first published in *Ambedkar Journal of Social Development and Justice*, Vol. 3, March 1993. The author is grateful to Dr Baba Saheb Ambedkar National Institute of Social Sciences, Mhow for allowing him to reproduce it in this collection.

1. These issues have been discussed on the basis of the exploration of the available literature on women. Some of the important contributors in this regard are: Ahmed, Iftekhar (1985), "Rural Women and Technological Change: Theory, Empirical Analysis and Operation Projects", *Labour and Society*, Vol. 10, No.3, September; Ahooja-Patel, Krishna (1979), "Women Technology and Development Process", *EPW*, Vol. XIV, No. 36, September 8; Desai, Neera (1985), Caste, Class and Gender (paper presented in 17th All India Sociological Conference, Surat, South Gujarat University); D'souza, V.S. (1975), "Family Status and Female Work Participation: An Empirical Analysis", *Social Action*, Vol.25, No.3, July-September; Jain, Devaki (1979), *Women's Quest for Power: Five Case Studies*, Sahibabad, Vikas Publications; Mies, Maria (1984), "Capitalism and Subsistence: Rural Women in India", *Development*, December, No.4; Mukerji, Vatsala (1986), "Status of Women: Economic Policy for Developing Countries", *Economic Times*, January 18; Patel, Vibhuti (1985), "Women and Work", Bombay, SNDT Women's University; Sarafati, Hedva (1985), "Job Equality for Women: Progress, Problems and Perspectives", *Labour and Society*, Vol.10, No.3, September; Sharma, Miriam (1985), "Caste, Class and Gender in Production and Reproduction in North India", *Journal of Peasant Studies*, Vol. 12, No.4, July.

2. Census of India, 1981, Primary Census Abstract, Scheduled Castes.
3. More working hours of the labourers in a situation of a lack of forced labour may not necessarily be a sufficient indicator of their exploitation. It can only be stated in terms of the farmer-worker relationship, which has an inbuilt element of exploitation. Furthermore, the incentive system, either consciously introduced or a part of system, as is the case at present, does not exclude exploitation.
4. The data for the present study were collected in 1985–86. Since then the wages might have gone up.
5. The area of the present study has proximity with the Shivalik hills. It is known as Kandi area. The minimum wage rates fixed by the Punjab government for the Kandi area are lower than the rest of Punjab.
6. The categories 'migrant labourer' and 'local labourer' should be understood in the following manner: The migrant labourer means the person who has come from any other state or region to a particular workplace. Local labourer works in his/her own villager within the region where daily commuting is possible.
7. As such, it is very difficult to characterise a particular activity as semi-gainful. Theoretically speaking, the activity of a person should either generate income in which case it becomes gainful work or not have income, which makes it non-gainful work. However, non-gainful work may consist of domestic work and other work, like collection of fuel wood and/or animal fodder. The categorization of non-gainful work is for the purpose of having an estimation of women's work without remuneration which–nay not entirely be a domestic work. It can be further argued that a woman who is doing her domestic work cannot be characterised as gainfully employed. On the other hand, the collection of wood, making dung cakes and bringing animal fodder has potential of being considered as gainful employment. In case either of these items is sold in certain conditions, may be in the fog in of distress sale. It is within this context-limited though as it may seem, these activities have been termed as 'semi-gainful'.

References

Berreman, G.D. 1979. *Caste and other Inequities: Essay on Inequality*. Meerut: Folklore Institute.

Brandzaeg, B. 1979. *Women, Food and Technology: A Case of India*, *EPW*, Vol. XIV, No. 47, November 24.

Government of Punjab. 1985. *Statistical Abstract of Punjab*, Chandigarh: Government of Punjab.

Omvedt, Gail. 1980. *We Shall Smash This Prison.* Delhi: Orient Longman.

Rudra, A. 1970. "In Search of the Capitalist Farmers", *EPW*, Vol. V, No. 26, June 27.

Sethi, R.M. 1982. *Female Labour in Agriculture.* Chandigarh: Panjab University.

Sharma, M. 1985. "Caste, Class and Gender: Production and Reproduction in North India", *The Journal of Peasant Studies*, Vol. 12, No. 4, July.

Singh, K.P. 1980. "Economic Development and Female Labour Force Participation: The Case of Punjab", *Social Action*, Vol. 30, April–June.

5

Emerging Trends in the Caste Structure of Punjab

This paper seeks to examine the changing conditions of social, political and economic living of scheduled castes in Punjab. Certain developments in the recent past demand an investigation in the light of the dynamics of Punjabi society. These include the electoral success of Bahujan Samaj Party (BSP) in the recent Lok Sabha elections, and the conversion of some scheduled castes to Buddhism in Phagwara. These occurrences have a sociological context which requires exploration. The following questions may be raised with regard to the dynamics of caste structure of Punjab: Which are the dominant castes in Punjab? What are the various forces that have led to changes in the lives of scheduled castes? Are these changes confined to a few castes among them?

The succeeding discussion is aimed at answering these questions. It is worthwhile to note that part of this paper is based on an empirical investigation conducted in Hoshiarpur district. The purpose of the presentation of data is to highlight the changing socio-economic life of the scheduled castes and to examine the structure of economic and political dominance at the micro level. It may be further added that the analysis and findings are based on the social reality of the rural Punjab.

The discussion is divided into four parts. The first part provides the theoretical context. Part two includes the empirical context. The third part describes the various changes that have taken place in Punjab. And, the last part concludes the discussion.

Theoretical Context

Explanations of social change broadly identify three alternative strategies. These are causation, intervention and collective action (Judge and Bal, 1996). Change can be brought about by certain forces at work in society. Sociologists identify various such forces, some of these are urbanisation, industrialisation, etc. In recent times, the political system has begun to intervene more actively in the social structure to bring about transformation. In India, examples of such intervention are the abolition of untouchability, reservation policy and land reforms. What is noteworthy is that these interventions have occurred through legal rational action. At the same time, people themselves have been making collective efforts, particularly through social movements, to change the conditions of their lives. Moreover, for a change to occur, more than one strategy may be at work at the same time.

Social change has both macro and micro contexts. There may be a change taking place within and outside the society. A large number of sociological village studies have vividly examined micro-level changes. Both levels of change have distinctiveness as well as interconnections. To understand macro-level changes, an examination of the mode of production is essential. When these changes take place, new relations of production emerge. We know from the debate on the mode of production in Indian agriculture that its identification has been a matter of controversy. However, with regard to Green Revolution areas, changes in the mode of production have occurred.

In a way, the mode of production is dynamic, and certain changes through modifications in the means of production take place. But if society has moved from a patron-client relationship to wage labour, then the change in the mode of production is self-evident. However, the problem arises when both forms of relationship begin to co-exist. How should we characterise such a mode of production? This calls for an examination of the micro reality.

It helps us to understand the plausibility structure of persistence of some social formations even when the mode of production undergoes a change. It has been observed that the effect of change on various caste groups, who occupy the same position in their relation with the forces of production, is not always uniform. It is this lack of uniformity in the change among various castes which leads a social scientist to examine certain key components of the superstructure. Consciousness, culture, tradition and values acquire a significant place in intercaste comparisons when all other indicators of change are shared by all castes.

In the light of the above theoretical perspective, we will examine changes in the caste structure of Punjab with special emphasis on scheduled castes. Owing to the limitation of empirical investigation, the analysis will remain confined to a few castes among them. To be more precise, this paper examines the differences in the responses of two scheduled castes, viz., Chamars and Bhangis or Churhas, to the changing conditions in Punjab.

Empirical Context

According to the Census of India, 1991, the scheduled castes constitute 28.31 per cent of the population in Punjab, whereas at the all-India level, their share in the total population is 16.73 per cent. Punjab has the highest proportion of the scheduled castes compared to any other state in the country.

However, there are inter-district variations in their population size. Before the creation of new districts, those with a percentage of scheduled castes higher than the state average were Jalandhar (39.08%), Faridkot (34.08%), Hoshiarpur (33.32%), Patiala (29.27%) and Bathinda (29.2%). At the same time, the two scheduled castes under discussion are not uniformly distributed in the state (Pimpley, 1980). We find that Jalandhar, Hoshiarpur and Kapurthala districts have a preponderance of Chamars (Briggs, 1920), whereas Bathinda and Amritsar districts have a concentration of Churhas. In other districts too, such variations can be observed. For our present analysis, the main focus of investigation is the Doaba region[1], which consists of Jalandhar, Hoshiarpur and Kapurthala districts. The empirical study was conducted in the five villages of Hoshiarpur district.[2] The data presented here provide comprehensive information regarding the socio-economic and political characteristics of scheduled castes in these villages.[3] The size of the sample was 400. The selection of the sample was based on the stratified proportionate random sampling method. Of the total respondents, 86.25 per cent belonged to the Chamar caste. Among others were Balmikis or Churhas (10.50%), Bazigars (2.75%), Bhanjara (0.25%) and Julaha (0.25%). In other words, Chamars were in an overwhelming majority. As already noted, the Chamars constitute a higher proportion than any other caste among the scheduled castes in this region[4].

The data shown in tables on education, occupation and other related socio-economic variables indicate changes among the scheduled castes. The Chamars are the most mobile caste. The following findings emerge from the data:

- Tables 1 and 2 show the education levels of both respondents and their children. It is clear that considerable number among the scheduled castes has received formal education. Even more revealing is the tremendous increase in the education of their children.

Table 1
Education of the respondents

Level	*Number*	*Percentage*
Illiterate	235	58.75
Upto primary	35	8.75
Upto middle	74	18.50
Upto matric and Other Professional training	46	11.50
College	10	2.50
Total	400	100.00

Table 2
Children's education

Education of children	*Number*	*Percentage*
All educated	214	53.50
Some educated	83	20.75
All illiterate	35	8.75
Not applicable	68	17.00
Total	400	100.00

- The data on occupation (Table 3) have been categorized into occupational prestige categories as provided by D'souza (1985) in his study of Punjab villages. There is evidence of occupational diversification among the scheduled castes under investigation. At the same time, one finds that 49.25 per cent of the total respondents are engaged in labour. It is noteworthy that a sizeable proportion has moved to higher prestige occupations compared to their traditional caste calling. As compared to their fathers (Table 4), 21.75 per cent have got a higher occupation, which shows a degree of occupational mobility.

Table 3
Occupation

Category	*Occupation*	*Number*	*Percentage*
III	Flour miller	1	0.25
IV	School teacher	6	1.50
V	Panchayat secretary	2	0.50
	Shopkeeper	to	2.50
	Shopkeeper-cum-labourer	1	0.25
	Carpenter	1	0.25
	Carpenter-cum-labourer	1	0.25
	Blacksmith	2	0.50
	Own cultivator	5	1.25
	Own cultivator-cum-labourer	1	0.25
	Clerk	10	2.50
	Mechanic	4	1.00
	Mechanic-cum-Labourer	1	0.25
	Roadways conductor/driver	4	1.00
VI	Weaver	29	7.25
	Weaver-cum-machine-operator	1	0.25
	Weaver-cum-labourer	17	4.25
	Jute spinner	2	0.50
	Jute spinner-cum-watchman-cum-labourer	4	1.0
	Toymaker	2	0.50
	Tailor	4	1.00

cont'd...

cont'd...

	Sharecropper-cum-labourer	4	1.00
	Police/armyman	8	2.00
	Mason	5	4.25
	Tinner	1	0.25
	Band master-cum-labourer	4	1.00
	Machine operator	2	0.50
	Painter	2	0.50
VII	Cobbler	7	1.75
	Cobbler-cum-labourer	5	1.25
	Vendor	2	0.50
	Horse cart driver	1	0.25
	Peon-cum-labourer	5	1.25
	Postman	1	0.25
	Watchman	2	0.50
	Ward boy	1	0.25
	Washerman	2	0.50
	Rickshaw puller-cum-labourer	6	1.50
	Agricultural/casual labourer	197	49.25
	Sweeper-cum-labourer	5	1.25
VIII	No occupation	32	8.00
	Total	400	103.00

Table 4

Father's occupation

Occupational level	*Number*	*Percentage*
Same	295	73.75
Higher	18	4.50
Lower	87	21.75
Total	400	100.00

- One indicator of economic condition of scheduled caste families is the number of rooms by family size (Table 5). We find that a majority live in hard conditions. At the same time, 16.25 per cent among them have three or above rooms.
- It has been found that only 24 scheduled caste respondents owned land, of which one each was a medium and semi-medium farmer.

The implication of this lack of landownership for their social mobility is their relatively greater ability to move out of the agriculture.

Table 5

Family size and number of rooms

Family size	Number of rooms				Total
	One	Two	Three–Four	Four & Above	
2–5	84 (58.33)	84 (43.97)	17 (30.90)	5 (50.00)	190 (47.50)
6–8	50 (34.72)	94 (49.21)	28 (50.90)	4 (40.00)	176 (44.00)
9 & above	10 (6.94)	13 (6.80)	10 (18.18)	1 (10.00)	34 (8.50)
Total	144	191	55	10	400

- With the exception of one village, in all others, scheduled castes constitute more than half the population. Since democracy is sometimes reduced to a numbers game, it was worthwhile to examine the caste structure of village panchayats. It was found that four villages had been consistently electing upper caste Sarpanchs. Most of the panchayat members belonged to the scheduled castes. Only one village had elected a scheduled caste Sarpanch three times. The Sarpanch of this village is better off than his fellow caste members. However, it was found that the number of scheduled caste panchayat members is rising.
- It is clear from the findings of the study that the social and political situation of scheduled castes is changing. What are the implications for the caste structure of Punjab? Two issues here require analytical treatment. These are forces of change in Punjab and the identification of those scheduled castes which have experienced these changes – more than others. The data appear to suggest that the maximum change has occurred within the Chamar caste. Its manifestation is the formation of classes within a caste group. We would do well to historically trace the manner in which the caste structure of Punjab has evolved and continues to do so as a result of a large number of factors.

Changing Caste Structure of Punjab

A typical construct of caste structure of Punjab would correspond to the varna hierarchy. Accordingly, we can place Brahmins, Rajputs,

Khatris, Banyas, Jats, artisan castes and the scheduled castes in a descending order. However, Punjab's social structure underwent major changes which can be traced back to the medieval period. Sometimes it is argued that caste has lost its rigidity in Punjab (Narang, 1982). This is an erroneous observation. Many a time this idea is articulated in order to emphasise the egalitarian impact of Sikhism. What most writers on the caste structure of Punjab have failed to highlight is the religious divisions in Punjab within which caste hierarchies evolved. Even here the lowest of the low remained at the bottom as despised groups. Moreover, caste hierarchies are observed in terms of the intensity of the practice of purity and pollution by ignoring certain regional variations. Exclusion is perhaps the appropriate criterion to assess the strength of the caste system in Punjab or elsewhere.

In an inegalitarian system supported by the ideology of karma, the arrival of the notion of equality of any kind was an important event. It provided the possibility of change in status which was hitherto absent. In this regard, Islam played a pivotal role. However, it also became the basis for comparison at a large scale which resulted in the Bhakti movement. In the context of Punjab, the Sikh movement was a vehicle of change in the caste structure. Many castes were able to improve their status. It is interesting to note that the egalitarian appeal of Sikhism drew within its fold those caste groups which were denied social status in accordance with their economic achievements. Habib (1976) has examined the case of Jats of Punjab in the light of this historical condition. Jats, who were originally a pastoral community, settled as peasants in Punjab and Sindh. Through their hard work they were able to improve their condition, but they could not get higher status within the fold of Hinduism. The Sikh movement provided them with the platform for social mobility. Now, they are the dominant caste in Punjab. Habib, however, has not explained the conversion of Jats to Islam in the light of this thesis. The other castes, which have improved their status and no longer belong to the lower castes, are Ramgarhias and Ahluwalias.

Saberwal (1990) considers Ramgarhias as the most mobile caste. As blacksmiths, they were village artisans. They were given a lower caste status. Their conversation to Sikhism played an important role in raising their status.

In recent years the Ramgarhias have been the most enterprising among Sikhs (Bal, 1995). Ahluwalias were originally liquor distillers and were known as Kalals. The Sikh movement afforded them the opportunity for capturing political power and improving their social status.

However, the Sikh movement failed to help the Churhas – the lowest among low castes – to enhance their status. Singh (1985), who treats the Sikh movement as a plebeian revolution, found that in the initial stages the Churhas were christened as 'Rangretas'. Nowadays, Sikh Churhas are known as 'Mazbis'. They are still excluded from social interactions which characterises a religious community.

The beginning of British rule in Punjab coincided with the end of Sikh rule. By the second half of the 19th century, the effect of the Raj could be discerned in various forms. According to Oberoi (1994), the conversion to Christianity of some persons evoked a tremendous response among the three religious communities of Punjab. We find that among the convertees, the Churhas form such a sizeable proportion that Christian and Churha have become synonymous in Punjab. The major response to such conversions came from the Arya Samaj movement in the 19th century. The Arya Samaj introduced the Shudhi movement with the purpose of bringing back to the fold of Hinduism families who had converted to other religions, particularly Islam. Sharma (1985) has examined the effect of reconversion on the status improvement of such families. He finds that Shudhi failed to enhance the status of these families who belonged to scheduled castes. Obviously, no such effort could be observed among the Sikhs and Muslims. Their egalitarian claims would have stood in contradiction to any such effort. It would have amounted to an acceptance of the existence of castes among these religious groups. However, caste stratification among all the religious communities continued to exist at the turn of the 20th century. For example, the Bhangi was known as Balmiki as a Hindu, Mazabi as a Sikh, and Mussali as a Muslim. His conversion to Christianity gave him another name, i.e., Masih. Such change of names had no implications for the improvement of his status.

The initiative to change the caste status from within came from the Chamar caste in the Doaba region. What is known as Ad-dharma movement was led by Mangoo Ram, an ex-Gadharite, who belonged to a village in Hoshiarpur district. In the late twenties he was able to mobilise a larger number of Chamars. His strategy centred on evolving a separate identity for the scheduled castes from the major religions of the state. In the process, large-scale mass mobilisation took place, with the participants being enumerated as Ad-dharmis in the Census of 1931 (Juergensmeyer, 1982). However, the movement remained confined to Chamars. They became Ad-dharmis, but there was no change in their status. Still, the Ad-dharma movement raised the level of consciousness of at least one caste, the impact of which was felt after independence. One such consequence was, as Juergensmeyer has pointed out, their migration to western countries.

After independence, the abolition of untouchability and the reservation policy introduced by the government were major forces of social change. In his study, Bains (1994) has noted that scheduled castes failed to fill the reserved seats in the case of Class I posts, whereas they were overrepresented in the III and IV class posts. More significantly, among those who utilised the reservation policy, the Chamars were the most numerous. One of the fallouts of the reservation policy was the reaction of the non-scheduled castes as a result of which caste-based boundaries have become firmly demarcated.

In the case of Punjab, the major source of change has been the agricultural development of the state. What is popularly known as the Green Revolution is a phenomenon of high agricultural growth rate which began in the late sixties. Experts have identified many factors which made the Green Revolution possible. These included HYV seeds, chemical fertilisers, mechanisation, irrigation infrastructure, provisions for institutional credit and the ready acceptance of the new technology by farmers. The Green Revolution led to two important processes with regard to the increase in the production of a number of crops grown in a year as well as the area under cultivation. Consequently, the need for labour rose from a few days during the seasons to throughout the year. Since the crop needed to be harvested as quickly as possible so that the land could be released for the next crop, labour intensity also increased. We find that during peak seasons migrant labour from other states could be easily absorbed by the local agricultural operations. In spite of the efforts of landowners to depress wages through migrant labour, the wage rates increased. One may question whether real wages have increased or not. However, a recent study conducted by Shergill and Singh (1995) shows that there is no rural poverty in Punjab.

The scheduled castes belonging to the class of agricultural workers have been able to improve their economic conditions by crossing the line of absolute poverty. Relative poverty probably continues. What have been the social implications of this improvement in economic conditions? Here, we may recall our comparison between the two prominent scheduled castes in Punjab, viz., Chamars and Churhas. From the perspective of the Green Revolution both castes should have benefited equally. To an extent, this is what has happened. However, we find that the Chamars or Ad-dharmis have been able to extend their newly-acquired economic clout to the political arena. The rise of the Bahujan Samaj Party (BSP) in Punjab is mainly a consequence of the mobilisation of this caste. There does not seem to be a wider coalition of dalits in Punjab. Omvedt (1994) is of the view that there is a commonality between the Mahars of Maharashtra and the Chamars of Punjab. She considers both of them to have been small landholders. This is not true in the case of Chamars. The only commonality seems to be that some families of this caste have recently converted to Buddhism.

The political leadership provided by the BSP aims at capturing power through electoral politics. This implies that the aspirations of the Chamar caste have grown from achieving equal status to attaining elite status. The election of Kanshi Ram from the Hoshiarpur Lok Sabha seat, which is not a reserved constituency, indicates this trend. At the same time, some cases of conversion to Buddhism show that there is an underlying current of rejection of previous identities. How can we analyse these changes? In the concluding part of the paper an attempt will be made to answer this question.

Conclusion

In this part we will try to examine various changes in the caste structure in the light of the theoretical discussion in the first part. The history of change in the caste structure of Punjab shows that certain castes were able to improve their status by joining the Sikh movement. However, improvements were also made possible by the fact that these castes had either enhanced their economic condition or captured political power. The notable exception to this phenomenon was the Mazabis who were unable to improve their caste status mainly due to the fact that there was no change in the collective life of this caste as compared to Jats and other castes. Moreover, the Mazabis were part of the untouchable castes which the others were not.

The data provided in the second part indicate that a lot of changes are taking place among the scheduled castes. The findings also suggest intercaste variations. We find that the Chamars are more mobile than the Balmikis. Part three also reinforces this conclusion on the basis of other studies. The reasons for greater mobility among Chamars may be located in the manner in which they have evolved through their collective experience of movements. In Punjab the Chamars form an exception as a caste. They are the only caste to have waged a movement for higher status. The members of this caste have been able to exploit various opportunities after independence. As a result, there is a process of class formation within this caste, with its elite striving to compete with the upper caste power holders. The Green Revolution has improved the condition of the non-elite among Chamars. This has provided the material basis for their electoral aspiration. The conversion to Buddhism is limited. If it acquires a mass character, the lag between social and economic conditions in a situation of rising political aspirations will become a decisive factor.

In the end, we may argue that because of its dynamic character, the mode of production does not have uniform consequences for all social groups. The capitalist development of agriculture in Punjab has affected its two main scheduled castes differently. In addition to the opportunities provided by the new mode of production, the history and level of consciousness of a caste plays an important role in its response to the changing socio-economic scenario.

Notes

This article was originally published in *Administrator*, Vol. XLII, No. 1, January–March, 1997.

1. Three broad regions of Punjab are Doaba, Majha and Malwa.
2. These five villages are Badowal, Bajwara, Methiana, Phuglana and Sahri.
3. The data, which were collected in the late eighties, give insight into the changing scenario in Punjab under the impact of Green Revolution. They point to the growing mobility among Chamars. Since this preceded the emergence of the Bahujan Samaj Party, the data throw light on the factors which led to its success.
4. Chamars are also known by various names such as Ramdasyas, Ravidasyas and Ad-dharmis.

References

Bains, Ravinder S. 1994. *Reservation Policy and Anti Reservationists.* Delhi: B.R. Publishers.

Bal, Gurpreet. 1995. *Development and Change in Punjab,* Delhi: National Book Organization,

Briggs, Geo, W. 1920. *The Chamars.* Delhi: B.R. Publishers.

D'souza, V.S. 1985. *Economic Development, Social Structure and Population Growth.* New Delhi, Sage Publications.

Habib, Irfan. 1976. "Jats of Punjab and Sind" in Harbans Singh and N.G. Barrier (eds.), *Punjab Past and Present: Essays in Honour of Dr. Ganda Singh.* Patiala: Punjab University.

Judge, Paramjit S. and Bal, Gurpreet. 1996. *Strategies of Social Change in India.* Delhi: M.D. Publication.

Juergensmeyer, Mark. 1982. *Religion as Social Vision: The Movement Against Untouchability in Punjab.* Berkeley: University of California Press.

Narang, Amarjeet Singh. 1982. "Punjab: Development and Politics", in Gail Omvedt (ed.), *Land, Caste and Politics in Indian States.* Delhi: University of Delhi.

Oberoi, Harjot. 1994. *The Construction of Religious Boundaries: Culture, Identity and Diversity in Sikh Tradition.* Delhi: Oxford University Press.

Omvedt, Gail. 1994. "Kanshi Ram and the Bahujan Samaj Party" in K.L. Sharma (ed.), *Caste and Class.* Jaipur: Rawat.

Pimpley, P.N. 1980. *A Profile of Scheduled Caste Students.* Chandigarh: Punjab University.

Saberwal, Satish. 1990. *Mobile Men: Limits to Social Change in Urban Punjab* (Revised). Delhi: Manohar.

Sharma, Satish K. 1985. *Social Movements and Social Change.* Delhi: B.R. Publishers.

Shergill, H.S. and Singh, Gurmail. 1995. "Poverty in Rural Punjab: Trends over Green Revolution Decades", *Economic and Political Weekly,* Vol. XXX, No. 25, June 24.

Singh, Jagjit. 1985. *Perspectives on Sikh Studies.* Delhi: Guru Nanak Foundation.

6

Green Revolution and the Bahujan Samaj Party in Punjab

Recent electoral successes of the Bahujan Samaj Party (BSP) in northern India have drawn the attention of social scientists, and various theoretical assumptions will be made to analyse and understand the numerous factors and processes behind this success. Kanshi Ram originally hailed from the Ropar district of Punjab. His ability to mobilise electoral support among the dalits in other states seemed to be an indicator of a wide coalition of the depressed communities in India to articulate their interests through formal political processes. The criticism of Gandhi and Ambedkar by Mayawati in 1994 indicates a different kind of politico-ideological orientation of this party. It is all the more important when it is realised that among the supporters of the BSP the members of only one dalit caste are more vocal and active both as leaders and voters. Certain issues with regard to the BSP phenomenon acquire a great significance for a political sociologist. For instance, is it a dalit movement for caste equality? Why has the BSP gained more popularity in northern India? Does BSP represent the interests of all the dalit castes in northern India?

The forthcoming discussion aims at answering these questions rather tangentially, in the sense that an attempt has been made to highlight the relationship between the economic development, particularly the Green Revolution, and social and political mobility. We have examined the issues in the context of Punjab only. For this purpose we have divided the discussion into four parts. The first part provides the theoretical perspective of this study. It also mentions other similar studies. The second part deals with the socio-historical background of the Chamar caste. In the third part, we shall focus on the socio-economic changes experienced by this caste as a result of the Green Revolution. The fourth part provides certain tentative conclusions.

Theoretical Perspective

The theoretical perspective of this study can be stated in terms of the relationship between economic development and social change. The emerging economic reality influences other facets of people's life. The Green Revolution in Punjab has been the development of capitalism in agriculture. This was a new mode of production which changed the mode of agriculture and it affected the different social groups in various ways. Theoretically, the effect of economic development on different caste groups may vary even when they occupy common social position. The scheduled castes, who are largely the landless agricultural labourers, might not have evenly received the benefits of the Green Revolution. Furthermore, the improvement in the economic conditions changes the political behaviour and aspirations of a caste. Once, a caste might be struggling for equal status, but later on, it may be aspiring for a share in power. Struggle for status and striving for power sharing are two different dimensions in the political behaviour of a caste, because these two are separate goals. The transformation in the existing conditions contributes towards the transformation of the aspiration of a caste.

In sociological literature there are certain important studies, which discuss the effectiveness of the strategy of political mobilisation for the improvement of the status of the lower castes. For example, Rao (1979) has studied Sri Narayana Dharma Paripalana Movement among the Izavas of Kerala and Yadava movement. Similarly, Zelliot (1970) and Hardgrave, Jr. (1970) have shown in their studies that the use of political means is the effective method for status improvement. Other scholars, such as Rudolph and Rudolph (1967), and Lynch (1969), have also highlighted the same phenomenon. All these studies have a historical context. For example, the Nadars, the Mahars and the Izavas began their struggle during the British rule. In a way, these movements were waged in a colonial situation when the influence of Western liberalism could be felt but the development of the Indian society was slow, which left it socially traditional and economically backward. Even then, these castes carried on their movements for better status – a result of certain distinct characteristics which were linked with the existential conditions of those castes. In the case of the Nadars education and economic autonomy, in the case of the Mahars the status of watchman and small peasant, and in the case of the Jatavas the shoe trade became the main source of emergence of consciousness, with which they strived for their relative economic independence to political mobilisation for better social status.

Bailey (1972), in his study of an Orissa village, has shown the ways the sociologist must investigate the form and content of change among castes. Three castes of this village (all the three being low castes) improved their economic conditions through the liquor trade. After the economic betterment each of the castes followed its distinct strategy for the improvement of its status. In a way, this study highlights the possibility of diverse strategies for the improvement of the status. In this context political mobilisation becomes one of the strategies for the status enhancement of the dalits. This leads us to examine the conditions under which political mobilisation is an effective strategy. At this juncture, it would be worthwhile to quote Rudolph and Rudolph (1967: 70) at length thus:

> The relationship of caste to social and political change and to the conduct of government and politics varies more than the examples of the Nadars and Vanniyars suggest. Some of the factors that effect its role include: (1) the number and size of other caste actors; (2) regional differences and their effect on the caste profile of particular states; (3) differences in the level and characteristics of relevant political systems; (4) the relative significance of dominant and subject castes and the related propensities toward vertical and horizontal mobilization; (5) changes over time in the social and political environment in which particular castes operate; (6) the degree of self-consciousness and cohesion that characterize particular castes; and (7) the countervailing power of other castes, interest groups, and integrative forces, particularly political parties.

In contrast to these general factors, Seth (1987: 47), on the basis of an empirical study of two villages in Uttar Pradesh, puts forward extreme poverty, illiteracy and absence of politicisation as the basis of the failure of lower castes to protest against caste oppression. Rudolph and Rudolph have contextualised the relationship between economic, social and political dimensions of caste in both time and space. In addition to that, the size of a caste and its level of consciousness have been taken as important variables. It may be further argued that the relative economic independence of a caste is an important factor which influences its political action.

On the basis of the above discussion, we can identify the following features which form the basis of a caste's political behaviour:

(a) Size of the caste in a region.
(b) The relative economic independence.
(c) Level of consciousness through education or traditions of collective mobilisation.
(d) The orientation for goal attainment has historical specificity in the sense that with the changing historical conditions any lower caste may shift its goal from better status to equal share in power for itself only though it may seem to be involving other underprivileged castes.

The above mentioned general features require an investigation into the regional features of the caste which effectively uses political mobilisation strategy.

Chamars/Ad-dharmis/Ramdasya

There has been a degree of confusion in the nomenclature of the Chamar caste. Though, traditionally, a leather working caste, Chamars over a period of time have been changing their caste identity. As we shall see a little later, these changes have been influenced by various historical circumstances. It may be added further that in the census of India referring to various scheduled castes in Punjab, these names have been listed as representing different castes. However, the village level reality provides a different picture. The upper castes club these categories to designate most of them as Chamars in private and Ad-dharmis in public. Saberwal (1990) has noted that some Balmikis claimed the Ad-dharmi status in 1920s, but this may rather be treated as an exception if such cases are identified. For our present purpose, we shall club together all the three caste names to designate them as Chamars. To begin with, let us have some knowledge of this caste.

The Chamar caste is the most numerous castes among the scheduled castes in North India. In the opinion of Briggs (1920), the pioneering authority on the subject, the Chamar includes some castes which seem to have emerged as separate castes with distinct identity. In this way, Mochis, Julahas and Koris can be primarily included under the umbrella name of Chamar. Of the various states, the Chamars are highly concentrated in Punjab. According to the 1911 census figures, the total number of Chamars was 1,139,941. In addition to that the Mochis were 4,19,378, Julahas were 6,35,044 and Koris were 18,050. Very few Chamars were Muslims and 1,75,379 of them were Sikhs. Most of them were Hindus. According to Fuchs (1981), the Muslim Chamars called themselves Mochis. Here, we are primarily concerned with the population designated as Chamars who were either Hindus or Sikhs.

At present, according to the 1991 census, the scheduled castes constitute 28.31 per cent of the total population of Punjab. There are lot of variations in the distribution of the scheduled castes population according to the district. Some districts, such as Jalandhar, Hoshiarpur, and Faridkot, have a higher proportion of the scheduled castes than the state average (for details see Table 1). Of the various scheduled castes in Punjab, Chamars and Balmikis/Mazabis are the most numerous.

Table 1

District-wise age distribution of scheduled castes in Punjab, 1991

District	*Percentage*
Gurdaspur	24.70
Amritsar	28.00
Ferozepur	21.80
Ludhiana	24.74
Jalandhar	39.08
Kapurthala	29.46
Hoshiarpur	33.32
Rupnagar	24.57
Patiala	29.27
Sangrur	26.83
Bathinda	29.27
Faridkot	34.08
Punjab	28.31
All India	16.73

Source: Census of India, 1991.

In the discussion of the location of a caste in the social hierarchy caste occupation is an important dimension. Since we are aware of the fact that the Chamars are an ex-untouchable caste, it becomes very important to know their economic activities. Ideally, it is understood that a caste performs only one occupation which is hereditary. In actual practice, a caste may always be performing more than one occupation. Numerically speaking, the Balmiki/Mazabi is an equally important caste. This quantitative fact in the social context transforms into a quality in the democratic context when the reservation policy and elections are linked with this dimension. We would do well to discuss the occupational features of both Chamars and Balmikis.

The traditional occupation of a Chamar is leather work, but he has been performing various occupations in Punjab. According to Fuchs (1981: 198–99), the Chamar "is the general servant and field worker in the villages; he does all the work requested from him by the high castes, often without getting the payment, or such work as cutting grass, carrying wood and bundles, acting as watchman and the like; he plasters the houses with mud or whitewashes them when they need it. The Chamar takes the hides of all dead cattle and the flesh of all cloven-footed animals, leaving the others to the Churhas. He makes and mends shoes, thongs for the cart, and whips and other leather work".

In Punjab, the Balmikis or Churhas are scavengers. Like Chamars, they also have other occupations. We again depend upon Fuchs (ibid., 240) thus: "their traditional occupation is scavenging, sweeping the houses and streets, cleaning the stables of carrying to the fields and distributing manure, and in cities and village houses where women are secluded, removing night soil". He further enlists, keeping and rearing impure animals like pigs and fowls, serving as village menials and messengers for the upper caste to carry the news of death and working as agricultural labourers. Still another significant dimension linked with their survival is the recruitment to the army of the Mazabis and they make 'excellent soldiers'. There is a distinct regiment in the Indian Army known as Sikh LI, which is comprised of the Mazabis.

It may be noted that even in contemporary Punjab most of these occupations are still carried out by these two castes. It simply implies that though there could be a caste occupation, yet the occupational variations had always existed and the hereditary character of an occupation was basically prevailing at the level of the family. Omvedt (1994) regards Chamars as a small peasant caste among the scheduled castes. It may be true for other parts of India, but in the contemporary Punjab the Chamars are not small peasants. In fact, a very small number of Chamars and Balmikis can be found cultivating land as sharecroppers at a low level. The distinctive character of Chamars has been their keeping and rearing cows/buffaloes at a small level. Cattle rearing and selling milk was done simultaneously by most of the Chamar families. In the process, many individuals among them have moved upward by becoming cattle traders. What made Chamars different from the Balmikis was the level of their mobilisation in the 20th century in the form of Ad-dharma movement, which raised their consciousness and brought qualitative changes in their social and political life (for details, see Juergensmeyer, 1982).

The Ad-dharma movement, led by Mangoo Ram, an ex-Ghadarite, was contemporaneous to the Mahars movement led by Ambedkar. It was a movement, which rejected Hinduism, Sikhism and Islam and made an effort to establish a distinct identity of the dalit castes. However, it could only mobilise the Chamar caste. The movement reached its peak in the late 1920s and got intensified at the approach of the 1931 census operations. In the 1931 census most of the Chamars in Hoshiarpur, Jalandhar and Lyallpur (now in Pakistan) districts got themselves enumerated as Ad-dharmis. It may be worth noting that they were mobilised on the issues of caste equality. One of the songs which became popular in 1920s can be translated as: "We dig the wells for the upper castes; we give them water; but the same water is not available to us. We are not allowed to draw water from the same well." In the post-1931 phase till independence, the Ad-dharma movement lost its momentum. It was successful in raising the awareness among the Chamars as well as in giving them a distinct religious identity. In this new religious identity, the famous medieval saint, Ravi Das, became their Guru and his writings as included in the Guru Granth Sahib, the sacred book of the Sikhs, became the textual identification for the new religious identity. In spite of all the limitations, the formation of a new religious identity further fostered a new unity among the Chamars who now began to call themselves Ad-dharmis. Much before the Green Revolution, they had already begun to acquire education and among the various scheduled castes in Punjab they got the maximum benefits of the reservation policy.

Impact of Green Revolution

The phenomenon of Green Revolution which began in Punjab in the late 1960s involved high agricultural production due to HYV (high yielding varieties) seeds, chemical fertilisers, institutional credit and irrigation facilities. It was not simply the high output of crops which had been sown traditionally in Punjab, but the cropping pattern, its extensity as well as intensity, everything, underwent radical changes. One of the instances is paddy cultivation, which earlier was confined to the river bank areas, has now become a major crop in Punjab. The penetration of capitalism started at a large scale when the Punjabi farmers began to grow crops exclusively for the market. For our purpose three things are of great significance as features of the Green Revolution. First, new crops were introduced the purpose of which was profit for the farmer. Second, there was an increase in the cropping intensity in the sense that three to four crops a year were taken. Thirdly, in spite of mechanisation, these crops remained labour intensive. The influx of migrant labour from Uttar Pradesh and Bihar has contributed to the depression of daily wages, but over the years, the wages have been on the rise in Punjab. There has been a controversy among social scientists regarding whether the wage workers have benefited from the Green Revolution or not. Instead of discussing various arguments offered by them for and against the issue, we would rather like to present the actual empirical situation the purpose of which is to locate economically in the agrarian structure those Chamars, who are still wage workers. Among the Chamars who are landless, agricultural labourers are in a majority.

The following arguments are based on a data collected from a village in Hoshiarpur district. The village is located at a distance of 15 kilometres from Hoshiarpur and borders Jalandhar district. The village has Jat Sikhs as the dominant caste who own 90 per cent of the agricultural land of the village. The scheduled castes who constitute 70 per cent of the village population own less than 2 per cent of the agricultural land. Among the scheduled castes the Chamars are 70 per cent. The other numerous scheduled caste is that of Balmikis who rank second in terms of their population size (25% of the scheduled castes population).

The major crops in this village are wheat, maize, sunflower, potato and peas. Among the minor crops are paddy and sugarcane. On an average, three to four crops per year are taken as a result of which the labour requirements of the farmers have gone up. Most of the agricultural operations, such as harvesting, threshing, weeding, potato digging and pea picking require extensive labour, that too within a specified period. In the process labour is required throughout the year. On a conservative estimate a male agricultural worker is employed for eight months and female worker for seven months a year. In the case of men, casual work in the construction sector in the city may supplement his income during the non-work period in the village. At the time of data collection daily wage for men is Rs 50 and for women Rs 30.

On the basis of above, we may work out the income level of these families with a minimum of statistics. Let us take a nuclear family in which only husband and wife are working as agricultural workers. It may, however, be added that proceeding estimates are equally applicable to other scheduled castes families who are working on daily wages. The difference between Chamars and Balmikis particularly lies in the fact that a substantial number of the former are already employed in formal sector. Furthermore, more Chamars have recently migrated to Gulf countries than Balmikis. Taking into consideration the daily wages of the couple and working day's per year, we find that the husband earns Rs 12,000 per annum and the wife Rs 6,300 per annum. In sum the annual income of a family from wages is Rs 18,300. This income is supplemented by selling milk to the village milk cooperative. In this case if we assume that two litres of milk is sold for six month every year at the rate of Rs 7 per litre, then the annual income from milk is Rs 2,520. Thus, the total annual income of the family comes to Rs 20,820. This conservative estimate of the annual income of the family at least establishes one simple fact, i.e., it has income above poverty line even if we assume that in addition to husband and wife there are three minor children. This has been convincingly demonstrated by Shergill and Singh (1995) with the help of data on rural Punjab. The benefits of Green Revolution have reached the working class. It is also evident from the fact that none of the Chamar families in this village is living in *kutcha* house. All of them have been able to construct brick houses with their own resources. This fact is important in the light of government scheme to construct houses for the scheduled castes.

Should we expect that the change in the economic conditions of Chamars combined with objective factors would have brought changes in their political behaviour and collective assertion in terms of better status and more share in the political power structure at various levels? In the last state assembly, panchayat and Lok Sabha elections, the electoral results may further enlighten us in this regard. The village falls under Sham Chaurasi (reserved constituency) for state assembly and Phillaur (again reserved) for Lok Sabha elections. Before we provide the information, a succinct description of the contemporary political dynamics is required as a background.

It was worth mentioning that Punjab underwent a long spell of political uncertainty created by terrorist violence for a period of fourteen years. During this period, the formal democratic process was repeatedly suspended in the state. The imposition of governor's rule for a long period introduced a process of domination of the bureaucracy, both administration and police. The police organisation was given unlimited powers through the Terrorist and Disruptive Activities Act (TADA). The violation of democratic rights of the people became a routine phenomenon. In such an environment, it seemed natural that all sections of society would have suffered because of either the terrorists or the police.

Before the advent of terrorism, whose objective seemed to be the realisation of a separate state of Khalistan, the nature and character of the state politics had been exhibiting both some specific as well as general features. In the general sense of the term, there were numerous political parties of the left, the right and the centre. However, the structure of alliances revolved around a national level party and a regional party which were the dominant parties and competing for power in the state. Like most of the states in the country, the Congress Party was the major contender for power. The specificity of Punjab politics can be located in the internal as well as the external dynamism of its regionally dominant political party, viz., the Akali Dal.

Internally, the Akali Dal is dominated by the Jat Sikhs who constitute a majority in the total population of Sikhs. Among the Sikhs are also included certain scheduled castes, such as Mazabis, Julahas and others including Chamars. The interests of these castes are hardly represented in this political party. A powerful nexus between Shiromani Gurdwara Prabandhak Committee (SGPC) and the Akali Dal and the power struggle among the major leaders have always kept the party faction-ridden. Externally, it always articulates and aggregates two kinds of interests. First, most of the issues it takes up, whether in power or not, are related with the economic interests of the Jat peasantry like, crops, credit and water distribution among states among others. Secondly, by narrowly defining the interests of Punjab as interests of Sikhs it takes up various issues which directly and/or indirectly concern the Sikhs. In these narrowly defined issues we have slogans like 'threat to the unity of Sikh Panth', 'inclusion of Punjabi speaking area', 'promotion of Punjabi', etc. Such a political dynamics does not provide any ideological and programmatic political space to the dalits. Thus, the domination of the Akali Dal signifies the domination of the Jat landed peasantry in which the dalits are more or less marginalised.

The policy of the Congress party in Punjab had no regional autonomy since the formation of Punjabi Suba in 1966. The Congress leadership at the Centre always approached Punjab politics as a counter-struggle to the Akali Dal. However, owing to its legacy of the nationalist movement, the Congress party had its strongholds among the dalits. Interestingly, if a comparative study of the socio-economic background of the leaders of both the parties is made, then we may find only marginal difference. This does not only indicate the common origin of elites (this is perhaps true even for both the communist parties), but also emphasises the fact that for dalits who aspire for elite positions the struggle would be hard if they attempt by joining any of these parties. We are here not referring to the Bhartiya Janata Party (BJP) whose social base has been the urban upper trading castes.

In the backdrop of this political reality, it should be remembered that all these political parties tended to react to terrorism differently. The Akali Dal, after the assassination of Sant Longowal in 1985, became more conciliatory towards terrorists and some of its leaders openly supported them. Among the leaders of Akali Dal, a majority either did not venture to speak against terrorism or supported it. The Congress leadership at certain levels did not openly oppose terrorism excepting a few. Some of the Congress leaders protected terrorists and gave them patronage. It were the communist parties which openly opposed terrorists and became the major target of terrorist attacks.

The State Assembly elections in Punjab were held in February 1992. The terrorists opposed them. The Akali Dal, except for one leader and his supporters, did not contest elections as a result. One of the parties which fought elections and is having the second largest number (9) of MLAs in the state assembly is the Bahujan Samaj Party. Then followed the Lok Sabha and panchayat elections in the state.

At this moment it is relevant to discuss the empirical situation. It is worth noting that in the Sham Chaurasi constituency of State Assembly a BSP candidate was declared elected whereas in the Phillaur Parliamentary constituency a Congress candidate was elected. In the panchayat elections of the village referred to here the candidate who was elected the Sarpanch, had been holding this position for the last 20 years. The political affiliation of the Sarpanch, who is Jat Sikh and a big farmer, has been shifting between terrorists and Akalis. Recently, he has joined the Congress (T). In the history of the village only once a member of the Chamar caste was elected to the post of Sarpanch. In the composition of the panchayat a majority of the members is invariably from the Jat caste. In spite of the rise in the popularity of the BSP among the Chamars, no class or caste issue has come to the fore in the village as well as in the region.

There seems to be two levels of political perceptions of the more aware Chamars compared to other dalit castes. At the local level, economic dependence plays an important role in creating political subservience. It should be noted here that in recent elections, members of the dalit castes have become Sarpanchs in various villages in this district. A dalit's becoming a Sarpanch in a village, however, does not simply relate to the economic logic. One may find that a large number of them are economically prosperous. There are also certain other caste-related dimensions involved which covertly acquire great importance. A point in argument is made by providing a parallel instance of a practice which in modem times may not be acceptable, but is going on in other parts of the country. The village, we are referring to as a case, was originally inhabited by Muslim landowners. They had donated some land to a Brahmin, as an occupancy tenant (the family now owns that land) in lieu of his services to them. Of his various services one was to provide meals to the Hindu and Sikh government officials who used to visit the village. This continued till 1947. In the contemporary situation, the dalit Sarpanch has to depend upon Jat landowners for a similar purpose, failing which, the upper caste officials may just avoid visiting the village. This gives a degree of advantage to the Jat landowners in terms of influence in the bureaucracy. However, at the state and national levels, the local dependence does not remain that central. The Chamars have been using political influence for various purposes. As an instance the following case of Bajwara village near Hoshiarpur which occurred a few years back may indicate an aspiration of a different kind among the Chamars.

A family belonging to the Chamar caste was cultivating a piece of land it leased from a landowner who belonged to the Ramgarhia caste and was settled abroad in England. After 15 years he returned to the village and asked the tenants (members of the family) to buy that land as he did not intend to settle in his village. He did not have much time and wanted to return to England as early as possible. However, the family members were not interested in anything as the record of crops (girdawari) of the land they were operating as tenants was in their names. Upon their evasion of the proposal to buy his land, the landowner began to look for other buyers. The state was under governor's rule at that time, and bureaucracy was supreme. A big landowner of the nearby village, a senior administrative officer and a police official joined together to buy the land. They made the payment to the landowner who disappeared from the scene. Next evening the police raided the village, arrested a male member of the tenant's family and forcibly ejected them from the land. Perceiving themselves to be in a helpless situation they decided to approach Kanshi Ram, the leader of the BSP. The result of this approach was that their man was released from police lock up and they got back their land.

The pattern, which emerges from the above case, does not indicate any dalit movement for social equality as Omvedt tends to suggest. In context of Punjab, the BSP seems to be providing the platform for articulating the aspirations of the emerging elite in the Chamar caste.

Conclusions

The rise of the BSP is linked with improvement in the economic conditions of the scheduled castes, particularly the Chamar/Ad-dharmi caste. The above hypothesis seems to be plausible for which further empirical evidence is required. There is no denying the fact that as the most mobile caste among the scheduled castes, the Chamars/Ad-dharmis have benefited from the development process in which new occupations have emerged, but the improvement in the living conditions of most of the Chamars has occurred as a result of the Green Revolution. This economic change has created classes within the caste and the elites among the Chamars seem to the skilfully using dalit issues for their aspirations. In UP, BSP formed the government and that, too with the help of the Bharatiya Janata Party (BJP). We know that the BJP has Hinduism as its ideological base which is also the basis of caste inequality. In the 1996 Lok Sabha elections, BSP has formed an alliance with the local communal Akali Dal. Though the Sikh religion strongly emphasizes caste equality, yet in actual practice the ex-untouchable castes are still excluded from the mainstream Sikh society, which is dominated by Jats and Khatris. This alliance is basically anti-Congress and is for the purpose of acquiring influence, however limited it may be.

Finally, there is the need to explore the issue related with the BSP and the dalit movement. Kanshi Ram, who began his activities from the organisation of Backward and Minority Communities Employees Federation in 1978, and Dalit Shoshit Samaj Sangarsh Samiti in 1982, belongs to a different period of India's social and economic development. A democratic polity with a degree of public posture towards social justice has contributed a lot in bringing about changes in the approaches to struggles for social equality. Development programmes aiming at poverty eradication and land reform policy have effected changes in the Indian society irrespective of their complete success. The democratic processes have not only initiated a process of ethnic assertion, but also a movement towards capturing formal power positions. In the process, we find the dalits forming their own parties and fighting elections by making alliances with other parties. One may question the logic of alliance with communal parties like the BJP or the Akalis on the part of the BSP, but the fact remains that it is an alliance for sharing power. What has emerged as a significant dimension of struggle for status is another approach of power orientation, which is different from the social movement approach.

In this struggle for formal power at different levels, the better off among the scheduled castes have started dominating the political process. This case is very close to the example of Akali as a representative of the Sikhs, but which largely articulates the interests of Jats. It is the Chamar caste which dominates the political process amongst the scheduled castes.

Note

This article was first published in Judge, Paramjit S. and Satish Kumar Sharma (eds.), *Dimensions of Social Change: Essays in Honour of Professor P.N. Pimpley.* Jaipur: Rawat Publications, 1997.

References

Bailey, F.G. 1972. *Caste and the Economic Frontier: A Village in Highland Orissa.* Manchester: The University of Manchester Press.

Briggs, G.W. 1920. *The Chamars.* Delhi: B.R. Publishing Corporation.

Fuchs, Stephen. 1981. *At the Bottom of Indian Society: The Harijan and Other Low Castes.* Delhi: Munshiram Manoharlal.

Hardgrave, Jr. Robert L. 1970. "Political Participation and Primordial Solidarity: The Nadars of Tamilnad", in Rajni Kothari (ed.), *Caste in Indian Politics.* Delhi: Orient Longman.

Juergensmeyer, Mark. 1982. *Religion as Social Vision: The Movement Against Untouchability in Punjab.* Berkeley: University of California Press.

Lynch, O.W. 1969. *The Politics of Untouchability: Social Mobility and Social Change in a City of India.* New York: Columbia University Press.

Omvedt, Gail. 1994. "Kanshi Ram and the Bahujan Samaj Party", in Sharma, K.L. (ed.), *Caste and Class Movements in India.* Delhi: Manohar.

Rao, M.S.A. 1978. "Social Movements among the Backward Classes and Blacks: Homology in the Sources of Identity", in M.S.A. Rao (ed.), *Social Movements in India.* (Vol. 1), Delhi: Manohar.

Rudolph, L.I and Rudolph, S.H. 1967. *The Modernity of Tradition: Political Development in India.* Chicago: The University of Chicago Press.

Saberwal, Satish. 1990. *Mobile Men: Limits to Social Change in Urban Punjab.* New Delhi: Manohar.

Seth, V.N. 1981. *Sociological Study of Harijan Protest.* Ph.D. thesis (Unpublished) Department of Sociology, Panjab University, Chandigarh.

Shergill, H.S. and Gurmail Singh. 1995. "Poverty in Rural Punjab: Trends over Green Revolution Decades", *Economic and Political Weekly,* Vol. XXX, No. 25, June 24.

Zelliot, Eleanor. 1970. "Learning the Use of Political Means: The Mahars of Maharashtra" in Rajni Kothari (ed.), *Caste in Indian Politics.* Delhi: Orient Longman.

7

Punjabis in England

The Ad-dharmi Experience

The primary purpose of this paper is to highlight the international migration of the scheduled castes from Punjab with special reference to the Ad-dharmi caste. An attempt has also been made to examine the social dynamics of the Punjabi community in England for the purpose of locating the Ad-dharmis with regard to some indicators, like marriage, social interaction and discrimination. It may be noted that the main theme of various studies on Indian diaspora has continued to be the examination of the relationship between the immigrants and the host society. Some studies take stock of the history of migration of Indians to various countries of Africa, South East Asia, Europe and North America. Till recently, there was hardly any attempt to focus the analysis on the study of the marginalised groups among the Indians abroad. The recent studies in this context investigate mainly the issues concerning women. The general rise in the research in the area of women studies has also a spill over effect on the diaspora studies. It may be further noted that like the issue of integration and adaptation of the earlier period till the mid-1980s, the research has now overwhelmingly tilted towards the study of multiculturalism. Even multiculturalism as a policy in various countries of the west recognises the broad cultural units among the immigrants, like Chinese, Arabs, Indians including Hindus and Sikhs, Japanese, etc. For any policy package it is an extremely cumbersome job to work out strategies for each unit of the large group. As a result certain aspects of internal dynamics of Indians abroad have remained unexplored. In this regard, the dalits from Punjab, who constitute a significant section of the Punjabis abroad, have been ignored by nearly all. In fact, even when the proportion of the scheduled castes in Punjab is quite high, they remain invariably unattended by the scholars, including the non-resident Punjabi scholars even when their studies focus on issue of Punjabi identity.[1]

In addition to the general apathy towards the dalits, which till recently was an all-India feature of intellectual discourse, Punjab has one additional distinction. Owing to the hegemonic influence of Sikhism, particularly after independence, the distinctions of caste are treated as external to the scope of Punjabi society. This view is fallacious and it is evident from certain sociological studies that there is an existence of castes and caste hierarchy among the Sikhs.[2] There are 39 castes among the scheduled castes in Punjab. Earlier, there were 37 castes among them (Singh, 1999), but recently the government has added Rai Sikhs/Mahatms and Mochis to the list. All these castes are either Hindus or Sikhs. Owing to recent conversions, a few might have recorded their religion as Buddhism in the recent census enumeration (Judge, 1997). Of all the dalit castes the Chamars/Ad-dharmis and Balmikis/Mazabis are the most numerous in the state. Some of the studies indicate that Ad-dharmis are among the most mobile castes in Punjab (Saberwal, 1990; Judge, ibid.). In spite of such a general profile of the scheduled castes, they do not figure as a distinct sociological unit of analysis. Any reference to dalits abroad in the recent works is found in the works of Aurora (1967), McLeod (1986) and Juergensmeyer (1982).

The problem has been examined from the phenomenological perspective. In other words, it is assumed that the scheduled castes and the upper castes share a common stock of knowledge as a result of which they construct the intersubjective world after their migration to England. This intersubjective world is primarily based on their everyday experiences of interaction in Punjab. They face an altogether distinct social world in which both of them become strangers. Their being strangers situate them at the margins of the British society. It is therefore expected that the earlier intersubjective world would become irrelevant – totally or partially – to create a new social world in which both the groups might have altered their social spaces. In a way, the alteration in the position of the scheduled castes is likely to change for the better.

The fieldwork was conducted in two cities of England, namely, Birmingham and Leamington Spa. The case study method was used to collect data. In all 50 Punjabis were interviewed, out of which 25 belonged to the Jat caste, one was Brahmin, one was Khatri, one Ramgarhia, and 22 were Ad-dharmis. All interviews were recorded and in some cases a group of persons were interviewed together. All of them belonged to the Doaba region of Punjab. One of them was living and working in Amritsar, but he belonged to Hoshiarpur district. Before the description of the overseas migration of the dalits, it is appropriate to precisely discuss the emergence of a new caste/social identity known as Ad-dharmi in the Doaba region of Punjab.

Ad-dharmis

According to the Census of India, 1991, the scheduled castes constitute 28.31 per cent of the total population of Punjab. The districts, which have higher percentage of the scheduled castes than the state average, are Jalandhar (39.04%), Faridkot (34.85%), Hoshiarpur (33.32%), Kapurthala (29.46%), Patiala (29.27%) and Bathinda (29.27%). In all there are 29 castes among the scheduled castes out of which Ad-dharmi, Chamar, Balmiki, Mazabi, Dom, Kabir Panthi, Sansi and Bhanjara are among the most numerous (Juergensmeyer, 1982). It may be added that in Gurdaspur district a considerable number of the erstwhile Churha caste has converted to Christianity. Though there is a term 'Christian dalits' being used in the social sciences, yet in the light of the official classification they are categorised as backward classes. There is also a districtwise numerical spread of various dalit castes in Punjab. In Hoshiarpur, Jalandhar, Kapurthala and Faridkot districts the Chamars are preponderant, whereas in Bathinda, Patiala and Amritsar districts the Mazabis and Balmikis are numerous. It may be noted that it is the Doaba region consisting of Jalandhar, Hoshiarpur and Kapurthala districts (excepting the Faridkot district of Malwa region) that the dalits are highly concentrated.

The Ad-dharmi as a distinct social and religious group came to exist when the government accepted the demand of the leaders of the Ad-dharma movement to record them as a distinct caste in the census of 1931. The participants in the Ad-dharma movement belonged to

Chamar, Churha and other dalit castes. The Chamars dominated the movement numerically as well as ideologically. Mangoo Ram, who emerged as the leader of this movement, was among the pioneers of the dalit diaspora. In many ways the Ad-dharma movement was the expression of the need of social space for the economically better off Chamars. The domination of the Chamars in the movement was so strong that it came to be identified with them. In this paper the term 'Ad-dharmi' is used for the members of the Chamar caste. In addition to the widely recognised fact that the two names imply the same caste, there is still another reason for doing so. First, there is a tremendous diversity in the nomenclature of the Chamars, as they are also known as Ravidasya, Ramdasya, Mochis, etc. Second, the Chamars are a widely spread caste group cutting across the regional and cultural boundaries, whereas the Ad-dharmis are largely concentrated in a particular region of Punjab, i.e., Doaba. Their geographic spread is due to their mobility. Finally, the recent but limited conversions of the members of this caste to Buddhism has further contributed to the diversity though this time it is only the religious change and the new term is 'neo-Buddhism'. Since it is a recent phenomenon exhibiting the rising influence of the ideology of Ambedkar, the differences within the caste have not yet come to the surface.

Dalits among the Punjabi Pioneers

The Punjabi pioneers who went abroad were ex-soldiers and had already been exposed to various places in the country (and sometimes outside the country) owing to their service in the British Army. Most of these pioneers were Jat Sikhs and the information regarding the dalits among these pioneers is not available (Juergensmeyer, 1982). We may make a conjecture that the possibility of dalits going to overseas was remote owing to their low socio-economic conditions and lack of exposure to the outside world. Thus, we find that very few dalits went to North America in the beginning of the 20th century. One of them was Mangoo Ram and information about him is available due to his first participation in the Gadhar movement and then on his return leading the Ad-dharma movement. Juergensmeyer (ibid.), in his work on the Ad-dharma movement, has provided a biographical sketch of Mangoo Ram. He (ibid., 284) gives the following account of migration of Mangoo Ram to the United States:

> In 1909 America was in the air. Scores of upper caste farmers from Mangoo Ram's area of Hoshiarpur had gone to the United States, and those who had not gone were talking about it. Mangoo Ram decided to go also. He persuaded his father that it would be good for the business–he would send money back from America–and his father responded by giving him some of the savings from the family business. Amid assurances from the local *zamindars* ("landowners") that he would be employed by their relatives in America, Mangoo and two Chamar friends set off for the new world.

It is obvious from the above narrative that Mangoo Ram belonged to a well-to-do family of dalits. Juergensmeyer also informs that he also got some formal education. Only Mangoo Ram could make it to the United States, whereas the other two Chamar boys returned. In the United States he worked for the former zamindars of his village. On this issue Ronki Ram (2001) is of the view that Mangoo Ram remained within the confines of caste relations abroad. However, the list of his jobs at different places is quite long which implies that after the initial stage he became independent. As pointed out by Juergensmeyer (1982), for him joining the Gadhar movement was an experience of equality among his countrymen and we also come across a reference to some Chamars living in the United States in an interview with Mangoo Ram. Mangoo Ram returned to India along with the other Ghadar activists after the First World War broke out in 1914.

Kessinger (1974) has also noted the migration of the dalits to foreign countries during the first half of the 20th century. According to him (ibid., 166), 2 per cent of the Chamars and 1 per cent of the Julahas born in Vilyatpur were living abroad in 1898. In 1910 1 per cent of Chamars and 3 per cent of Julahas of the village were living abroad. Interestingly, in 1922, only Julahas showed any trend as 9 per cent of them were living abroad, whereas no one from among the Chamars had gone out of the country. Another important caste among the dalits of the village was that of the Churhas.[3] There was no tendency among them to migrate. On the other hand, McLeod (1986: 62–63) has provided castewise data of the Punjabis who entered New Zealand between 1912 and 1921. Out of the total 212 Punjabis who entered New Zealand during this period 133 were Jats and 24 were Chamars. Among the Chamars 22 belonged to the Doaba region, whereas the other two were from Majha. Interestingly, no Julaha is to be found among the Punjabis in New Zealand. While commenting on the caste background of the Punjabis in New Zealand in the early 20th century,

McLeod (1986: 65) opines: "Although this caste representation may seem surprising at first sight it is in fact entirely predictable. The figures reflect both the numerical dominance of the Jats in rural Doaba and the unusually high proportion of Chamars in the same area. They also bear a marked resemblance to the caste profile which Kessinger has drawn for Villayatpur".

The information provided by Juergensmeyer and Kessinger is in fragments, but still its relevance and significance cannot be ignored. It is interesting to note that the Chamars were more mobile than other dalit castes. The Julahas also showed ability to migrate overseas. Kessinger has made an interesting observation about the reasons for migration of various castes in his study village. He (1974: 166) writes:

> ... Property groups with more than ten acres of land migrated with less frequency than others because the land was sufficient to absorb the labour of all members, apparently no matter how many, particularly with the intensification of cultivation after 1920. The striking feature, however, is that there was little difference in the rate of migration between the landless, and the small, or middle-size land holders. Absolute economic welfare (the amount of land) cannot account for this lack of variation; neither can per capita land for adult males ... .

From 1890s through the 1930s wealth and incomes acquired outside Vilyatpur were used to advance in the village social system.

The explanation offered by Kessinger posits the Jats in the village hierarchy quite well, but it partially describes that given their economic disabilities how the dalits could manage to emigrate. In the case of the Chamars, who were to organise Ad-dharma movement in the 1920s, two explanations seem to be plausible. As a result of the British annexation of Punjab, the leather trade flourished which was the main factor in the relative prosperity of the Chamars. In the early 20th century Briggs noted the economic changes taking place among the Chamars thus:

> ... The recent increase in the value of farm products has resulted in some instances, in the substitution of cash for grain as wages. This will eventually help the Chamar. The increased value of leather has led the landlords, in some parts of the country, to question the Chamars, traditional right to raw skins. But the landlord has been obliged to offer another form of compensation, and this has been in cultivating privileges ... (ibid., 175–76).

Briggs (1920: 58) has pointed out various aspects of the probable mobility among the Chamars. It is not expected that all the Chamars might have experienced upward mobility in the beginning of the 20th century, but, as pointed out by Briggs, certain Chamars became rich in India. It may be reminded that Mangoo Ram's father made money in this trade that enabled him to migrate to the USA (Juergensmeyer, 1986). The second explanation could be that the landowners took them along with them. It seems to be a remote possibility. Probably, the Jat landowners became the source of information for them regarding the unlimited opportunities abroad. Among the emigrants, the proportion of the Chamars was considerably less than the Jat Sikhs. The economic capability of the Chamars in particular and dalits in general to migrate abroad was confined to a tiny minority. After independence in 1947 general conditions underwent a significant change which paved the way for the migration of the dalits to the western countries, particularly to England.

Ad-dharmis in England

The story of the migration of the Punjabi dalits has not been recorded the way it has been done in the case of the Jat Sikhs. Aurora in his pioneering study of the Punjabis in England has shown surprise at the presence of the Chamars in England. He (1967: 29) writes thus:

> Besides Jats there are also some other castes amongst the Indian immigrants. Chamars (leather workers) and Tarkhans (carpenters) being of some numerical significance. Chamars are an untouchable caste and their socio-economic status before World War II was so low that their presence among the Indian immigrants in England shows a surprising rise in their economic well being. [4]

Juergensmeyer has provided the limited but useful information on the migration of the dalits to England. According to him (1982: 246), approximately 3,00,000 Indians migrated to England during the first two decades after 1947. Among these Indians, most of them were Punjabis. The Jat Sikhs constituted an overwhelming majority among the migrants. For the dalits the migration was never an easier process, because, in addition to the economic resources, they were supposed to acquire necessary papers and documents for travelling. To get a passport was one of the most difficult things.[5] This hurdle was overcome when one dalit, Ishwar Das Pawar, became the

Under-Secretary for Passports. According to Juergensmeyer, he "helped five hundred Scheduled Castes applicants to emigrate every year". Juergensmeyer makes an estimate of the proportion of the dalits among the Punjabis, which is 10 per cent. It implies that the number of the dalits, particularly the Ad-dharmis, is quite large within the Punjabi community in England.[6] In India, the emigration of Punjabi dalits is not regarded as a factor in their mobility. For example, Saberwal's (1990: 82) study of the Ad-dharmis and the Balmikis does not take stock of the emigration of dalits as an important variable in the analysis. However, he has recorded the emigration of the dalits and has also observed that more Ad-dharmis have gone to England than the Balmikis. We are not informed whether the emigration is a cause or the consequence of the social mobility of the Ad-dharmis.[7]

The information gathered through the interviews indicates that the pattern of migration of the Ad-dharmis to England has been more or less the same as that of the Jat Sikhs. The migration of the Punjabis to the western countries has occurred in four phases explained by the author elsewhere.[8] The decline in their migration has taken place due to the strict immigration laws and policies of the British government. The restrictions on the immigration of the South Asians began in the 1970s and continue till today. These four phases may be described as follows:

- The first phase began with the Ad-dharmis who migrated to England as pioneers in the 1950s. They got employment as workers in the industry. When they saved sufficient money to buy a house, they started the process of either sponsoring their own families or getting married. In either case these pioneers lived for a decade or more and did not return till they had bought houses. They along with their upper caste counterparts laid the foundations for the evolution of the Punjabi community.
- In the second phase the families and spouses of the pioneers migrated as dependants. Though most of them were married and had children, yet a few of them also returned to get married. The latter category of the pioneers married late as they took a considerable time to be economically well off. In the 1950s and 1960s the migrants had to struggle a lot to be able to bring their families in England. It usually took ten to fifteen years for most of the people. In the case of the already married pioneers their children were grown up when they reached England, whereas the

unmarried migrants were in their late thirties at the time of their return for getting married. Thus, in the second phase were included spouses and children of the pioneers. In a majority of the cases the first two phases were complete by 1970.

— As the sons and daughters of the pioneers grew up, they were to be married in India. The spouses of these grown up sons and daughters reached England in the third phase. Third phase also included the parents of the wives of the pioneers. By 1977 there was a significant decline in the migration to England as a result of the restrictions.

— In the fourth phase we find that the migration is cyclical and acquires a never-ending character. It is always the parents migrating after their sons and daughters have reached England on marriage basis. In many ways the pattern of migration is taking place in an unbroken chain. In the recent years the Punjabis of all castes are migrating predominantly to Canada and Australia, whereas England has lost its place as the most desirable destination. The reasons are simple. The British government is persisting with restrictions on the immigration of the South Asians and England is no more the most developed country with unlimited opportunities.

The discussion of the pattern of migration of the Ad-dharmis clearly indicates that over a period of five decades since independence the Ad-dharmis have emerged as a sizeable and distinct social group within the Punjabi community. One interesting indication of this distinct character of Ad-dharmis is the existence of their separate gurdwaras from those of the Jats. It is pertinent to mention here that the Punjabi Sikhs are divided along the caste lines so far as the gurdwaras are concerned. Every caste seems to have its own gurdwaras. This is in spite of the fact that the basic tenets of Sikhism promote equality of castes. We find that in England as well as in other western countries each caste group has its own gurdwara. The existence of the gurdwaras according to the caste may not be regarded as a unique feature of the diaspora Sikhs. In a recent collaborative study of the author on terrorism, it has been found that there are two kinds of gurdwaras in the villages of Punjab (Puri, Judge and Sekhon, 1997).[9] There are historical gurdwaras, which are linked with the event associated with any of the ten gurus of the Sikhs. Most of these gurdwaras are under the control of the Shiromani Gurdwara Parbandhak Committee (SGPC).

The second kind of gurdwaras may be called social, as they are located in every locality (*patti*) of a big village. Each *patti* is homogenous in terms of caste. Thus, for social occasions, the caste-based gurdwaras are used. Since in England and other western countries there cannot be any historical gurdwara, the replication of the Punjab pattern has occurred in the construction of the social gurdwaras. In addition to the gurdwaras, the Ad-dharmis have also constructed 'Buddhistan' or 'Buddha Vihar'. It may be noted that there is no definite pattern in the evolution of Buddhism among the Ad-dharmis. They would go to both the places. However, the Buddhist leaders among them were of the view that the dalits hesitate to visit Buddhistan, as they want to hide their caste identity. The criticism of Sikh community is one of the common features of the Ad-dharmis. Interestingly, the argument put forward by them is common. When Sikhism emerged, it did not have caste inequalities. Now, the castes have emerged among them and we have Mazabi, Tarkhan, Kumhar, Jat and so on.

Punjabi Community in England

It was important to know the perceptions of both the Ad-dharmis and the non-dalits regarding the pertinent features of the Punjabi community. A summary of responses of both the groups is presented below:

— All the respondents were of the view that the Punjabis in England have been trying to maintain their culture. They have been partially successful.

— They opined that the Punjabis have made a lot of progress in England. At present, the Punjabi is found in every field of economic activity. They are in business, education and other professions. In other words, they have been a successful community.

— So far as the community as such is concerned, all the 20 Ad-dharmi and 15 Jat respondents pointed out that its internal division was a replica of Punjabi society. Owing to the Untouchability Offences Act, the discrimination on the basis of caste has been legally abolished and the practice of untouchability has been made cognisable offence punishable by law in India. It may not be inferred that caste-based discrimination has disappeared in the country. Even in Punjab, which is regarded as a state having a limited effect of casteism due to the Sikh movement, the stories of atrocities against dalits appear in newspapers. However, it has become difficult for an upper caste person to address the dalit by his caste name, as it is not legally permitted. In England no law prevents the upper caste persons to address the dalits by their caste name.[10] Each caste has its own gurdwara. The Ad-dharmi respondents were of the view that even the school-going kids were aware of the caste identity. The Ad-dharmi respondents were quite emphatic in the contention that in the Punjabi community the economic status is less talked about than the caste background. A Sikh does not meet the other Sikh with fraternal feelings. He is more bothered about the caste status. Three hundred years have passed since the formation of Khalsa, but the caste system has not been eradicated. The dalit respondents were of the view that in the land of Gurus the caste system should have been eradicated within three centuries. All the aspects of caste system are in existence in England.

— Ad-dharmi respondents further informed that casteism varies with the age and the number of years the person has spent in India before migrating to England. It however does not mean that some of the upper caste sections are free from it. In fact, they learn it from others. In spite of the fact that all upper caste Punjabis are aware of this, it is more prevalent among the elderly and middle aged Punjabis. The younger generation is not aware of the existence of such sharp divisions among the Punjabis. They are told about it, particularly about the 'Chamars'. The author interviewed a large number of Punjabis in England, Canada and the USA (Judge, 1999). Most of them belonged to the Jat caste and they thought differently. According to them, the younger generation, which has been born and brought up in these countries, is not aware of the caste status the way other Punjabis are. Even if they are told about it, they do not comprehend the ramifications of the caste status for them.

— The caste is one of the most serious issues in England. However, activities of the *Taraksheel* (Rationalist) Society and some others, such as socialists, have made an impact on the caste system. Casteism is on the decline. It may not be concluded from this that the caste system will be abolished. It cannot be abolished, because it derives its strength from Hinduism. Ambedkar understood this fact and he decided to move out of the fold of Hinduism. As a result of the influence of Hinduism, everybody, irrespective of his social and demographic characteristics, believes in caste system. The difference is only in degrees. What makes it a strong and a durable system is the practice of caste endogamy.

Intercaste Marriages and the Ad-dharmis

In all the interviews conducted in England one common response was regarding the rise in the incidences of intercaste marriages among the Punjabis. In England the Punjabis are now a well-settled community and its internal dynamics shows certain trends towards the weakening of the rules of endogamy. It is particularly visible in the case of non-dalit castes. The most prevalent among these intercaste marriages are between the Jats and the Tarkhans. The author attended one marriage in which the groom belonged to the Jat caste, whereas the bride was from the Nai caste. In the beginning there was a lot of opposition in those cases where the girl belonged to the Jat caste. The Jats in general have stopped objecting to those marriages in which case the girl belonged to any other non-dalit caste. It may be linked to the tradition of accepting women from outside through purchase or the practice of paying the brideprice among the Jats. This tradition has almost disappeared now. As the respondents pointed out, the Jats do not object to hypergamy, whereas hypogamous marriages involving Jat girls are resented by them. The tendency towards the acceptance of intercaste marriage in which the bridegroom is not a dalit is one of the major changes that have occurred among the Punjabis.

The problem emerges when the boy belongs to the Ad-dharami caste and the girl is from the Jat caste. It is pertinent to remark that in Punjab there are cases of a Jat girl marrying an Ad-dharmi boy. Such occurrences have been rare and in the 1970s there was tremendous reaction of the Jats when two lecturers in a college in Hoshiarpur district got married. They were dismissed from the college by the Jat-dominated management, but were taken back when the then Prime Minister of India intervened. Despite all such daring instances the cases of intercaste marriages involving a dalit boy and the upper caste girl are still rare. The Jats in England take special care to prevent such a possibility right from the beginning. As mentioned earlier, in accordance with the Untouchability Offences Act in India, addressing a dalit by his caste name is legally regarded as derogatory, but using caste names privately at home to inform the children about this cannot be avoided. In the case of diaspora communities the laws of the native land have no influence over them. Using the caste name to mention a particular caste group is one of the common occurrences in England. The best way to socialise the child about the caste identity is to impute on their minds the caste names in the everyday life interaction. This subtle way of making the child aware of differences among the Punjabis becomes effective in creating the inter-subjective world. Still, the caste differences are to be translated into a hierarchical order. As pointed out by one of the leaders of the Ad-dharmis in Birmingham, it may start with a casual remark, "You are free to marry any boy/girl when you grow up, but don't marry a dalit boy/girl". In fact, the expression used is the real caste name. In addition to creating the awareness of the difference, the attempt is made to make the child conscious of the content of the difference between his/her family and the dalits. It is difficult to make a sense of untouchability for them. Thus the best way to highlight the hierarchical difference is to say "We were landlords and they were labourers working for us".

The question was asked from all the Punjabis who were interviewed that whether there were cases of intercaste marriages in England in which one of the marrying couple belonged to the dalit caste. Everybody seemed to be aware of such marriages. In a group of six dalits who were being interviewed one of them informed that he had attended such a marriage. The boy was Ad-dharmi and the girl was Jat by caste. He told that it did not look like marriage celebration. It rather seemed as if the people were attending a funeral, he said. There was a commonly held view among the respondents that in such cases the parents do not accept the couple. As the law supports them, the parents think it prudent to let it happen. In some cases the Jat parents react sharply and physically torture the girl to force her to abandon the intention of such marriage. There are also instances of marriages between an Ad-dharmi girl and the Jat boy. The opposition to such marriages is also present, but it may not take the magnitude of resentment, which grows when the girl is from the Jat caste.

It may be inferred that intercaste marriages are not arranged, but the boy and the girl first secretly date and then tell their parents that they wish to get married. In a situation where the interaction is based on caste the conditions for love marriage are provided by non-community settings. In this regard, the school and the university provide the settings for interaction between the young boys and girls. Fearing such an eventuality some Jats discourage higher education among daughters. In the Punjabi immigrant literature this theme figures frequently. For example, in his story *'Panj Kalyani'*, Amanpal Sara (1993) has convincingly depicted the typical attitude of the parents of the girl. The father does not want her to go to college and expects her to marry the boy of his choice. The girl, however, does not want to marry. What Sara has depicted in this story is the dilemma of the parents who want that their children should excel without internalising the values of the host society. The education is located in an ambivalent situation in their perception. Without education it is not possible to achieve excellence, but at the same time the education and the educational institutions are the main sources of dissent against the authority of the parents. It was informed that in those cases where the boy is Ad-dharmi the educational level of the couple is high and it is quite probable that they are doctors or lawyers. This further corroborates the argument that education is the major source of change in marriage practices among the Punjabis in England.

Among the Ad-dharmis the pattern of most of marriages is not different from the other caste groups in the Punjabi community. All the Ad-dharmi respondents were in favour of caste endogamy. They said that one should marry in one's own caste, because it helped in the adjustment of the spouses. One major problem they pointed out in the case of an intercaste marriage was in the symmetrical interaction among the relatives. The upper caste relatives did not regard a dalit as equal. It also seemed that the perpetuation of kinship ties within the Punjabi community is an important basis of mechanical solidarity. Each segment within the ethnic community tended to continue its communitarian interaction within the framework of caste and kinship. To maintain their culture they also preferred marrying their sons and daughters in India. However, the cultural differences between the England and Punjab are coming in the way of marital adjustment. The respondents reported no specific case of marital tension among the Ad-dharmis. However, there seemed to be a consensus among them that the divorce rate is going up in the Punjabi community.

Caste and Race

Ostensibly, the issue of relationship between caste and race is not an important one. The two are regarded as different forms of social inequality. Interestingly, earlier anthropological writings on the origin of caste have taken up this issue into cognisance. Some well-known ethnographers, namely, Risley and Hutton, have given due considerations to the racial dimensions of caste. In the post-independence era this issue has become secondary and the domination of structural-functional approach in sociology changed the trend in the study of caste towards the analysis of functions and nature of dominance. In recent years the controversy has emerged between the dalit scholars and the Indian government with regard to whether caste is race or not (Pinto 2001). A section of the dalit intellectuals treats caste as race, whereas the Government of India refuses to accept this assertion, particularly in view of its international ramifications.[11] How does the dalit diaspora perceive the relationship between the caste and the race? In a way, they are an appropriate group to understand this issue as they have had the experience of both the worlds. The following responses were recorded:

> There is a basic difference between caste and race and the two should not be confused. However, the caste discrimination is worse than the racial discrimination. Over a period of time there has been a tremendous decline in racial discrimination, whereas the caste is permanently stuck with the dalits. The Ad-dharmis are facing two levels of subordination. One is racial and they share it with other Punjabis. The second is caste-based which is operating within the Punjabi community. They have no intention of moving away from their ethnic milieu in an alien environment, but the caste-based subordination must end.

In the Punjabi literature, which has been the outcome of the migration experience of the Punjabis abroad, the caste issue does not occupy the central position. The focus, as is the case with the social science literature, continues to be the migration experience and the encounter with the host culture and society. Even then we find attempts at comparing caste with race. Two such stories are worth mentioning, one is by Major Mangat (2000) and Jarnail Singh (1999) writes the other. It is worthwhile to precisely discuss the story by Major Mangat.

The word '*Trishankoo*' is used metaphorically to denote the position of a person who is located in between two worlds. The main character of the story is Gurdev Singh. He is middle-aged man and his son is a doctor. It is his son who encounters a racial attack when he goes in his sports car in the white-dominated area to meet his white girl friend. She is also a doctor and the both plan to marry in near future. For Gurdev Singh the interracial marriage is acceptable as both his son and future daughter-in-law will earn lot of money. He shares these thoughts with his friend who has come to inquire about the incident. Then he, asks Gurdev Singh about Punjab as he has just returned from there. At this juncture, another world is introduced that has no race but caste system. Gurdev Singh narrates how his sister's daughter wanted to marry a dalit boy. He felt ashamed and decided to kill the boy. However, the intervention of the mother of the girl saves the life of the boy. He tells his friend that earlier he wanted to settle in India, but now he cannot live there as he has lost his honour.

The story provides an understanding of the reaction of the Punjabi upper caste persons to the issue of race as well as caste. The diaspora Punjabis have maintained their caste consciousness and in certain situations it becomes more important than race.

Conclusions

The emigration of the Ad-dharmis (then Chamars) to western countries was a result of the change in their economic conditions in the second half of the 19th century. Though the caste-based discrimination has continued to exist in Punjab till today, yet the practice of untouchability declined considerably due to the effect of the Sikh movement in Punjab.[12] McLeod (1975: 84) has summed up the issue of the relationship between caste and Sikhism in the following manner:

> ... Entry to the Panth [Sikh religion] was open to all and within it caste was certainly discounted. It was, however, by no means obliterated. It survived in terms of commensality and marriage patterns, demonstrating in both respects that degree of tenacity that has proved so puzzling to successive generations of foreigners.

In another work, McLeod (1986: 111) has highlighted the prevalence of caste consciousness among the Punjabis in New Zealand.

Two factors seemed to have played a decisive role in the international migration of the scheduled castes. First, a section among them experienced prosperity as a result of changes in the economy. In this regard, the leather trade flourished due to which the Chamars experienced change. There seems to be an evidence of emergence of classes among the Chamars. Second, the Jat landlords played an important role in helping the Ad-dharmis to migrate to North America in the early 20th century. Their migration to England after independence in 1947 was more or less independent of the Jats. However, in certain cases, informal factors, such as friendship and patronage of the Jat landowners, might have facilitated their migration. The evolution of Punjabi community in England entails segmentation on the basis of caste. The social construction of everyday life of the Punjabis in England is characterised by both change and continuity. The change is pushing forward through the young generation, which despite all efforts of the parents has refused to accept the Punjabi values in totality. The reason is the influence of secular institutions of the host society, such as the schools and universities. The Ad-dharmi respondents seemed to be resenting casteism among the Punjabis in England, but showed inclination towards maintaining their caste identity. It is particularly evident from their support to caste endogamy.

It indicates that caste has relevance in providing a particular identity in the construction of their social world. At the same time, this identity should be without prejudice and discrimination. In other words, the dalits in England do not question the difference; rather, they are protesting against the inequality and discrimination that result from it. There is a need for looking into the plausibility of attaining equality without necessarily ending the differences. This raises normative issues of two kinds. First, since the caste consciousness is prevalent among the older generation, it may be argued that over a period of time the younger generation would be able to eradicate caste identity. It also assumes that caste-based identities cannot be egalitarian at the level of practice. Second, in a situation of the persistence of caste identities along with equality there is a need to reconceptualise caste. Is it possible for an inegalitarian system, which has been in existence for centuries in India to alter its character even for those who live in an alien society? It is difficult to ascertain at the moment.

Notes

This article was first published in *Economic and Political Weekly,* XXXVII (31) August 3, 2002. It was also published in Paramjit S. Judge et. al (eds.) *Development, Gender and Diaspora: Context of Globalisation,* Rawat Publications, Jaipur, 2003 under the title "Punjabi Scheduled

Castes in Punjab". The author is grateful to Jarnail Singh Bains and Lavkesh Prashar for their help in the collection of case studies. The critical comments of Dr Gurpreet Bal on the paper are gratefully acknowledged.

1. For instance, two books on Punjabi identity were published and both the works did not incorporate anything on dalit identity. Since three of the editors were non-resident Punjabi scholars living in England, they seemed to be oblivious of the fact that a considerable population of the dalits exists among the Punjabis in England. These works are Pritam Singh and Shinder S. Thandi (1996) and Gurharpal Singh and Ian Talbot (1996).
2. The present Punjab is divided into three regions clearly demarcated by the route of two rivers, viz., Beas and Satluj. The area lying between these two rivers comprised by Jalandhar, Hoshiarpur and Kapurthala (also the recently carved out district of Nawan Shahar) is known as Doaba. On the West of Doaba is Majha and on the south of it is Malwa.
3. Kessinger's (1974: 166) mention of the Julaha (Kabir Panthi) caste having migrated abroad makes an interesting case of analysis. Among the people of the village studied by Kessinger most of them seem to have migrated to Australia, New Zealand or Fiji. It may be pointed out that the Julahas belonged to the artisan caste as their caste occupation was weaving. However, unlike a majority of the artisan castes like Chhimbas, Tarkhans, Kumhars, etc. they were not included in the shudra castes.
4. Aurora (1967: 29) also provides a case of Nathu belonging to the scheduled castes hailing from village Shanker in Jalandhar district. He had never travelled beyond Delhi, but with the help a travel agent he reached England where a Jat family of his village helped him to find an accommodation. The arrival of Nathu in England after independence and Mangoo Ram in the USA in the beginning of the twentieth century have one thing in common, i.e., both of them were helped by their village fellows from the Jat caste.
5. In fact, getting the passport continued to be the major step towards achieving the objective of going abroad. Owing to the Indian government's efforts to simplify the procedure, it has now become relatively easy to get the passport.
6. At the time of the field-work the author asked a Punjabi upper caste regarding the total number of the dalits from Punjab living in England. His response was very interesting. He said the total number of dalits in England is equal to that of the Jats. The reason he gave was that there was higher population growth rate among the dalits than the other castes in England. He said, "If we have two children, then they have four". This response falls in the category of the attitudes that exist among the communal Hindus in India towards the Muslims. Not only that, there seems to be general pattern

of perception of the majority caste/religious communities towards the minorities.

7. Saberwal (1990: 82), the first edition of this work came out in 1976. There is also a section on the observations of the author in its revised edition in 1990. He revisited the place of study. He mentions the emigration of the Ad-dharmis and the Balmikis, but he does not regard it as a factor of social mobility.
8. For a detailed discussion on the pattern of migration of the Jat Sikhs, see Paramjit S. Judge (1992).
9. Puri, Judge and Sekhon (1999). The study was conducted in 28 villages of Amritsar and Gurdaspur districts. Some of the villages, such as Sur Singh, Butala and Sathiala, included in the sample were big having population of more than 5,000 persons. In such villages the caste basis of the gurdwaras was quite obvious.
10. The respondents have alluded to call dalits by their caste names, such as Chamar, Churha, etc.
11. It may be just pointed out that the Durban Conference did not recognise caste at par with race.
12. There is a need to make a distinction between untouchability and discrimination based on caste. In the case of the practice of untouchability the principle of purity and pollution is enforced in the form of commensal taboos. The touch of the person belonging to the impure caste can pollute the upper caste person. On the other hand, discrimination is a consequence of both the ideology of caste hierarchy and the exercise of power by the upper caste persons in various fields of social and occupational life. The prevalence of caste based discrimination is an indicator of the existence of caste consciousness in the society.

References

Aurora, G.S.1967. *The New Frontiersmen: A Sociological Study of Indian Immigrants in the United Kingdom.* Bombay: Popular Prakashan.

Briggs, G.W. 1920. *The Chamars.* Delhi: B.R. Publishing Corporation.

D'souza, V.S. 1985. *Economic Development, Social Structure and Population Growth.* New Delhi: Sage.

Judge, Paramjit S. 1999. *Parvas: Sabhiacharik Sankat,* (Punjabi). Jalandhar: NRI Sabha.

——. 1997. 'Green Revolution and Bahujan Samaj Party in Punjab', in Judge, Paramjit S. and Satish Kumar Sharma (eds.), *Dimensions of Social Change: Essays in Honour of Professor P.N. Pimpley.* Jaipur: Rawat Publications.

——. 1994. *Punjabis in Canada: A Study of Formation of an Ethnic Community.* New Delhi: Chanakya Publications.

Juergensmeyer, Mark. 1982. *Religion as Social Vision: The Movement against Untouchability in 20th century Punjab.* Berkeley: University of California Press.

Kessinger, Tom G. 1974. *Vilyatpur 1848–1968: Social and Economic Change in a North Indian Village.* Berkeley: University of California Press.

Mangat, Major. 2000. *Trishankoo.* Ludhiana: Aesthetic Publications.

McLeod, W.H. 1975. *The Evolution of the Sikh Community: Five Essays.* Delhi: Oxford University Press.

——. 1986. *Punjabis in New Zealand: A History of Punjabi Migration 1890–1940.* Amritsar: Guru Nanak Dev University.

Pinto, Amrose. 2001. "UN Conference against Racism: Is Caste Race?" *Economic and Political Weekly,* July 28.

Puri, Harish K., Judge, Paramjit S., and Sekhon, Jagrup S. 1997. *Terrorism in Punjab: Understanding Grassroots Reality.* New Delhi: Har-Anand.

Ronki Ram. 2001. "Untouchability and the Question of Dalit Identity: A Critique of Ad-Dharam Movement", Paper presented in National Seminar on Liberalisation, Dalits and State held in May 3–4, 2001, Department of Sociology, Panjab University, Chandigarh.

Saberwal, Satish. 1990. *Mobile Men: Limits to Social Change in Urban Punjab.* Shimla: Indian Institute of Advanced Study in association with Manohar, New Delhi.

Sara, Amanpal. 1993. *Sarad Rishte.* Ludhiana: Cooperative Publications.

Schutz, Alfred. 1980. *The Phenomenology of the Social World.* London: Heinmann.

Singh, Jarnail. 1999. *Do Tapoo.* Ludhiana: Aesthetic Publications.

Singh, K.S. 1999. *The Scheduled Castes.* Calcutta: Oxford University Press.

Singh, Gurharpal and Talbot, Ian. (eds.). 1996. *Punjabi Identity: Continuity and Change.* New Delhi: Manohar.

Singh, Harjinder. 1977. "Caste ranking in two Sikh villages", in Harjinder Singh (ed.), *Caste among Non-Hindus in India.* New Delhi: National Publishing House.

Singh, Indera Paul. 1977. "Caste in a Sikh village", in Harjinder Singh (ed.), *Caste among Non-Hindus in India.* New Delhi: National Publishing House.

Singh, Pritam and Thandi, Shinder S. (eds). 1996. *Globalisation and the Region: Explorations in Punjabi Identity.* Coventry: Association for Punjabi Studies.

8

Interrogating Changing Status of Dalits in Punjab

The pace of change in India really picked up after independence as never before. The committed leadership of the ruling party aimed at bringing 'socialism' in India whose social structure was marked by certain unique features of legitimacy of an ascribed system of social inequality. What is known as the caste system was and has remained the unique, undesirable and relatively unchanging system of inequality. In the light of reservation policy the social structure of India was consciously fractured. But caste reappears, sometimes with vengeance and in virulent form as the case of lynching of five dalits in Jhajjar in Haryana shows and sometimes with the dysfunctionally politicised mode. Rajni Kothari (1970) once characterised the persistence of caste in politics as politicisation of castes. However, at the level of social hierarchy, it still remains to be seen as to what extent the efforts of the modern Indian state have succeeded in bringing equality. The main objective of this paper is to examine, assess and analyse the changing status of the dalits of Punjab. Accordingly, the discussion in this paper has been divided into five parts. In the first part an effort has been made to look into the emerging issues in the study of dalits in general, the purpose of which is to contextualise and theoretically situate the discussion on the change and continuity among the dalits. The second part provides an accurate but general description of certain unique features of the dalits of Punjab[1]. Parts third and fourth respectively delineate and examine the change and continuity among the dalits of Punjab and the discussion is concluded in the last part of the paper.

Contextualising the Issue

At the outset, it may be pointed out that though the term 'dalit' signifies a broad canvass, yet in the present analysis we mean only the scheduled castes (SCs). The usage of the term 'dalit' also presents another set of problems. This refers to Shah's (2002) insightful observations regarding differentiation of the dalit category. He observes: "... One can understand if politicians use the category in an undifferentiated manner on account of their vested interests. One can also understand if journalists use it in a facile manner on account of their superficial knowledge of the society at the ground level. But it is difficult to understand how social scientists also use it in undifferentiated manner and make grandiloquent statements about the dalits" (ibid., 1317). He further argues with the help of various sources that there is differentiation among the dalits and it is hierarchical, that is, if we treat all the dalit castes as one whole, then it would exhibit all those features that characterise the Hindu caste system, particularly with regard to the marital practices. On the contrary, Bharati (2002: 4339–40) asserts that the term 'dalit' signifies unity, as it broadly covers all the people who have been at the lowest rungs of the Indian society.

Both Shah and Bharati are observing the social reality from different perspectives. Whereas Bharati is right in articulating the view that there should be unity in the identity of the dalits, Shah, on the other hand, rightly emphasises that as social scientists we should look into the hierarchy among the dalits and work out its implications. In this regard, Shah has a realistic view, which has tremendous implications for the recent discourse on dalit identity invariably created by the dalit scholars. We may point out that Shah's observations are equally valid for the dalits of Punjab. What has remained unexplored, unnoticed and unanalysed is the relationship between the hierarchy and the social transformation among the dalits. Once this aspect of the discourse on the dalit identity is taken into consideration, one may find that among the dalits there are 'oppressors' and 'oppressed'. Similarly, one may find a general observation in the existing literature that the better off among the dalits have benefited from the reservation policy. If we quantify this observation in the form of the actual identification of castes that got the maximum benefit from the reservation policy, then it is quite probable that single caste in a region emerges as the major beneficiary. In this regard, Bharati and others are wrong in their assertion to treat dalits as a single whole of the oppressed. As we would see little later, the hierarchical differentiation among the dalits is oppressive and is functioning on the principle of exclusion.

In the analysis of caste system in India, one of the prevalent discourses is the existence of caste stratification among the non-Hindus. Weber (1970) has dealt with the issue of caste among the non-Hindus and he makes it explicit that in this case the Brahmin has lost his significance. In the case of Hindus, the centrality of the position of Brahmins has remained unchanged. In spite of this limited insight that Weber provided, no attempt has been made to explore this further. The prevalent discourse thus makes an attempt to create a worldview that there is something specific about the Indian subcontinent that can be situated in the Indian civilisation. Thus, we have studies of empirical nature that affirm and substantiate the presence of caste stratification among the Sikhs, Muslims and Christians.[2] Such empirical observations draw strength from the historical fact that the Sikhs, the Indian Muslims and the Christians have their roots in Hinduism and their co-existence has been influenced by the Hindu ideology, way of life and worldview. Such a view has important implications for the understanding of the dalits of Punjab. It is a Sikh majority state, and the Sikh dalits are eligible for the benefits under the reservation policy. The politics of recognition has played a role in confusing the issue. Sikhism is an egalitarian religion, but caste stratification not only exists, it is also perpetuating in the Sikh community. However, the caste hierarchy is different from that of the Hindu. Among the Sikhs the castes that occupy the top positions may become lower in the Hindu caste hierarchy. In this regard, the caste system among the Sikhs is largely based on power and privilege paradigm, whereas the Hindu caste system has strong ideological basis, which supports and legitimises the given system of inequality. As a result, the position of the upper castes in the Sikh community has been facing constant challenges from the egalitarian ideology. The modern Indian state has decisively intervened in the evolutionary process in the Sikh community through an affirmative action programme. Contemporary writings during the 19th century tend to suggest that Sikhism was fast moving towards merger with Hinduism (Bingley, 1985). The Singh Sabha movement and the British colonial policies combined to create a Sikh identity along Khalsa lines for which the emphasis on equality among castes within the community became a rallying point to demarcate it from Hinduism. No wonder that Giani Ditt Singh, a dalit (Ramdasia), became one of the major ideologues of the Singh Sabha movement.

To further illustrate the issue of the dalits with regard to the religious communities, we may take the example of 'temple entry'. It is a well-known fact that the dalits were prohibited from entering the Hindu temples. Ambedkar organised the movement of the Mahars on this issue in the earlier stages of his struggle. This movement for temple entry met with strong resistance, opposition and violence from the upper caste Hindus in Maharashtra. Conversely, we do not find such struggle for the entry into the Sikh gurdwaras. There is no denying the fact that in villages of the present Punjab there are separate gurdwaras for all castes. However, a dalit is not prevented form entering the gurdwara belonging to the upper castes. Yet, another notable feature is that the priests in the gurdwaras may belong to the lower castes, particularly the backward classes, such as Chhimbas, Bhatras, etc., and one may occasionally find a dalit priest in the gurdwara belonging to the Jat Sikhs. While examining the status of the dalits within Sikh community, one has to keep a sense of balance to make a distinction between rhetoric and reality. The classical examples of the rhetoric of casteless Sikhism are found in Kahn Singh Nabha's work *Hum Hindu Nahin* that was published in 1898 and in the speeches of Sant Jarnail Singh Bhindranwale during 1982–84 (Judge, 2002b).

There are certain ways of investigating whether change has occurred in the status of dalits. One way is to identify the parameters of change in the caste system. In this context, it is to evaluate whether various features, such as endogamy, hereditary occupations and restrictions on interaction and food have changed. Whatever may be the degree of change in these features of caste system, the shift from the ideal construction could be regarded as an instance of transformation. If we take into account all these features, then we find that the major change has occurred in the hereditary character of occupations, whereas the practice of caste endogamy has not undergone much change so far as the dalits are concerned.

A considerable number of studies have been conducted on the effect of political mobilisation on the status of the SCs. An organised struggle for status has been recognised as the key variable in the success achieved in the enhancement of the status. Some of the examples of this path of change are Mahars of Maharashtra (Zelliot, 1970), Nadars of Tamil Nadu (Hardgrave, Jr., 1970), Izhavas of Kerala and Jatavs of Agra (Lynch, 1974). Some micro-studies at village level tend to suggest that organised protest plays an important role in changing the self-image and others' perception of the SCs (Seth, 1987). One positive element in this perspective is that the SCs themselves organise to wage a struggle to improve their status. However, this presupposes certain conditions without which an organised struggle is not possible. One condition that is referred to in the existing literature is the consciousness that emerges as a result of ideological codification of subordination, discrimination and oppression for which there is a need for leadership that could perform this task. In a strategy that is primarily based on the efforts of the dalits, the leadership has to be from within.

The meaning of political mobilisation is shifting towards empowerment through electoral politics. Mayawati, the Chief Minister of Uttar Pradesh and Kanshi Ram, the supremo leader of the Bahujan Samaj Party (BSP), represent this emerging trend. Instead of mobilising the dalit masses to collectively assert their identity and claim equality, this new perspective entails mobilisation for votes. In other words, the dalit leaders treat the dalits as vote banks and then become political actors as well as players at both the state and national levels. This perspective introduces new trend in the sense that it has all the ingredients and potential of providing better bargaining space to the dalit leaders. Moreover, after forming the government, the BSP could always initiate, revive or implement policies meant for the Dalits. For instance, the allotment of land to the dalits has been one of the successful ventures of Mayawati in her earlier stint as the Chief Minister. However, in the politics of coalition government, Mayawati has contributed to reinforce *Hindutva* forces that earlier were labelled as 'Manuwadi' by her. The implication of all this is quite clear. After a particular stage of development, capturing power becomes an end in itself rather than a means to an end of social equality.

The new electoral approach of empowerment is rooted in the perspective of change from above. Social reform and the reservation policy are two other well-examined efforts, which also aim at improving the status of the dalits in India. The reservation policy has given rise to an ambivalent situation, as the better off sections among the dalits have been able to make use of opportunities provided by it. At the same time, the division of society into upper castes, backward classes, other backward classes, SCs and STs has been created, reinforced and reaffirmed by the reservation policy. Within each category of people, there could be diversification, but we also witness "reverse status orientation in public" among the members of hitherto existing upper castes. The Jats of Rajasthan and the Ramgarhias of Punjab are now officially the other backward classes (OBCs). This reverse status orientation in public is characterised by 'double consciousness' to use the term coined by Du Bois (Watson, 2002). However, the content of this double consciousness is qualitatively different from what Du Bois had in mind with regard to the American Blacks. In this case, the members of the caste are aware of their dominant position in the region and it is clear that this position is unchallenged and irreversible. Thus, the redesignation as OBCs would only give them benefits in the form of reservations in government jobs. The latter aspect of consciousness that gives reasons for exploiting the electoral, constitutional and legal structures is a new emerging phenomenon in Indian society and it has all chances of picking up the momentum. Once the reservation policy is isolated from the birth-ascribed status, it turns into a populist political action. It may just be reminded that the basic premise of the reservation policy was that if the socially degraded castes could get political representation, education, government jobs, then the birth-ascribed status might be replaced by the achieved status. What has actually happened in India is that both kinds of status have begun to co-exist. The politically powerful groups are seeking to broaden the base of reservation policy, which, as it has started happening, may become the main impediment in the overall development of the dalits.

Describing Dalits of Punjab

Placed in the broader Indian context is the social structure of Punjab. The society in Punjab has certain unique features with regard to the dalits and the caste system. In fact, the issue is much more complex than one may anticipate. While discussing Punjab's social structure, there is a need to pinpoint certain distinctive elements, particularly with regard to the dalits. It may be appropriate to start the discussion by identifying such elements as under:

1. The proportion of the dalits in the total population of Punjab was 28.31 per cent according to the 1991 census and it is likely to increase further in the 2001 census. This proportion is the highest in the country if we compare it with other states.
2. Within Punjab, the population distribution of dalits is not uniform. Of all the districts, Jalandhar with 39.08 per cent of the total population has the highest percentage of the dalits, followed by Faridkot (34.08%) and Hoshiarpur (33.32%) districts. Ferozepur has the lowest percentage of dalits, i.e., 21.80 per cent, which is still higher than the all-India average.
3. According to the official list, Punjab has 378 castes of dalits. Among these, two are the most numerous castes. These are Chamars (leather worker) and Churhas (scavengers or sweepers). However, these two castes have experienced nomenclatural diversity over a period of time. Thus, Chamars are now Ad-dharmis, Ramdasias, etc., whereas the Churhas are Balmikis and Mazabis. In most of the cases the nomenclatural change has emerged from the interreligious interaction.
4. It may be further noted that various castes of the dalits are unevenly distributed in the state. In Jalandhar, Hoshiarpur, Gurdaspur, Ropar and Faridkot districts, the Chamars are most numerous, whereas in Amritsar, Bathinda and Mansa districts, Churhas are most numerous. One common aspect of these castes is that despite their concentration in certain pockets, they are found in all the districts of the state. Other castes are small in size and thus confined to a particular region of Punjab. For example, the Doms are largely confined to the Gurdaspur district.
5. The most significant dimension of the dalits is related with the religious composition of present Punjab. In Punjab, the Sikhs are the majority community both in terms of political domination and numbers, as they constitute 62.95 per cent of the population. The Hindus come next being 34.46 per cent of the population of the state. Both the Christians and Muslims are considerably smaller in proportion than the Sikhs and Hindus. The Muslim and Christian dalits are not included among the SCs. They are identified as

backward classes. The Sikh dalits are officially recognised as the SCs as a result of which they are at par with their Hindu counterparts since both are eligible for benefits under the reservation policy of the government. Ironically, Sikhism claims, professes and preaches social equality among men. It is expected that caste equality be practised among the Sikhs. It seems that the politics and economics of reservation policy, combined with age-old traditions, customs and practices, have led to this paradoxical situation. It is all the more important in the light of the fact that in recent decades the Sikhs have fought and struggled for rewriting and revising of the Article 25 of the Constitution of India to recognise Sikhism as a religion distinct from Hinduism. No such attempt has been made in the direction of getting the dalits de-recognised as the SCs. On the other hand, the Ramgarhias have been accorded the status of OBCs.

The above description of certain distinctive features of the dalits of Punjab makes it obvious that for the understanding of the issue there is always a need to keep diversities in our focus of analysis. It has already been stated that Punjab has certain distinctive features so far as caste and untouchability are concerned. It is generally argued that in Punjab there is discrimination without untouchability. Such a general observation, or sometimes assumption, is based on the argument that Sikhism has significantly influenced the patterns of relations and interaction among various castes. Being an egalitarian religion, Sikhism does not believe, preach and practise caste-based inequality. Islam is also egalitarian. However, there is always a gap between ideal claims and empirical reality. At the empirical level, it is difficult to make generalisations either of the ways. Various references to the existence of castes among the Sikhs can be found in the sociological literature and other aspects of public life. There does not seem to be any need to go very far to examine whether or not castes exist among the Sikhs. An easy way to question the rhetoric of castelessness among the Sikhs is that the Government of India has recognised certain castes among the Sikhs as SCs, which are eligible for the benefits under the reservation policy. Interestingly, Kirpal Singh Badungar, the former President of the SGPC, belongs to a dalit caste. In recent years we have not found any leader of the Shiromani Gurdwara Parbandhak Committee (SGPC) or the Akali Dal asserting that since there is no caste among the Sikhs, the reservation policy should be discontinued. On the contrary, the Ramgarhias have been successful in getting being recognised as OBCs at par with their Hindu counterparts, largely known as Tarkhan and/or Lohar. Obviously, it would not affect their social standing, which they achieved due to Sikhism, in a negative or positive manner.

Mapping Change

Three major indicators of change among the dalits of Punjab, particularly the Doaba region, namely, education, emigration and empowerment, require serious scholarly attention. Among these migration to foreign countries is the distinguishing feature of Punjabi dalits. Nowhere else in India it would draw anyone's attention. Education is an integral part of industrial society. The evolutionary perspective emphasises the role of education in the social mobility of the SCs. In one way or the other, education is a prerequisite for social mobility in the modern society. The diversification of occupations that has followed industrialisation has instrumental rational basis. The knowledge, skill and attitudes required for the performance of a job are essentially acquired through modern education. Though education, emigration and empowerment may be regarded as the main indicators of the social mobility of the SCs in contemporary Punjab, yet an examination at the empirical level is still required.

Across disciplines, social, economic and political dimensions are recognised as primary factors of social change. It is alleged that with regard to change, the realm of values is the most difficult component of society. However, in the case of the dalits, it is both. Certain features of the caste system may not be adequate indicators of change. Quite often, endogamy is recognised as the basic feature of caste system. However, the frequency of intercaste marriages may not adequately show the degree of change in the caste system. The dominant form of mate selection in India is through preferential marriages within kinship networks or is arranged by the parents. In such a situation, marriages would tend to take place within the limited endogamous circle governed by traditions. Moreover, hypergamy has been one of the oldest forms of marriage. It may be reminded that the domain of marriage is either a part of customs and traditions or the individual's choice. The state cannot actively intervene in marriage as it either impinges upon the rights of community or violates the liberal tradition of individual choice. The state has successfully interfered in the family to uphold the rights of the individual, but the institution of marriage is an altogether different domain. Since the intervention of state is always expected to be formal, public and legal, it can only intervene if an individual complains that he/she is being married against his/her will. Even in the case of commensality, the state can act if members of a caste are discriminated against in hotels, restaurants and public places, but it cannot monitor the informal and private spheres of individual and social life. Thus, the indicators of change are expected to be visible, formal and public in which both state intervention and efforts of the dalits can be empirically observed, examined and evaluated. In this context, education, emigration and empowerment have formal and public spheres that could be investigated. The following discussion takes into cognisance these three indicators to assess the social change in Punjab with regard to the dalits.

Education

Sociologists have attached paramount importance to education in modern society. Education is multifunctional for the capitalist system. Capitalism has secularised occupational structure by removing, partly or completely, tradition, custom and inheritance from the choice of occupations. It has achieved diversification, multiplication and specialisation of occupations due to the intensification of industrial production. The occupational requirements were linked with specific skills that required training. Education and occupation have become inseparable, as the society endlessly requires more and more specialised services. The role of education in raising the consciousness is widely acknowledged in the contemporary world. The western world recognised the relevance of education in integrating individuals with the society and thus it progressively made it accessible to all sections of society. The leaders of independent India were largely educated in the western tradition and gave due weightage to education for the SCs as a means to improving their status. Immediately after the end of colonialism the literacy levels of people were low and the government undertook positive steps to make education accessible to all. It was not an easy task. Simultaneously, the Constitution of India provided for the reservation of a certain proportion of seats for the members of the SCs in the educational institutions.

What has been the performance of the Indian government in providing education to its citizens during the last fifty years? The data available show that though a significant improvement has taken place, yet 100 per cent literacy remains a distant dream. The literacy level of the SCs is still low. The data in Table 1 indicate that in comparison with 10.27 per cent literacy rate of the SCs in 1961, it has gone up to 37.41 per cent in 1991. In this regard, the change is noticeable but below expectations. In Punjab, the literacy rate of the SCs in 1991 was 33.35 per cent, which is less than the all-India average. Interestingly, in Hoshiarpur district, 52 per cent of the SCs are literate (Chandra, 2000).

Table 1

India: Urban and rural literacy rates of the scheduled castes, 1961–1991

Year	*Rural*	*Urban*	*Total*
1961	8.89	21.81	10.27
1971	12.77	28.65	14.67
1981	18.48	36.60	21.38
1991	33.25	55.11	37.41

Source: Online. File: // A: I Ministry of Education.

Table 2

Number of districts of Punjab according to literacy percentages of the scheduled castes, 1991

Literacy slabs (in %)	*Number of districts*
20–30	4
30–40	2
40–50	2
50–60	3
60–70	1
Total	12

Source: Online. File: // A: I Ministry of Education.

Table 2 provides an interesting insight into the district-wise pattern of literacy in Punjab. According to the data, there is only one district in which the literate SCs constitute between 60 and 70 per cent of their total population. Obviously, this refers to the Hoshiarpur district. Later on, at the turn of the century, Hoshiarpur district became the first district of Punjab to have 100 per cent literacy.

In a study of five villages in the Hoshiarpur district, in which 400 households of the SCs were studied, the educational characteristics provided some insights into the changing scenario. Table 3 shows educational level of both husband and wife and it is clear from the data that 41.25 per cent husbands and 11.95 per cent wives were educated. However, it was found that there was significant upward trend in the education of their children(Judge, 1993, 1997). In spite of the fact that the education levels of the SCs show an upward trend, the years of schooling remains still low.

Table 3

Education by sex in five villages of Hoshiarpur district

Level of education	*Wife*	*Husband*
Illiterate	354 (88.5)	235 (58.75)
Upto primary	24 (6.00)	35 (8.75)
Upto middle	18 (4.50)	74 (18.50)
Upto matric	4 (1.00)	46 (11.50)
College	–	10 (2.50)
Total	400 (100)	400 (100)

Figures in parentheses indicate percentages.

Acquiring education is generally perceived as a means to get white-collar jobs, which in the case of the dalits is an important element in their efforts to move away from their traditional occupations. Various studies (Bains, 1994; Jodhka, 2000) indicate that whereas the SCs are over represented in Class IV category of government jobs, they are under represented in all other categories. It also shows that despite the reservation for the SCs in the educational institutions and government jobs, they have failed to make full use of it. In this context, we have to make a distinction between availability, accessibility and utilisation. On top of this underutilisation of reserved seats in the educational institutions and government jobs, the non-SCs have sharply reacted against the reservation policy (Bains, 1994). The upper caste students of medical colleges were in the forefront of the agitation against reservation in Gujarat and Punjab.

Further, we may take up yet another important issue, which refers to what Shah (2002) calls hierarchical differentiation among the SCs. One may ask which castes among the dalits have benefited from the reservation policy? What seems obvious in the case of Punjab is that the Ad-dharmis (Chamars) have made the best use of the reservation policy. This fact has to be seen in comparative perspective. The other dalit caste that is numerically preponderant, namely, Balmiki/Mazabi has not been able to keep pace with the Ad dharmis. While commenting on the patterns of mobility among the Ad-dharmis, Saberwal (1990: 73) writes:

> ... among the Ad Dharmis, hereditarily the weavers and leatherworkers, many were by early 20th century beginning to enlarge the scale of their earlier interests. A substantial business in hides-and-skins, taking one over a large region, enabled one to observe, learn, and transmit to one's children some standard urban norms, for example, those concerning food, dress, speech and education; for his sons, the mobility train would that much be easier to enter.

The above comment was made by Saberwal while comparing Ad-dharmis and Balmikis. In a way, he establishes causal connection between emerging capitalist mode of production under the British rule and certain flourishing trades that were regarded as unclean and polluting by the upper castes. Such a transformation during the colonial period paved the way for international migration and struggle for status improvement among the Chamars who later on took up the different identity, that is, Ad-dharmis.

Emigration

International migration of Punjabis began in the 19th century and accelerated in the early 20th century. In the post-independence period, the emigration of Punjabis has been phenomenal, as they have virtually spread all over the world. In India, the Gujaratis have outnumbered the Punjabis in emigration. In both the cases, the landowning castes, namely, Jats of Punjab and the Patidars of Gujarat, are most numerous among the emigrants.

The emigration of the dalits has a history older than that of the Jats and Patidars. The migration of the tribals and the poor from Chhotanagpur area and Tamil Nadu under the indentured labour system to plantation colonies was the major phenomenon of the movement of the people from India during the colonial period. However, it is not known how many dalits emigrated as indentured labourers. Conversely, the migration of Punjabis was voluntary and in search of rich pastures, which could add to their prestige in the native villages. Various studies of the emigration of Punjabis emphasise two important aspects of the migrants. First, in the beginning, the emigration began from Majha and Malwa, but later on it became prominent from the Doaba region consisting of Jalandhar, Hoshiarpur and Kapurthala districts (McLeod, 1986). What has remained unexplored and unanalysed is the emigration of dalits to Australia, New Zealand, USA and Canada at the beginning of the 20th century. Kessinger (1974) has listed various dalit castes, which sent their members abroad. McLeod (1986) has given a detailed caste background of the people who reached New Zealand. He has also narrated a case of Dr Baldev Singh Share, who was son of Giani Ditt Singh of the Singh Sabha fame. As is well known, he was a Ramdasia – a dalit caste among the Sikhs. It is notable that Dr Share was not only the son of a prominent leader of the Singh Sabha movement, but also a medical doctor by profession. Another notable figure among the dalits was Mangoo Ram who was Chamar by caste and emigrated to the USA. He belonged to village Mughowal in Hoshiarpur district.

One common element in the emigration of dalits in the beginning of the 20th century is that the Chamars were numerically preponderant among them, which seems to be a result of their economic improvement (Judge, 2002). However, in actual numbers and in comparison to the Jats, the emigration of the dalits from Punjab was quite low.

In the post-independence period, the emigration of Punjabis accelerated and Canada and England were the major destinations. Both these countries needed manpower to strengthen their economy. The emigration of the people from the Doaba region continued unabated and a significant dimension was the presence of dalits among them. According to Juergensmeyer (1982), the Ad-dharmis accounted for 10 per cent of the total emigrants to England. This rough estimate of the proportion of the Ad-dharmis in England provides us a reasonable understanding of their presence. Being 10 per cent of more than half a million Punjabis is a substantial size.

The change in the economic conditions of the dalits is both a cause and consequence of emigration. There is hardly any research conducted on the emigration of the dalits. In a recent study (Judge, 2002a) of the Ad-dharmis in England, it has been found that though little is known about the impact of emigration on the dalits in Punjab, yet considerable changes have occurred among the dalit diaspora in

England. In Midlands we find that Balmikis/Mazabis and the Ad-dharmis are economically as active as the Jats and other non-dalits are. They are largely doing the same jobs and visit the same pubs in the evenings. This has, however, not eliminated casteism among the diaspora Punjabis. At certain levels, caste identity is being reinforced. For example, owing to the Untouchability Offences Act, a person belonging to a dalit caste cannot be addressed by his caste name, which is considered derogatory in India, whereas in England calling somebody as 'Chamar' has no such legal implications.

When the diasporic dalits come to Punjab for some days or weeks, they invariably exhibit behaviour similar to that of the Jats. What distinguishes them from the Jats is that emigration enables them to become elites within the caste and their pattern of interaction undergoes a change. Since there is no empirical study on this issue, it is based on personal observations of the author. The dalits who joined the bureaucracy, those who become traders and those who became political leaders comprise the elites among the dalits. The immigrant dalits to the western countries are the fourth type of the dalit elite. Following the classical model of the characteristics of elites, they have one important feature, namely, intermarriages. Thus, directly or indirectly, there is some degree of interchangeability of positions. The sons and daughters of the officers are married into the emigrant families. There is also a great degree of orientation towards settling in the cities. The formation of classes within the dalit castes is not a recent phenomenon. As Saberwal (1990) has pointed out, the flourishing hide-and-skin trade gave the impetus to the emergence of rich dalits, particularly belonging to the Chamar caste.

The emigration to the western countries is limited and confined to better off sections among the dalits in Punjab. On the other hand, the migration to Gulf countries has an altogether different character. The Punjabi migration to the Gulf countries has not drawn the kind of attention that the emigration from Kerala has drawn. Whatever is being stated here is more in the nature of conjectures, which are based on observations. When the migration to the Gulf countries, generally called Dubai in Punjab, began in 1970s, the western countries had started restricting immigration through stringent enactments. Thus, all castes and classes of people from rural areas, that is, the Jat landowners, artisan Ramgarhias and the dalit agricultural labourers migrated to the Gulf countries. The fundamental difference between the migration to the West and the Gulf countries was that the emigrants had no choice of settling permanently in the latter.

In Hoshiarpur district, where international migration has now become a part of culture, Gulf migration has also made entry into the folk consciousness as is evident from the following couplet:

> *Bareen barsin khattan gia si, khatt ke liande rambe; Dubai lai gai lut ke, sare ronki bande.*
>
> (Dubai has snatched all the lively men from the village.)

In a study of village Ajram in Hoshiarpur district, conducted by this author in 1984, the change in the conditions of the dalits was visible from the houses as they had started constructing *pakka* houses, but still many houses were *kacha* or semi-*pakka* at the time of the fieldwork (Judge, 1985). A revisit to the village after seven years revealed that all the houses of the dalits were *pakka*. Emigration to the Gulf countries partly contributed to that change. In the third visit in 2000 it was found that most of the dalits who had returned from the Middle East had opened shops in the village.

In the end, we may return to the dalits, particularly the Ad-dharmis, in England to examine whether the Punjabi community is still practising caste. It was found that caste awareness still persists among the Punjabis. There are no restrictions on dining together and friendly interaction, but intercaste marriage in which the boy is Ad-dharmi is resented and discouraged. In order to prevent such an occurrence, caste consciousness is intentionally imputed on the young generation through the socialisation process. Interestingly, even the Ad-dharmi respondents were in favour of caste endogamy (Judge, 2002a).

Empowerment

The expression 'dalit empowerment' has two-fold meaning. First, it implies the efforts of the dalits to empower themselves in the political process. Second, it means that they are provided with opportunities through the state efforts to occupy formal positions of power in the political process. As discussed earlier, any attempt at change must entail the analysis of agency, that is, the agents who aspire to bring change would do so by acting upon the rules and resources in the institutional context that persist over a period of time in a space. Empowerment is basically a consequence of an act of an individual, a collectivity or an institution. Weber (1970: 180) defines power as "the chance of a man or a number of men to realize their own will in a communal action even against the resistance of others who are participating in the action". It is well known that Weber makes a distinction between power and authority whereby the latter refers to legitimate act of power. For the present purpose, the state, that is, constitutionally legitimate agency to exercise force, would empower a section of people through legal rational action, i.e., enactment.

The two dimensions of empowerment of the SCs can be characterised as empowerment 'from below' and 'from above'. The empowerment from below refers to the efforts of the SCs to assert and capture power through political mobilisation and social movement approach. In this regard, various studies have indicated that political mobilisation has proved to be an effective strategy of the dalits in India. The Mahars of Maharashtra (Zelliot, 1970), the Jatavas of Agra (Lynch, 1974) and the Nadars of Tamil Nadu (Hardgrave, Jr., 1970) are some of the examples of this dimension of empowerment. In the 1950s, when the Constitution of India had already guaranteed equality, the formation of the Republican Party of India by Ambedkar was the beginning of a new era of dalit empowerment, through participation in the formal political process. In fact, this formal participation was a culmination of the Poona Pact, when Gandhi went on fast to virtually force Ambedkar to withdraw the demand for separate electorate for the depressed castes. In Punjab, Mangoo Ram organised and led the Ad-dharma movement, which aimed at giving a new identity to the dalits. The movement remained largely confined to the Chamar caste, but it succeeded in acquiring new identity for its participants, namely, Ad-dharmis. In the 1931 Census, the Ad-dharmi emerged as a new caste. Later on, Mango Ram supported the movement of the dalits led by Ambedkar. The Ad-dharma movement had its impact on a section of dalits and the empirical studies show that the Ad-dharmis have been the most mobile caste among the dalits (Juergensmeyer, 1982; Saberwal, 1990). Thus, in the post-independence period, these Ad-dharmis joined the Republican Party of India. The real presence of dalits as a political force could only be felt after Kanshi Ram's BSP emerged on the political scene. Chandra has examined the rise of the BSP in India in general, and in Hoshiarpur in particular. It is worthwhile to quote her (Chandra, 2000: 35) thus:

> The early cadre base of the BSP in Hoshiarpur, as elsewhere in India, came from BAMCEF (Backward and Minority Communities

Employees Federation), an organization of government employees founded in 1978 by Kanshi Ram to prepare the ground for a political party. Affirmative action policies had produced a concentrated pool of Scheduled Castes in government jobs who were educated, organized into professional unions, and financially better off than other scheduled castes. These employees offered Kanshi Ram, himself from among their ranks, a concentrated pool of resources with which to launch a political party.

Unlike Uttar Pradesh, the BSP failed to make a significant impact in the already existing political configuration in Punjab. It began a system of alliances that proved to be of minor political gains, because the BSP soon faced split and two parties emerged that dissipated all its advantages. Though the BSP could not become a force to reckon with, but it always had the potential to be so if we keep in mind that the SCs constitute nearly one-third of the population of Punjab and in Jalandhar district they are two-fifths of the population. In a recent work, Gupta (2000) has argued that caste constituency in electoral politics is a myth. There is a reasonable basis to accept what Gupta has said in the case of Yadavas. In the case of the dalits of Punjab the caste factor or, to use Shah's impression, hierarchical differentiation among them has played an important role in preventing them from becoming a major political force in Punjab. The BSP is generally identified with the Ad-dharmis. Thus, the rest of the castes feel threatened by the increasing influence of the Ad-dharmis though the BSP is aimed at creating a broad front of the dalits. In spite of all this, the BSP has better prospects of becoming an important player than parties other than the Congress and the Akali Dal. The major shift from grassroots level movements to the formal political participation in elections as a means to empowerment is quite visible among the dalits.

In the formal political process the efforts of the Indian government to empower the dalits have taken a new turn when it introduced the 72nd (Panchayats) and 73rd (Nagarpalikas) constitutional amendment bills. These came into force as the Constitution (73rd Amendment) Act and the Constitution (74th Amendment) Act in 1993. In the light of these amendments there is a provision for reservation of seats in local bodies in rural and urban areas for women and the SCs. In a way, these constitutional amendments are aimed at empowering the women and the dalits at the grassroots level. After a decade of these amendments one may take note of the changes. One of the major changes is that all the seats of the Sarpanchas meant for reserved category have been filled, as has been the case with the reservation for the SCs in Lok Sabha and the Vidhan Sabha. Following the Weberian model it becomes clear that the dalits have acquired legal rational authority. But, the important question is whether the occupants of these positions have been empowered. Or, have the women and the dalits got power? Viswanathan (2002) has brought out a case of resignation of two dalit Sarpanchas in Tamil Nadu two weeks after their election and has shown that no empowerment has taken place.

Referring to the empirical situation, the five villages of Hoshiarpur district were revisited (see Judge, 1997) to examine the situation after the reservation in panchayats. In all the five villages the Sarpanchas belonged to the SCs. It was only in one village, namely, Sahri, that the Sarpanch seemed to have some autonomy and was independent of the influence, threat and coercion of the Jat landowners. In all other four villages, the power has remained in the hands of the upper caste landowners constantly reminding us of the useful conceptual distinction between power and authority made by Weber.

The case of Onkar Singh, the Sarpanch of village Sahri, is somewhat different. In the recent Vidhan Sabha elections, he was a candidate from Sham Chaurasi (reserved) constituency. He was the candidate of the Bahujan Samaj Morcha (Kainth). Though he lost the election, yet his party's alliance with the then ruling Akali Dal gave him influence and power. The second aspect of his empowerment was that in the village the SCs constitute more than half of the population and most of them belong to his own caste, that is, Ad-dharmi. The Jat landowners have failed to effectively fracture his power at the local and the regional levels. Most of the SC Sarpanchas have not been as resourceful as the above case shows. The instance of village Wadala Kalan in the Amritsar district provides an insight into the way the formal and political dynamics works at the village level.[3] In this village, the Sarpanch belongs to Ramdasia caste and he originally hails from the Hoshiarpur district. One Mazabi family was economically better off. The head of the family was a contractor of the Food Corporation of India (FCI). He was in conflict with the Jat landowners and started saying that after he became the Sarpanch he would set the Jats right. The Jats decided that the Mazabi would not become a Sarpanch and they asked the head of the only Ramdasia family to fight the elections.

In sum, the agenda of empowerment is in existence without sufficient base for it. The Ad-dharmis are emerging as a politically active and dynamic caste. It has the needed aspirations, resources and mobilisation. However, everything has not changed at the expected level. The continuity in and of structural inequalities based on birth and ascription shows the other face of the reality. The next section aims at exploring this continuity.

Mapping Continuity

The main impediment to the change in the status of the dalits is the presence, persistence and sometimes reinforcement of the caste system, casteism and articulation of caste identities. Since the caste identity draws its strength from the traditions, religious ideology and the economic and political inequalities, the likelihood of its disappearance seems less probable in the near future. On may argue from the postmodernist perspective that even if caste differences in the form of articulated identities in the social and political spaces continue to persist, one should aim at achieving equality among them. In this regard, the role, relevance and exercise of power occupy centre stage. In a society in which the major religion, that is, Sikhism, claims to be egalitarian in ideology and practice, equality with difference may seem easier to achieve. However, such expressions, ideas and desires are to be seen in the light of the ground reality. At the empirical level, the social dynamism may be operating at an altogether different level.

In the light of the above, two questions may be raised. Have the atrocities on and the discrimination against the dalits come to an end? What is the role of hierarchical differentiation among the dalits in perpetuating caste? To the first question we may add what Chandra (2000) calls "humiliation of and discrimination against" a small section of dalits who are doing white-collar jobs. Chandra (2000: 36) narrates the case of Rattan Ram, who was a clerk and joined the BSP in Hoshiarpur, thus: "… When I met him in 1997, he narrated numerous incidents of discrimination throughout his career, ranging from passing remarks about his lack of 'merit' to being passed over for promotions because of his caste identity." It may be pointed out that in the Punjab villages the locality of the dalits is still called *Chamarhli* if the Ad-dharmis live there and *Thathi* if the Mazabis live there. This seems to have remained unchanged. Jodhka (2002) also mentions the ecological segregation of the dalits in his recent study, which reconfirms the already existing fact. Interestingly, the *Chamarhli* or *Thathi* is invariably located towards southwest of the village.

Jodhka (2000) has gathered information of the reported cases of atrocities on the SCs in Punjab from 1995 to 1999. It is interesting to note that the number of reported cases have been increasing, which indicates the growing awareness of the dalits on the one hand and rising cases of caste conflict on the other. Still another source of having a fairly good idea of atrocities and discrimination is the newspaper reports. Three such cases, which appeared in *The Tribune* from 2001 to 2002 and show various atrocities committed against them, are discussed here.

The first news referred to the temple entry of the dalits thus: "Dalit devotees coming to Sidh Baba Baal Jati Rupal Temple at Rakhra village, near here (Patiala) are not allowed even at the platform leading to the sanctum sanctorum. They must offer obeisance from one end of the platform. Similarly, those who want to take *langar* must use separate utensils kept for them and be seated separately. Both Sikhs and Hindus visit the temple."[4] This case is a clear-cut violation of the constitutional provisions and uniquely different from other cases in the sense that in other cases the caste and class combine to create an environment of oppression. In this case, only the caste status comes into play. The news reporter also informed that even the rich dalits were not allowed to go beyond that point.

The second story refers to village Balamgarh in Malerkotla where a 14-year old dalit girl was raped. The girl was a domestic helper in the house.[5] In an earlier study (Judge, 1994), it was mentioned that sexual exploitation of the dalit women was common. In a revisit to the field, the informants were of the view that it had substantially declined. However, it cannot be generalised in terms of caste and the region. It is quite possible that in the region in which the Ad-dharmis are numerous such incidents have declined, but the same may not be applicable to the Mazabis and Balmikis or some other dalit castes in other regions, particularly the Malwa region. Some areas of Punjab, such as Bathinda, Mansa, Firozepur and Sangrur districts, are relatively different from the rest of Punjab. These areas have relatively low literacy rate and remnants of landlordism, which often result into the transformation of woman's sexuality into commodity.

The story of village Todarwal in Kapurthala district does not only indicate caste-class nexus, but also exposes the efforts at empowerment from above. The Village Panchayat was dominated by the SCs, but when about 30 families of dalits raised their voice against some rich families who were illegally occupying some land, all the upper caste families turned against them and boycotted them. "An open announcement about the boycott by the upper class families using a loudspeaker was made: 'Our people were not allowed even to go to fields to answer the call of nature. Our families have no work to do', she (Shanti Devi, the Sarpanch of the village) alleged." What was significant to note was that even the upper castes of the adjoining villages started refusing to employ them.[6] The day after this report appeared in some newspaper, the officials visited the village and told the press that the situation in the village was tense.[7]

The strategy of the upper caste/class landowners to ban entry of the dalits in the fields seems to be an old strategy. It is well known that most of the dalits in Punjab are landless and agricultural labourers. However, they had certain rights over the land as a part of the village community. The Mahalwari system of revenue collection in Punjab held every villager responsible for its payment. Under this system, families could own the land yet others could use it only after harvesting would be over. All this changed with modernisation and the right of the individual ownership was recognised. The landowners started using this strategy to control and suppress dissent and protest. It was found that in village Ajram in Hoshiarpur district the same strategy was employed by the landowners when the dalits went on strike demanding higher wages (Judge, 1985). The strikes of the dalits who were primarily agricultural workers signified a change in the relations of production in the 1970s. There was a change from the feudal to the capitalist mode of production and these series of strikes in various villages of Punjab highlighted the labour-capital conflict. There was also something unique to this conflict. In addition to class positions, it was superimposed by the caste relationships in which the working class also meant the dalit castes.

Another story of the dalits of Moondkheri village in Patiala district, reveals how even the formal channels at the local level can be effectively used against them in a situation of conflict. "Dalits protesting against having been made bonded labourers in this village have been penalised by the panchayat. As many as 15 of them have been blacklisted and list of names have been distributed among all traders including milkmen in the village as well as the nearby half a dozen villages." The situation precipitated when many landowners received legal notices that they were keeping bonded labourers. "Landowners are, however, emphatic that this has been done to identify 'mischief makers' in the village because they had filed false complaints against various landlords. They said all dalits had taken money in advance in lieu of their payments for the whole year or for six months and had stopped working claiming that they were being made bonded labourers."[8] The story refers to a Phillaur-based NGO[9], which has been working against the practice of bonded labour. The tradition of having bonded labour was prevalent in Punjab in a limited form. Since the traditional *jajman* and *siri* relationship in the village was characterised by durability and generational continuity, it involved a system of obligations and mutual responsibilities with the advantage and power to the former. The Green Revolution broke all such traditional relations and transformed them into instrumental relations. The influx of migrant labour into Punjab, in fact, provided opportunities to the dalits to move out of the traditional relationship and to become independent. Obviously, the bondage caused by indebtedness is still going on in some parts of Punjab and invariably the man in bondage is a dalit.

We may now turn to the understanding of the implications of the second question that we raised in the beginning of this section regarding the hierarchical differentiation among the dalits. One may call it the power of Hindu ideology or something else, but the existence of castes among the dalits cannot be wished away or put aside while discussing change in their status. Some of the notable and numerically large castes in Punjab are Ad-dharmi, Balmiki/Mazabi, Julaha, Sansi and Doms. They all are endogamous groups and tend to exclude each other in the construction of their identities. They have differentially benefited from the affirmative action of the governments thus resulting into bigger gaps among them. In fact, all the indicators of social mobility are leading towards emergence of the privileged and the underprivileged from within the dalits.

To conclude the discussion, the story of village Ajram in Hoshiarpur district provides an insight into how the caste system operates within the dalit castes.

> A young Ad-dharmi girl fell in love with a Balmiki boy. When their parents came to know about it, the girl eloped with the boy. Her

parents followed them and finally they were caught. The girl was brought back to village where she was virtually confined in the house. The girl's parents told her that she would not be married to the Balmiki boy as he belonged to the lower caste. After a few days the girl burnt herself to death.

This indicates that the caste system exists in virulent form among the dalits and we have still a long to way to go to achieve caste-free society.

Conclusions

The changes that have occurred among the dalits of Punjab are visible but lack uniformity. Some of the dalit castes, such as Ad-dharmis, have experienced tremendous change in their conditions after independence, whereas some others, particularly Balmikis, Mazabis and Sansis, have not improved their status. In the already stratified dalits, the uneven development has further led to the sharpening of differences among them. This hierarchical differentiation, which is marked by contradictions, is a major obstacle in the way of any dalit unity for social equality and justice. The second important aspect of the changes among the dalit castes is the emergence of economic inequality and the formation of elites within the castes. Once this has happened, the dalithood as an identity formation basically becomes an ideological tool in the hands of the dalit intelligentsia to be used as a means to have political space through negotiation and contestation. Empowerment in the real sense of the term is absent for the majority of the dalits. Thus, the subaltern dalits have been pitted against their own caste elites, as well as the upper caste landlords. The contestation between these groups is unequal. In spite of this general trend, the change in the living conditions of the dalits is progressively becoming visible, but one should not look into the issues of endogamy and commensality to map change, because to a considerable extent these are informal, private and invariably not open to negotiation till the actors involved in the situation choose to do so. For example, no law can force a family of upper caste people to invite dalits for dinner so long as it does not choose to do so. Similarly, the arranged marriage cannot be forced to be intercaste in practice by any law. By the same logic it may be argued that in public and formal situation, the commensality, and in love marriages the different castes of the couple may fall within the legal space. The social change experienced by the dalits is at two levels. Whereas the overall development of the society has affected the conditions of the dalits, the affirmative action programmes of the government have contributed to the improvement of their conditions. It may be concluded that if the dalits are as divided by caste as the society is, then there is a need to rethink caste and its significance in the Indian society.

Notes

This article was earlier published in Harish K. Puri (ed.), *Dalits in Regional Context.* Rawat Publications, Jaipur, 2004.

1. In this paper, an attempt has also been made to examine the changing status of the dalits in the diasporic Punjabi communities abroad. Thus, we have used the expression 'dalits of Punjab'.
2. Some of the studies are Singh (1974), Ahmad (1973), and Wiebe and John-Peter (1974).
3. The information provided by Dr J.S. Sekhon is gratefully acknowledged.
4. Jangveer Singh, "Dalits barred from temple", *The Sunday Tribune,* May 20, 2001, p. 1.
5. "14-yr-old Dalit raped", *The Tribune,* August 17, 2001, p. 5.
6. "Dalits allege persecution by upper castes", *The Tribune, May 16, 2002.*
7. "Tension in village, says report", *The Tribune,* May 17,2002, p. 2.
8. Jangveer Singh, "Panchayat blacklists Dalits", *The Tribune,* August 3, 2002, p. 3.
9. This refers to Volunteers for Social Justice (VSJ) and it is headed by Jai Singh. This voluntary organisation largely takes up the cases of the bonded labour in Punjab.

References

Ahmad, Imtiaz (ed.), 1973. *Caste and Social Stratification among the Muslims.* New Delhi: Manohar.

Bharati, Sunita Reddy. 2002. "'Dalit': A Term Asserting Unity", *Economic and Political Weekly,* Vol. XXXVII, No. 42, October 19–25, pp. 4339–40.

Bingley, A.H. 1985. *The Sikhs.* Delhi: National Book Shop.

Chandra, Kanchan. 2000. "Transformation of Ethnic Politics in India: The Decline of Congress and the Rise of the Bahujan Samaj Party", *The Journal of Asian Studies,* Vol. 59, No.1, February, pp. 26–61.

Gupta, Dipankar. 2000. *Interrogating Caste: Understanding Hierarchy and Difference in Indian Society*. New Delhi: Penguin Books.

Hardgrave, Jr., Robert L. 1970. "Political Participation and Primordial Solidarity: The Nadars of Tamil Nad", in Kothari, Rajni (ed.), *Caste in Indian Politics*. New Delhi: Orient Longman, pp. 102–28.

Jodhka, Surinder S. 2000. " 'Prejudice' without 'Pollution'? Scheduled Castes in Contemporary Punjab", *Journal of Indian School of Political Economy*, Vol. XII, Nos. 3–4, July–December, pp. 381–404.

——. 2002. "Caste and Untouchability in Rural Punjab", *Economic and Politically Weekly*, Vol. XXXVII, No. 19, May 11, pp. 1813–23.

Judge, Paramjit S. 2002a. "Punjabis in England: Ad Dharmi Experience", *Economic and Political Weekly*, Vol. XXXVII, No. 31, August 3–9, pp. 3244–50.

——. 2002b. "Religion, Caste and Communalism in Punjab", *Sociological Bulletin*, Vol. 51, No.2, September, pp. 175–94.

——. 1997. "Emerging Trends in the Caste Structure of Punjab", *The Administrator*, Vol. XLII, No. 1, January–March, pp. 55–66.

——. 1993. "Scheduled Caste Women in Work Force in Rural Punjab", *Ambedkar Journal of Social Development and Justice*, Vol. 3, March, pp.65–90.

——. 1985. "Class Analysis of Scheduled Castes in Ajram (A Punjab village)", in Pimpley, P.N. and Sharma, Satish K. (eds.), *Struggle for Status*. New Delhi: B.R. Publishing Corporation.

Juergensmeyer, Mark. 1982. *Religion as Social Vision: The Movement Against Untouchability in 20th Century Punjab*. Berkeley: University of California Press.

Kessinger, Tom G. 1974. *Vilyatpur* 1848–1968: *Social and Economic Change in a North Indian Village*. Berkeley: University of California Press.

Kothari, Rajni. 1970. "Introduction", in Kothari, Rajni (ed.), *Caste in Indian Politics*. New Delhi: Orient Longman, pp. 3–28.

Lynch, Owen M. 1974. "The Politics of Untouchability: A Case from Agra", in Rao, M.S.A. (ed.), *Urban Sociology in India*. New Delhi: Orient Longman.

McLeod, W.H. 1986. *Punjabis in New Zealand: A History of Punjabi Migration 1890–1940*. Amritsar: Guru Nanak Dev University.

Saberwal, Satish.1990. *Mobile Men: Limits to Social Change in Urban Punjab* (revised edition). Shimla: Indian Institute of Advanced Study in association with Manohar, New Delhi.

Seth, V.N. 1987. "Caste System and Status Change: A Study of Harijan Protest in Banda", in Sharma, S.K. (ed.), *Reform Protest and Social Transformation*. New Delhi: Ashish Publishing House.

Shah, A.M. 2002. "The 'Dalit' Category and Its Differentiation ", *Economic and Political Weekly,* Vol. XXXVII, No. 14, April 6–12, pp. 1317–19.

Singh, Harjinder. 1977. "Caste Ranking in Two Sikh Villages", in Harjinder Singh (ed.), *Caste Among Non-Hindus in India (1984–90).* New Delhi: National Publishing House.

Singh, K.S. 1999. *The Scheduled Castes.* Calcutta: Oxford University Press.

Weber, Max. 1948. *From Max Weber: Essays in Sociology (*tr. and ed. by H.H. Gerth and C. Wright Mills). London: Routledge and Kegan Paul.

Wiebe, Paul D. and S. John John-Peter. 1974. "The Catholic Church and Caste in Rural Tamil Nadu", in Harjinder Singh (ed.), *Caste Among Non-Hindus in India (1984–90).* New Delhi: National Publishing House. pp. 37–49.

Zelliot, Eleanor.1970. "Learning the Use of Political Means: The Mahars of Maharashtra", in Kothari, Rajni (ed.), *Caste in Indian Politics.* New Delhi: Orient Longman, pp. 29–69.

9

Caste Conflicts in Punjab

An Examination of Recent Jat-Dalit Clash in a Punjab Village

The violent clash between the Jats and the dalits in village Talhan in Jalandhar district has drawn the attention of everybody. Punjab has been regarded as one of those few states, which were free from such tensions. This was in spite of the fact that sociological studies have always revealed the contrary picture (Judge, 1985). Being predominantly a prosperous state Punjab earned many distinctions in eyes of the intelligentsia. Added to this was the fact that a majority of the people belonged to Sikh religion, which has been regarded as an egalitarian in both theory and practice. Most of such viewpoints, impressions and opinions have been invalidated by the clash between the Jat Sikhs and the dalits in a village in Jalandhar district. This process of demolition and demystification of the prevailing impression and views has also raised a plethora of issues with regard to the future of the dynamics of the relationship between the dalits and the upper castes in Punjab as well as India.

In this paper, an attempt has been made to understand and analyse the clash between the Jats and the dalits that occurred in the village Talhan. Since there are two actors, namely, the Jat Sikhs and the dalits, and their orientation towards the situation involved a shrine locally called either Gurdwara Baba Nihal Singh (henceforth the shrine), it is important and necessary to examine all the three components of the clash in the backdrop of the social setting of the village. The discussion in this paper has been divided into five parts. The first part is theoretical in nature and delineates various perspectives on social conflict, whereas the second part provides a panoramic view of the dalits of Punjab. The third part attempts at situating the emergence of contestation in the village social reality. The fourth part is the narration of the unfolding of the events leading to the clash and the negotiated settlement of conflict. The final part is aimed at making sense of the clash from the sociological perspective.

Understanding Social Conflict

In sociological literature, the conflict perspective is generally associated with the Marxist theory despite the fact that some of the theorists understand social conflict as an integrative and functional process. Weber (1962: 85) defines it as a social relationship, "insofar as the behaviour of one party is oriented purposefully toward making his own will prevail against the resistance of other parties or another party". A closer look at this definition would make it clear that conflict essentially involves power. In general terms, the conflict perspective understands conflict as an outcome of struggle over the scarce resources, but the views vary with regard to what the meanings of 'scarce resources' are. For Marx the relationship between the classes of bourgeoisie and proletariat is characterised by antagonistic interests. Thus conflict is inherent in the class relations, but it does not imply that it would turn into a struggle. For the conflict to manifest itself there has to be class consciousness, which is a result of ideology, and organisation of the working class.

Dahrendorf (1976) regards authority as the defining criteria of conflict as it divides members of an 'imperatively coordinated association' into positions of domination and subjection. He also makes a distinction between latent and manifest conflicts. The conflict is manifest when quasi-groups turn into interest groups implying that the members are able to articulate their interests. In contrast to the resolution of conflict in Marxist theory, Dahrendorf argues for the 'regulation of conflict', but conflict could lead to radical change irrespective of its pace and degree of violence.

There is a degree of complexity involved in the understanding of the caste conflicts. Any theoretical perspective in the understanding of caste conflict would take into consideration the nature of caste hierarchy with regard to power, privilege and ownership of means of production. The perspective of exclusion and inclusion tend to take care of three dimensions of the caste hierarchy, as the level of exclusion from power, privilege and ownership of means of production is linked with the caste hierarchy, and both theoretically and empirically the dalits constitute the 'excluded'. The principle of exclusion is based on discrimination and disabilities that are supported and sustained by coercion and ideology. The struggle of the excluded is invariably aimed at becoming equal partners in a non-hierarchical way. The exclusion based on birth is one of the most contested social spaces as it involves caste, race and gender. One of the important features of exclusion is its durability and perpetuation at the level of consciousness and practice even when the excluded have been able to achieve a degree of mobility in economic and other fields. This durability of the exclusion is one of the major reasons for the manifestation of conflict in certain circumstances, as it tends to block opportunities for the excluded, particularly when they have already achieved a degree of mobility in some walks of life.

The process of inclusion entails the collective assertion of the excluded as well as the intervention of the state. In the case of dalits the state intervention has taken place in the form of recognition of constitutional rights of freedom, equality of opportunity and justice, legal enactments to end all kinds of caste-based discrimination, and, finally, reservation policy in education, employment and political sphere in elected bodies. However, the collective assertion for inclusion involves contradiction that generally remains unresolved at the theoretical level. A movement of the dalits for equal participation in all walks of life may remain successful only in the public and formal structures of society, but it cannot compel or force the people to allow them to participate in private and informal structures of everyday life. For example, the dalits may be successful in achieving entry into restaurants and hotels, but the upper castes may continue to exclude them from their kitchens. Thus, there is a limit to the principle of inclusion through collective assertion and the state intervention. In spite of the fact that there is an increase in the rate of intercaste marriages, the caste endogamy continues to be the governing principle. The strength of caste endogamy lies in the method and mode of mate selection, which is based on the practice of arranged marriages. Can the state force an individual of a particular caste not to practice caste endogamy by discontinuing and violating the tradition of arranged marriage? The answer is no. If we take into consideration the views of Berreman (1979) that caste system is also characterised by cultural plurality, then the implications of this fact are that each caste would like to exclude the other and the caste endogamy is also based on this cultural exclusion. At a particular level, the process of inclusion is likely to take place through negotiation and consensus instead of confrontation and contestation in the political space.

To turn to equal participation, which is the rationale of state intervention and is also the prerequisite of inclusion, it may be stated that it depends on how the exclusion is articulated in the structures of everyday life and what are the markers of difference and similarity between the two groups. However, it is a long drawn process and the presence of conflict and its manifestation at certain points of time is likely to be the essence of the relationship between the privileged and the underprivileged.

There are five components of exclusion each of which presents a complex set of interactions. The struggle for inclusion, therefore, is not a simple process as there is also a dialectical reverse of this process. The social group, which excludes certain others, is also getting excluded from them. In such a situation there is a need to know whether these social groups wish to end their own exclusion and what would they achieve by doing so. These five components are: ecological, social (including cultural), religious, economic and political. The examination of the caste clash would be examined in the light of these five components of exclusion. There is however a need to know the distinctive and unique features of the dalits in Punjab, which is agriculturally the most developed state in the country.

Dalits of Punjab

The proportion (30%) of the scheduled castes (SCs) in the total population of Punjab is the highest of all the states in the country. There are however districtwise variations in the distribution of their population. In the Doaba region, consisting of Hoshiarpur, Jalandhar, Kapurthala and Nawan Shahar districts, the number of the scheduled castes is considerably high in comparison with the other regions.

However, in the Gurdaspur district of Majha region and the Faridkot district of Malwa region their percentages are higher than the state average. The Jalandhar district has the highest percentage of the dalits in the state.

There are also a large number of castes among the dalits of Punjab. There are 37 castes among them, but few castes are numerically preponderant, e.g., Ad-dharmi/Chamar, Balmiki/Mazabi, Julaha/Kabir Panthi, Dom and Sansi. In comparison with other states the proportion of dalits among the agricultural workers has been as high as 70 per cent (Reddy, 1978). There is a reasonable basis to argue that after the enactment of the tenancy reforms in Punjab as well as PEPSU[1] a large number of dalit tenants were evicted and dispossessed from their operational holdings and they swelled the ranks of the agricultural workers.

The dalits of Punjab also have religious diversity, which, interestingly, is also accompanied by the change in the name of some castes. The Christian dalits belong to the Churha or Bhangi caste, but now they have been classified as backward class. The Ramdsias, Sansis and Mazabis are Sikhs, whereas the Balmiki could be called Hindus. Mahashas, the ex-Dom, are Aryasamajis, and we also find some of the dalits have converted to Buddhism. One of the notable religious groups among the dalits is that of Ad-dharmis. The emergence and evolution of the Ad-dharma is a 20th century phenomenon. The British Raj recognised the Ad-dharmis in the census enumeration of 1931 as a distinct group, because they agitated to get this status under the leadership of Mangoo Ram (Juergensmeyer, 1982). The Ad-dharmis recognise, venerate and worship Ravidas – a medieval saint – as their Guru and his writings in the form of hymns occupy the holy status.

The fact that all the hymns of Guru Ravidas are included in the Guru Granth Sahib, the Ad-dharmis generally use it for their religious purposes. The religious place of worship is called Ravidas Mandir or gurdwara and in most of the cases the Guru Granth Sahib is used to read hymns of Guru Ravidas. Since for the Sikhs the Guru Granth Sahib is not merely a sacred book, but also as per the orders of the tenth Guru personifies the Guru, the Shiromani Gurdwara Prabandhak Committee (SGPC) – the highest governing body of the Sikhs – has formulated the rules to keep it. What is known as *Rahat Maryada* is a set of written rules that inform of the conduct of the true

Sikh. It also involves the rules as how to conduct oneself in matters regarding the maintenance and keeping of the sacred books. It is important to note and emphasise that the Ad-dharmis constitute a distinct caste and religious group (in the list of the scheduled castes of Punjab, the Ad-dharmis have been recorded/denotified as a caste). In the local setting at village level, the Ad-dharmis are generally known, called and mentioned as 'Chamars' by the upper castes though, as informed by Saberwal (1990), some other castes also joined the Ad-dharma movement.

For a researcher studying the dalits in Punjab, the understanding of significance, relevance and role of Green Revolution, emigration and education/employment is indispensable. It has also been frequently argued that the role of Sikhism in affecting the caste structure is equally crucial in Punjab. The Green Revolution phenomenon brought overall prosperity in Punjab villages contributing to the tremendous decline in the poverty among the working class. Though their turn came in the end, yet the dalits were able to draw certain economic benefits from it. These benefits might not be understood in term of increase in wage, but more as a consequence of expansion and diversification of occupational activities at the low level, which were undertaken by the dalits.

A fact unique to the dalits of Punjab and has remained least noticed is their international migration in the beginning of the 20th century (Judge, 2002). The emigration of the dalits has been going on unabated since the first decade of the last century and it has led to the prosperity of some of them. As a consequence of this, there is phenomenon of emergence of classes within the dalits. The third important development in the post-independence period has been the educational and occupational changes among the dalits. Owing to the reservation policy, a section among the dalits has been able to enter the formal, public sector after attaining education. It may however be mentioned that all these changes have not reached all the dalit castes. Some of them have benefited more than many others. In this regard, the caste that emerges at the top of hierarchy is that of Ad-dharmi. Still all the Ad-dharmis have not been able to change their living conditions.

An invariably ignored or unattended fact with regard to the dalits is that there are regional variations in the changes that have occurred among them. The dalits in the Doaba region have experienced more social mobility than those of Majha and Malwa. The uniqueness of Doaba lies in the fact that it has been having a strong tradition of international migration. The dalits, according to Juergenmeyer (1982), constitute 10 per cent of the total Punjabi emigrants during two decades immediately following independence in 1947. The undoubted and undisputed fact about the dalits of Punjab is that the Ad-dharmis of Doaba region are the most mobile in social and economic sectors. It is the area of political dominance that requires closer and in-depth scrutiny and examination. In the understanding and analysis of the clash in Talhan it may be kept in mind that we are essentially talking about the Jats and the Ad-dharmis. Without specifying the word 'dalit' the investigation and analysis would remain vague and unfocussed. The underlying message in this observation is that we are talking about the clash between the most dominant caste of Punjab and the most mobile and dynamic caste among the scheduled castes, i.e., the Jats and the Ad-dharmis.

The Village[2]

Talhan is a big village in Jalandhar district and is located at a distance of 10 kilometres from the district headquarters towards southeast. Sandhu (2003) recently remarked that it is not a typical Punjabi village. This, he stated on the basis of the fact that there are big and modern houses in the village. He is partially wrong in the sense that whereas it is true in the case of Punjab as such, it is wrong in the case of Doaba region. A visit to the villages of Doaba, particularly the area in which Talhan is located, would show that the ecological segregation has virtually ended and disappeared at the level of appearance as there is no way of identifying the houses of the upper castes from the dalits. They all look alike and Talhan is no different from this common pattern.

In spite of the fact that certain forces of development, such as Green Revolution, education and employment, and emigration, have blurred ecological segregation, a sense of distinction and separation continues to exist and perpetuate. There are some houses that have been constructed at locations that are at a distance from the main locality of the Jat Sikhs, but the dominant settlement pattern of the village continues to be the caste-based clustering of the houses. This pattern is not unique but can be monotonously observed in every village in Doaba. At the same time, the settlement of the dalits is still called 'chamarhli', which literally means the locality of the Chamars. There are two contradictory and simultaneous processes that are operating in the villages with regard to the settlement pattern. First, there is a process of reinforcement of the clustering of caste in one locality, because the upper castes do not sell their plots, even if available, to dalits. As a result one finds that there are two prices of the house plots in the villages. In and around the dalit locality prices are high due to heavy demand. Most of the sellers are landowning upper castes and they are willing to sell land to the dalits for house construction, but they would not do it in their own locality. Secondly, the emigration of Jats is leading towards the stagnation or very low increase in their population. In most of the cases all family members emigrate to any of the English-speaking western countries. In such a situation, they generally leave their houses in the care of a dalit family. Since the rate of emigration of the dalits is far less than the Jats, we find a process in which there is a high concentration of the population of the dalits in one part of the village, whereas the locality of the Jats is experiencing the reverse process.

As the contested space is a gurdwara, it is adequate to give a description of the religious places in the village Talhan. It has six religious places of worship. These are: the *mazaar* of a Sufi Pir Baba Fateh Shah, the shrine, two gurdwaras belonging to the Jats Sikhs, one Ravidas gurdwara, and one Jogi Pir Mandir. The last two belong to the Ad-dharmis. This kind of distribution is quite typical in Punjab except for the *mazaar* of Baba Fateh Shah, which indicates that Talhan had sizeable population of the Muslims before 1947. The village however belonged to the Jat Sikhs of the Bains gotra. Some of the Jats had also migrated to canal colonies (now in Pakistan) from where they returned to their native village. The Jats originally belonging to the nearby village Kotli also came from the Canal Colonies and were allotted land by the government and their gotra is Sandar. The existence of distinct gurdwaras from the shrine is not an unusual occurrence in this village. There are gurdwaras, which perform social functions for the village, such as, marriage and death ceremonies, and observation of *sangrand* – the first day of the month according to the Bikrami calendar, and Gurpurabs – the days on which the gurus born or martyred or died. Most of the times, the number of the gurdwaras is an indication of the number of localities. There is the second type of gurdwaras that have links or relation with the Sikh religious history. These gurdwaras are associated with the Sikh gurus or some Sikh saint (Puri, Judge and Sekhon, 1999). The shrine in Talhan belongs to the second variety. In 2002 the management committee of the shrine donated three lakh rupees for the construction of the Ravidas gurdwara. However, the construction of Jogi Pir Mandir disturbed the Sikh management of the shrine, which according to them was a typical Hindu temple with the bell installed there. In spite of the impression that the Jat Sikhs are orthodox in their religious practices (and this may be reinforced by the subsequent narration of the events), the tradition of ancestor worship, which seems to be pre-Sikh practice, is still going on. Thus, there is also an ancestral place of worship of the Bains gotra called in Punjabi *Jatherian di Matti* and it is a three-storey building.

It is clear and evident from the types of religious places of worship that Talhan is basically a Sikh and Ad-dharmi village. The worshipping of the *mazaar* of the Muslim Pir is an indication of the typical composite tradition of religious practices. Since this *mazaar* occupies the centre stage in the clash, it reaffirms the dialectics of the interaction between organised and folk religions at the level of common people and their consciousness. The following data provides us the information regarding the proportion of the scheduled castes in the village population:

Total population of the village	2946
Total population of the scheduled castes	1772
Percentage of the scheduled castes	60.15

Source: Census of India 2001; FPT. Punjab.

It is evident from the above that the scheduled castes, largely belonging to the Ad-dharmi caste, constitute an overwhelming majority in the village. The second numerically large caste group is that of the Jat Sikhs These two principal actors are the main constituents of the village. Whereas the Jats are the landowners, the Ad-dharmis are mainly landless but numerically more preponderant. About 10 Ad-dharmis own land and none of them owns above 10 acres. All these Ad-dharmis were involved in the business of skin and hides in Kolkata.

In spite of numerical preponderance of the Ad-dharmis, the Sarpanch of the village belonged to the Jat caste at the time of clash. It has been observed that even if a dalit becomes the Sarpanch of the village, the political power continues to be in the hands of the landowning Jats (Judge, 1985). In this village there are people belonging to the other backward classes (OBCs) called Ramgarhias and Jheers. Both the caste groups are Sikhs, but they seem to be outside the domain of contentions. Interestingly, in the management committee of the shrine, there is one member belonging to the Ramgarhia caste. The Ramgarhia caste has been recently declared as the OBC though it is one of the most mobile castes of Punjab. Besides, some families of the Bhatra caste, which is a backward caste whose traditional occupation has been begging also live. For some of them it still continues to be so though after their conversion to Sikhism they have become butchers in the cities and *granthis* or *pathis* or gurdwara priests known as *bhai* in the villages.[3] Talhan is an ideal place for the Bhatras to work as *granthis.* They get employment in the shrine and gradually some of them have started residing in the village. They are living in the houses that are unoccupied due to the emigration of their owners to the western countries.

In the absence of the exact information, it may be stated that there is a high degree of emigration of both the Jats and the Ad-dharmis. The emigration of Ad-dharmis is one of the distinctive features of the Doaba region (Judge, 2002). In this region, it is generally alleged that virtually every family has a relative in any of the western countries. The emigration has brought prosperity to the villages of this region. In Talhan, about 20 families of the Jats have completely migrated to the western countries, particularly England and the USA, and have permanently settled there. There are 15 families, which have one or two members emigrated to any of these countries. Among the Ad-dharmis about seven have emigrated to England and five to Canada and the USA. However, a large number of Ad-dharmis have gone to the Middle East countries. A noticeable effect of the international migration is the construction of big houses with all the modern facilities.

In the economic field there is an evidence of declining dependence of the Ad-dharmis on the Jat landowners. It also implies that the Ad-dharmis have moved out of the agricultural labour and have joined the urban formal or informal sector. It has been facilitated by the proximity of the village with Jalandhar. However, in bringing the prosperity to the homes of the village in general and Ad-dharmis in particular, the shrine has played a decisive and formidable role. Most of the diaspora villagers, irrespective of their caste, donated money to the shrine. The shrine in turn expended and spent a major portion of its income on improving the physical conditions of the village. It is the employment of the people of the village in the shrine that has also contributed to the improvement of the life of the Ad-dharmis. There are three kinds of employees working in the shrine, namely, the *sevadars*, *granthis* and those who cook *langar*. It was found that the Ad-dharmi women constituted the major proportion of the cooks. The *langar* is served throughout the day and its timings are from 6 am to 9 pm. For the preparation of langar, particularly on Sundays, more than 30 women were employed. Since the cooking of *chapattis* in this shrine is a major work, the employment of women was an important dimension of the village life. Each of the women was paid Rs 70 per day plus the cooked food in abundance, which she could carry home. There are also other kinds of activities in which the Ad-dharmis were employed. Moreover, there are shops opened in front of the shrine that are doing good business. In the backdrop of various objective conditions of the village, it is worthwhile to narrate the story of the clash between the Jats and the Ad-dharmis.

The Clash

The manifestation of conflict between the Jats and the dalits has not been a new phenomenon in the villages of Punjab. To understand this conflict, it is necessary to point out that the Jats and the dalits are not occupying just two positions in the hierarchy, but also belong to different positions in the process of production. The Jat, at the same time, is a landowner – an oppressor, whereas a dalit is an agricultural worker – an oppressed. The landowner of another upper caste may replace the Jat, but the relationship does not alter with such a change. The functionalists talk about the economic interdependence among various castes, but it may be reminded that it is equally oppressive in content. The domination of the landowner is invariably expressed in political, cultural and sexual exploitation. The *local* nature of relationship (though postmodernists celebrate local in contrast to universal) renders it so powerful that there is a little escape out of it. However, the revolt, opposition, or resentment of the dalits has also remained unabated and in the post-independence period there has been four major areas of open conflict between the landowning upper castes and the dalits. These were conflict over agricultural wages, conflict over formal power particularly during panchayat elections,[4] indecency shown to a dalit woman, and addressing a dalit by an insulting remark.

The conflict between the landowners and the dalit agricultural labourers has been one of the most common occurrences in Punjab. In one such event the dalits went on strike and the Jats resorted to what they called *nakabandi*, i.e., they banned the entry of the dalits into their fields. This continued for some days and the matter was resolved through the intervention of district administration (Judge, 1985). Such kinds of conflict had been quite common at the time of wheat harvesting, but started declining with the influx of migrant labour from Bihar and Uttar Pradesh. The arrival of the migrant labour contributed to the depression of daily wages in Punjab.

The conflict for power has continuously and uninterruptedly remained a live issue till the recent panchayat elections held in June 2003. In the absence of reservation of seats, the post of Sarpanch becomes highly contentious and even if the dalits constitute a majority in the village, the Sarpanch would invariably belong to the upper and dominant castes, particularly from the class of landowners (Judge, ibid.). As the panchayat elections have been postponed in Talhan, we find that the Jat Sarpanch continues to occupy his position. After the clash the elections were held in December and an SC woman became the Sarpanch, because the post was reserved for the scheduled caste woman.

Talhan also has a history of manifest conflict between the landowners and dalits. Though the informants could not remember the year, but in the early 1970s the conflict between the Jats and the dalits broke out when a Jat had beaten an Ad-dharmi woman alleging that she was ruining his paddy field. The district authorities intervened in the matter and resolved the conflict. In general, an insult to a dalit woman is the third most common cause of conflict.

However, over a period of time the content of the manifestation of conflict has undergone a qualitative change. Recently, the story of the dalits of Moondkheri village in Patiala district reveals how even the formal channels at the local level can be effectively used against them in a situation of conflict. "Dalits protesting against having been made bonded labourers in this village have been penalised by the panchayat. As many as 15 of them have been blacklisted and list of names have been distributed among all traders including milkmen in the village as well as the nearby half a dozen villages". The situation precipitated when many landowners received legal notices that they were keeping bonded labourers. "Landowners are, however, emphatic that this has been done to identify 'mischief makers' in the village because they had filed false complaints against various landlords. They said all dalits had taken money in advance in lieu of their payments for the whole year for six months and had stopped working claiming that they were being made bonded labourers."[5] In such a situation, the administration becomes helpless in intervening into and resolving the conflict, because the social boycott operates at informal level. The clash between the Jats and the dalits in Talhan is still different from the typical conflicts observed earlier. In the centre of the conflict is located the shrine and it is important for us to understand the politics and economics of the sacred place for which the story of its origin may be the right beginning.

The Jat Sikhs who came from Canal Colonies, originally belonging either to Talhan or Kotli, inform that in 1947 there was no gurdwara. There were just two graves, one of which was of Baba Nihal Singh and the other was of Harnam Singh Granthi. However, there has been a strong belief that the sacred place dates back to the sixth Guru of the Sikhs. The managing committee was formed in 1961 and in 1962–63 the gurdwara had been constructed and the Guru Granth Sahib had been installed. When the gurdwara was constructed, its impact increased and the number of people visiting the place to pay their obeisance started rising. At present, it is a big place and in the hall at the second floor 40 copies of the Guru Granth Sahib have been placed. At the time of the visit of this author, the 29 copies were occupied as the *granthis* were reading them uninterruptedly, which is known as Akhand Path in Sikhism. On Sundays the people in thousands come to this shrine to pay obeisance and make a wish. It is a popular belief that if you make a wish at the place of Baba Nihal Singh, it is fulfilled. Such kinds of beliefs are generally associated with the *mazaars* of the Muslim Sufi saints. In the newspapers that covered stories of the clash designated the shrine as *samadh*-cum-gurdwara.

With regard to the shrine we may raise two questions that are central to the understanding of the conflict. Is it a sacred place of the Sikhs only? Are the Ad-dharmis Sikhs? If we answer the first question by saying 'no', the second question becomes irrelevant. In case the answer is 'yes', the Ad-dharmis can only make a claim on the gurdwara if they are Sikhs or *claim to be Sikhs.* Interestingly, this issue has not yet been raised by anybody in the print media. A visit to the place gives an overwhelming and doubtless impression that it is a Sikh religious place. In fact, the status of this place may be understood from the perspective of the composite religious tradition of Punjab. As such, the Sikh religious tradition, which has been constructed by the Singh Sabha movement, prohibits the Sikhs from worshipping the graves, but this has never happened. The shrine is neither a social gurdwara nor a place of historical importance though an attempt has been made to connect, associate and relate it to the sixth Guru of the Sikhs. The shrine is a place developed, nurtured and controlled by the local Jat Sikhs, but it could have belonged to anyone. Since the Sikhs have been controlling it since 1961, they have imposed their own rules that have now become non-negotiable and unalterable.

It is now a well-known fact that the annual collection of the shrine in the form of donations and offerings is six crores of rupees. The impact of this money is visible in the form of beautifully paved metalled streets and the big school building, and the grandeur of the shrine itself. The Jat Sikhs of the village attribute the beginning of the conflict to the panchayat politics and the money collected at the shrine, but it seems that the immediate and precipitating cause of the conflict was the termination of the services of the local dalit women who were cooking *chapattis* and the work of preparing *langar* was handed over to a party from Goindwal on contractual basis. It was alleged that they were not performing their duties well and were disrespectful to the management. The termination of these women's services created conditions for the confrontation.

So far the issue remained confined to the village, but as the elections of the management committee approached the situation started changing radically. Since the elections are held on the first day of the month of *Magh* (January 14) in Bikrami calendar every year, the Ad-dharmis came prepared and told the previous committee that they had already constituted it, but however sent back. Three days after this event the Ad-dharmis reached the shrine and declared that they had constituted their managing committee, which would like to look after the shrine. It led to a clash between the two parties and some people were injured. The matter went to the court. The Jat Sikhs saw it as interference in their affairs and organised themselves. They resolved, recorded and handed over their social boycott to the Ad-dharmis without realising the fact that they had committed a legal offence punishable under law. When they came to know of this, they retracted their steps and some kind of agreement was reached with the involvement of the district administration. However, the social boycott of the Ad-dharmis at the informal level continued. As the time passed, the desperation of the Ad-dharmis increased and they started approaching the political parties. The news of the boycott also appeared in the newspapers. However, the matter remained unresolved in spite of the keen interest of the state government in it. It may be reminded that the caste politics being played by Kanshi Ram's Bahujan Samaj Party (BSP) has not been very successful in Punjab. Dhaliwal (2001: 3) reported that "to rejuvenate the party, obviously with an eye on the coming Assembly elections, Kanshi Ram has launched a massive political and social campaign in the state. He is not holding political rallies but also has asked his party cadres to wage war against casteism and fight for the rights of contractual farm labourers, called 'siri' in local parlance". The results of State Assembly elections of 2002 amply demonstrate that the casteist card of Kanshi Ram failed to enthuse the dalits of Punjab, particularly in the light of their proportion in the total population of the state. Even, the Bahujan Samaj Morcha of Satnam Singh Kainth – a break away group of the BSP – could not do much despite the fact that it had alliance with the Akali Dal (Badal).

In the political dynamics of Punjab there are two major players and contenders of power, namely, the Congress and the Akali Dal. All other political parties, namely the BJP, BSP and the Communist Party of India (CPI) are minor players and become effective only if they fight elections by forging an alliance with any of these two parties. The Congress being the centralised party does not form any alliance except for the understanding with the CPI. The CPI though once formed an alliance with Akali Dal, but it has a secular ideology, invariably forms a durable alliance, and does not muddle with the politics of caste and religion.

What happened in Talhan put both the major parties into a dilemma. As a ruling party, the approach of the Congress was towards reconciling the two parties and thus diffusing the situation. It was evident from the way the district administration tried to work out some kind of agreement between the two groups. The Akali Dal (Badal) remained ambivalent towards the entire contention, as it involved a dispute over a shrine, which till this date was controlled by the Sikh. It was a kind of catch–22 situation for the Akali Dal (Badal). Supporting decisively the Jat Sikhs meant alienation of the dalits from the Akalis and they could not afford to annoy the Jats who form the base of their power in the state. The way the situation emerged, it paved the way for the entry of the minor players, namely, the BSP and the BJP, to politicise and draw the focus of the general public at the state and the national levels. Under the patronage of the state vice-president of the BJP, Mr Vijay Sampla, the Dalit Action Committee was formed with dalit, namely, Chanan Ram as its president. This committee staged protest on May 17, 2003 at Jalandhar when the Chief Secretary of Punjab was holding a meeting of the senior civil and police officials "against the failure of the state government to initiate action against those who were booked for atrocities on Dalits and had given a call to boycott the Dalit community of Talhan village, owing to a dispute over the management of a shrine about four month ago".[6]

Towards the end of the month of May another player entered (rather brought in by the Jats of Talhan) the political and religious space, namely, Mohkam Singh of Damdami Taksal.[7] The interest shown by Bhai Mohkam Singh might have warned the district officials, but they undertook no step that could give an iota of indication of such kind. The stage was set for the clash, but there had to be a provocation and ironically it came from a very different source. The clash between the Jat Sikhs and the Ad-dharmis occurred on June 5, 2003. As the people of the village informed, it began at 2 pm and continued till 8 pm without any loss of life. Let us look into the occurrence and the nature and sequence of events that led to the clash.

As stated earlier, there is a *mazaar* of Sufi Pir, Baba Fateh Shah. Every year a fair is organised at this *mazaar* in the month of June by an NRI S. Singh, who lives in the USA and belongs to the Jat caste. His father has six brothers and all of them live in the USA. In actual number, one may estimate that about 40 persons of these seven families live in the USA. S. Singh has been organising these fairs for many years after wheat harvesting in the adjoining fields to the *mazaar*. The land belongs to his brother. He believes that if he organises the fair, he does well in business that year. When he reached his village, he found the situation tense and some people advised him not to organise the fair this time. However, he announced the fair and it was to be held on June 5–7, 2003. The Jats allege that the provocation came from the Ad-dharmis, which is refuted by them. There are two factors that seem to suggest that the Jats might be right. The provocation came from the

Ad-dharmis in the form of the Ad-dharmi boys passing some comments on the Jat girls who were singing devotional songs on the stage. The Jats allege that at that time there was no Ad-dharmi woman present in the crowd in the fair and as they told, when they tried to stop those boys, they attacked and the clash began.

Let us look into the two evidences that seem to be in the favour of the claim of the Jats. First, from a nearby house, the Ad-dharmis started pelting stones at the Jats. Ironically, the house belongs to the family of diaspora Jats and they have put it in the care of an Ad-dharmi family, which was attached to them under the jajmani system. The fact that a large number of stones had already been collected shows that there was an intent, planning or anticipation. Secondly, immediately after the violence broke out in Talhan, there were disturbances in a locality, namely, Boota Mandi, in Jalandhar city. Those who do not know the geography of the area may understand and interpret this information that the village Talhan is close to Boota Mandi. In fact, the two are located at a distance of more than 15 kilometres and there are many localities of the dalits in Jalandhar.[8] The violence or disturbances did not spread to other localities of the dalits in Jalandhar. There is a reasonable basis to argue that some of the residents of Boota Mandi were prepared for it.

In the clash at Talhan, 12 persons belonging to both the groups were hurt, whereas the agitated mob in Boota Mandi set a bus on fire. A young dalit boy, Vijay Kumar was allegedly killed in police firing. Next day violence spread to other areas. Phagwara witnessed violent agitation of the dalit youth. The traffic on many roads remained disrupted for many hours. The curfew was imposed in Talhan as well as Boota Mandi. During the curfew in the village, both the Jats and Ad-dharmis blamed the police for its partisan attitude and behaviour. During the curfew another drama was played in the village. The activists of the Damdami Taksal managed to enter the shrine and meanwhile the management committee announced that it was handing it over to the Taksal. At this juncture, the Sikh leaders at the state level and some officers managed to diffuse the situation and the activists of the Damdami Taksal came out of the shrine. All this happened when the curfew was on. The Government of Punjab acted in a predictable manner. It transferred the district level officers from both the administration and the police.

It seems that the appearance of the Damdami Taksal on the scene, which gave danger signal to all vested interests, was the main reason for the concerted efforts to resolve the conflict. The agreement was reached between the two groups according to which two persons from the Ad-dharmis were to be inducted into the management committee of the shrine, but the condition was that both of them must be complete Sikhs (*Puran Gursikhs*). At present, two persons from the Ad-dharmi caste are members of the management committee and they have now become complete Sikhs.

Conclusion

Making Sense of the Conflict

Strasser (1976) has examined and evaluated the normative structure of sociology by making a distinction between conservative and emancipatory themes in social thought. He makes it clear that,

> Social scientists have to realize that explanations are set up and value judgements are made for the same aim, namely, to fulfil human purposes. In practice, the universe in which man lives is factually created by him and not discovered, while in science we discover, and in so far help to recreate, the factual order; we set it up conceptually; we uncover the structure of reality. In sociological terms, the *theory* of society, or of man-in-society, thus becomes a function of *the problem* of order (Ibid.: 12).

Once we structure the sociological explanations into normative concerns, then the question of the position one takes with regard to the issue becomes crucial. In this regard, Becker (1974) has made it clear that it is not important whether we are neutral or not, but "rather whose side we are on". Becker makes a distinction between political and apolitical situations taking into account the hierarchy of credibility. As we are examining a political situation in which, to use Becker's expression, subordinates (dalits) were organised, it may be adequate to quote him (ibid.: 115) thus:

> It is no secret that most sociologists are politically liberal to one degree or another. Our political preferences dictate the side we will be on and, since these preferences are shared by most of our colleagues, few are ready to throw the first stone or are even aware

that stone throwing is a possibility. We usually take the side of the underdog; we are for Negroes and against fascists.

Becker's explicit position with regard to the dilemmas faced by the researcher clears many mists. What he does not state clearly is the underlying universal principles of justice and equity that have been cherished all over the world after their entrenchment in the western tradition. The basic reason for raising the entire issue of values in social sciences is that empirical reality we aim at interpreting and analysing here entails two sets of paradoxes, which seem to have emerged from the story of clash between the Jats and the dalits.

The first set of paradox is that the trajectory of contestation is religious in content, whereas the conflict has occurred between two caste groups. The paradox can be resolved if both the caste groups belong to the same religion. Or, one of the contesting parties believes to be the original or the real claimants for the shrine. This is not so though the shrine has all the features that lead us to believe that it belongs to the Sikhs. If the Ad-dharmis are Sikhs, then their demand and assertion that turned into clash is understandable. In fact, there is no way to establish that the Ad-dharmis are Sikhs. Now, the issue is why they wanted to be a part of the shrine when they were not Sikhs.

The second paradox is that the Ad-dharmis, traditionally recognised as oppressed and economically subservient, constitute a social group that has been able to improve its conditions. The nature of clash also indicates that they want representation in the management of the shrine for which they have confronted and fought the upper caste Jats. This clearly shows that the theoretical perspective of empowering the poor and oppressed is not operating in this situation. When we say dalits of Talhan, the impression it would give is different to people in the country from what their actual sociological profile is.

Let us try to remove these paradoxes from the perspective of inclusion and exclusion. Empowerment, education and employment are the policies of the government that may bring the dalits at par with the upper castes in political and economic fields, but it will not end their exclusion. The process of inclusion has to operate at both formal and informal, public and private spheres and the government cannot enter and intervene in the private and informal spheres. The religion of the Ad-dharmis may not be seen as a space with rigid boundaries. In view of the fact that in all Ravidas Gurdwaras the Guru Granth Sahib is placed and we can hardly make a distinction between a Ramdasia and an Ad-dharmi in social terms, the latter may like to claim to be part of the Sikh tradition. Moreover, the shrine is a part of the composite tradition, which has remained the dominant feature of the folk religion in Punjab. One can also raise a question with regard to the *mazaar* and the *jatherian the matti* as what business the Sikhs have with these, as one is a part of Muslim and the other pre-Sikh tradition (Judge, 2004).

In fact, the struggle and assertion of the Ad-dharmis is based on the principle of inclusion. The removal of their women from the employment of the shrine was not simply an economic action, but it was also an act of removing the dalits from participation. In the process of its conflict the Sikhs defined the Sikh identity in the light of singular tradition that was constructed by the Singh Sabha movement, that is, the Khalsa identity. It is interesting to note that the struggle for inclusion on the part of the Ad-dharmis also contributed to the reinforcement of the Sikh orthodoxy in the form of Khalsa identity.

Eagleton (1996: 122), while criticising the postmodernist emphasis on difference, remarks, "If postmodernism is a form of culturalism, it is because among other reasons it refuses to recognize that what different ethnic groups have in common socially and economically is finally more important than their cultural differences". In spite of the fact that at empirical level ecological spaces have not changed, the differences between the two have disappeared in the village. Though less in comparison with the Jat Sikhs the Ad-dharmis have also experienced the international migration and, in this village, they have sent the money back to their families. There have been a lot of changes in the educational and employment patterns, which are making differences between the two groups irrelevant. On top of all we find the prevalence of the common folk religious beliefs and practices that could become the basis of ending the differences. However, the process of inclusion has also a lot to do with the end of difference in consciousness and practice in the private sphere. It is here that the upper castes are blocking the way for total inclusion. One should rather be pessimistic about the future despite the positive observations, because there is an area in the process of inclusion that has to evolve and it may take a long time.

Notes

This paper was first published in *Man & Development*, Volume XXVII, No. 3, September 2005.

1. PEPSU (Patiala and Eastern Punjab States Union) was formed immediately after the princely states were merged with the Indian Union. Later on, PEPSU became the part of Punjab.
2. The data about the village and other information have been largely gathered from the newspapers, namely, *The Tribune* and the *Hindustan Times.* In addition to this, the author visited the village and stayed there for the whole day talking to the people. Further, in case of certain inquiry and doubt, some of the people were contacted on phone.
3. The *granthi* or the *pathi* is one who recites the gurbani.
4. In the recently held panchayat elections many incidents of the conflict between the Jats and dalits have come to the fore. The elections were held on June 29, 2003.
5. *The Tribune*, Thursday, August 3, 2002, p. 3.
6. *The Tribune*, May 18, 2003, p. 3.
7. *The Tribune*, May 27, 2003. This Taksal is associated with the name of Jarnail Singh Bhindranwala – the extremist Sikh leader. In an interview with a Jat leader, he told that Bhai Mohkam Singh's help proved to be the most vital for the Jat Sikhs.
8. Some newspapers reported that the disturbances in Boota Mandi began after the people saw clippings of the clash on television.

References

Becker, Howard S. 1974. Whose side are we on? In Gresham Riley (ed.), *Values, Objectivity and the Social Sciences.* Reading: Addison-Wesley Publishing Company. pp. 107–21.

Berreman, Gerald D. 1979. *Caste and Other Inequities: Essays on Inequality.* Meerut: Folklore Institute.

Dahrendorf, Ralph. 1976. *Class and Class Conflict in Industrial Society.* London: Routledge and Kegan Paul.

Dhaliwal, Sarbjit. 2001. "BSP's Bid to Re-establish Itself", *The Tribune,* Thursday, June 14, p. 3.

Eagleton, Terry. 1996. *The Illusions of Postmodernism.* Oxford: Blackwell.

Juergensmeyer, Mark. 1982. *Religion as Social Vision: The Movement against Untouchability in 20th Century Punjab.* Berkeley: University of California Press.

Judge, Paramjit S. 2004. "Recent Caste Clash in Talhan in Punjab", *Dalit–International Newsletter*, Vol. 9, No. 1, February.

Judge, Paramjit S. 2002. "Punjabis in England: Ad-dharmi Experience", *Economic and Political Weekly*, Vol. XXXVII, No. 31, August 3–9, pp. 3244–50.

Judge, Paramjit S. 1985. "Class Analysis of Scheduled Castes in Ajram (A Punjab Village)", in Pimpley, P.N. and Sharma, Satish K. (eds.), *Struggle for Status*. New Delhi: B.R. Publishing Corporation.

Puri, Harish K., Paramjit S. Judge, and Jagroop S. Sekhon. 1999. *Terrorism in Punjab: Understanding Grassroots Reality*. New Delhi: Har-Anand.

Reddy, T. Naggi. 1978. *India Mortgaged: A Marxist-Leninist Appraisal*. Anantapuram: Tarimela Nagi Reddy Memorial Trust.

Saberwal, Satish. 1990. *Mobile Men: Limits to Social Change in Urban Punjab* (Revised Edition). Shimla: Indian Institute of Advanced Study in association with Manohar, New Delhi.

Sandhu, Kanwar. 2003. "Warnings Went Unheeded as Talhan Blew up", *Hindustan Times*, June 10, p. 1.

Sandhu, Nirmal. 2003. "Why Talhan Happened", *The Tribune*, Tuesday, June 17, p. 9.

Singh, Jangveer. 2002. "Panchayat Blacklists Dalits", *The Tribune*, August 3, p. 3.

Strasser, Hermann. 1976. *The Normative Structure of Sociology: Conservative and Emancipatory Themes in Social Thought*. London: Routledge and Kegan Paul.

Weber, Max. 1962. *Basic Concepts in Sociology*. London: Peter Owen.

10

Dalit Assertion in Punjab

Examining New Trends and Emerging Dilemmas

Mapping the changing character of collective responses of the dalits of Punjab in the post-independence period implies capturing the diverse trajectories of their political and social actions. The Punjabi dalits could be distinguished from their counterparts in rest of the country in terms of certain features. One of the distinctive features that has been identified by most of the writers on the scheduled castes of Punjab is the egalitarian influence of the Sikh movement in the Punjabi society. Such a view is partly erroneous, because there is a basic difference between community and religion and in a multi-religious society it becomes all the more difficult to accept such a view. This is in spite of the fact that the influence of the caste ideology has not been successful in creating rigid restrictions on some aspects of intercaste interaction in Punjab. In spite of this presence of flexibility that has been invariably highlighted by the ideologues of religious discourses, the caste inequality and caste-based discrimination have remained the order of the day. Two major movements that addressed the question of caste and untouchability in the 19th and early 20th centuries were the Arya Samaj[1] and the Singh Sabha[2] movements.

In the present attempt to map the dalit assertion in the post-colonial Punjab, the discussion has been divided into five parts. The first part is an effort to look into the theoretical context in which the dalit assertion could be situated, whereas the second takes stock of the hierarchy and differentiation among the dalits in Punjab. The third part outlines some movements of the dalits against caste system in the colonial period and the fourth examines the post-colonial assertion of the dalits. The final part makes an appraisal of the factors which have both impeded and facilitated collective responses of the dalits the purpose of which is to identify the basis of the changing character of their assertion.

Theoretical Context

Caste has been conceptualised in sociological literature from various perspectives. From the structural perspective, the caste system has been constructed in the form of binary opposition of privileged/under-privileged, upper/lower, touchable/untouchable, etc. All these binary oppositions correspond with the division and opposition between manual and non-manual labour (Judge, 2002). All other oppositions have been constructed on this primary relationship marked by hierarchy, exclusion and plurality (see Berreman, 1979). It is hierarchical because the forms of labour have been graded socially in terms of power, status and privilege. It implicates a separation and exclusion of other castes in terms of interaction, interdining and intermarriages. Its plural character could be interpolated from the first two features of relationships among castes, namely, interaction and interdining. Owing to hierarchy and exclusion, each caste becomes an exclusive and insulated block and over a period time, it becomes the basis of distinct cultural traits as a consequence of which the caste system acquires culturally plural character. Cultural plurality is one of the major reasons for the perpetuation of caste and caste identity. In other words, the evolution of culture due to exclusion has reinforced the existing difference and its idea among castes.

Placing the opposition of manual and non-manual labour as the basic structure of caste system would turn its other dimensions into the components of superstructure. Dirks (2002) is of the opinion that the overlapping of the Indian society and caste system was a consequence of colonial discourse. However, he does not deny the existence and prevalence of caste even prior to the British rule. It may be added that caste system also survived and perpetuated due to the articulation of an ideology of dharma-karma. Owing to its ability to survive, the idea of revolt against such an exploitative system is regarded as, theoretically as well as historically, remote and far from satisfactory. Passive acceptance of the existential caste conditions has been considered to be the reality of the underprivileged. It may be mentioned that the underprivileged castes have constantly strived to achieve better conditions of life through various collective efforts, which have become visible because of their altered character in the 20th century in particular. Reservation policy of the Indian state after independence was not only an outcome of the welfare orientation and sense of guilt of the new leaders, but also the recognition of the ability of the dalits to take their grievances in the public sphere. In this regard, the Poona Pact was decisive in not only defining the future course of dalit movements but also the trajectories of religion and caste.[3]

What are various modes of protest and resistance available to the oppressed, marginalised and underprivileged to not only counter the oppression but also improve their conditions? Contrary to social conflicts that could be latent or manifest, protest is essentially an activity that is open and involves two parties, namely, the protestors and the authority. There are levels of protest – the extreme forms being the silent day-to-day resistance on the one hand and the violent revolt on the other. Most of the studies of protest tend to analyse the open and invariably violent protests the reason for which is that such cases are easy to notice, observe and examine. On the contrary, the everyday forms of resistance require a long-term observation and recording and identification of various activities of the underprivileged as resistance. Scott (1985) rightly regards them as weapons of the weak. However, the credit goes to Bloch (1966) for taking cognisance of certain silent forms of resistance of the peasantry in France, which, according to him, proved to be far more effective than the open violent revolts, because open rebellion invariably invited violent backlash from the state. It must not imply that open and violent protests do not take place and it is difficult to take a definite position with regard to the normative issue of whether these should take place or not. Open protest is an outcome of long and simmering discontent among the underprivileged.

Finally, it may be argued that the trajectory of the manifestation of discontent among the underprivileged may not necessarily remain the same over a period of time. Social change, emergence of new relations of production, and changing forms of political discourse and consciousness reorient, redefine and reshape the ideological codification of the prevailing conditions as well as the nature of the form of protest. If the incumbents in underprivileged positions remain unchanged implying that there is no or limited avenue of social mobility, then the protest has high probability of sustenance. Caste in this regard is an important basis of social grouping. Caste is determined by birth and owing to its hereditary character the underprivileged castes have remained unchanged. The Government of India, by designating them as the scheduled castes has made their identity permanent as social and cultural groups that belong to the lowest rungs of the Indian society. With such an official identity the scheduled castes have been struggling to get rid of various caste stigmas and in the process they have fought for their rights.

Hierarchy and Differentiation among the Dalits of Punjab

The fact that is generally ignored in the case of the dalits of Punjab is that in comparison with the other regions, the landlessness was widely spread among them. It was noted that among the agricultural labourers the scheduled castes constituted seventy per cent in 1960s (Reddy, 1978). Two facts are worthy of special mention regarding the socio-economic conditions of the dalits in the pre-independence period. First, a considerable number of them were involved in agriculture as tenant cultivators/attached labourers. As tenants, most of them were either tenants-at-will or sharecroppers, which implied that they did not have security of tenure. As attached labourers, they formed a durable and dependent system of relationships with the landowners under the sepidari or Jajmani system. Second, those who were involved in the leather trade experienced prosperity towards the end of the 19th century (Briggs, 1975), which facilitated their international migration in the beginning of the 20th century. Whereas in the former case different castes among the dalits were involved as cultivators, the leather trade remained confined to the Chamar caste.

The correspondence between caste and occupation could also be arranged in a hierarchy overlapping with that of castes among the dalits. This hierarchy was also a function of the political economy of agrarian structure in which each caste fitted into the production relations by performing specific jobs. Though for a majority of the dalit castes agricultural labour remained the main source of livelihood, yet their caste invariably denoted some specific economic functions. For example, Chamars were leather workers, Churhas were sweepers, Meghs were weavers, Dums were genealogists as well as jokers, Sansi were beggars and keepers of animals, Bazigars were acrobats, etc. Most of them would go for agricultural labour during harvesting time. Of all these castes, the Chamars distinguished themselves in terms of their economic persuasions in which they showed tremendous versatility. The following observations of Briggs (1975: 58) bring out the economic indispensability of the Chamar in the rural society:

> For five months, June to November, he works in the fields with a plough; for two months, November and December, he is engaged in reaping the *kharif* (the autumn crops); during January and February he is occupied with *kachcha* buildings and other forms of earth work; in March and April he is busy in gathering rabi; and in May he does a little earth work. Between times he does whatever work comes to hand.

Briggs also noted the occupational mobility of the Chamars in the early 20th century as he noticed that they were taking up jobs in railways and industry.

Despite their common status as dalits in relation to the upper castes, these castes accepted, maintained and perpetuated hierarchy. Some of them, such as Meghs, Julahas and Chamars perceived their own position as superior to other dalit castes. Ibbetson (1974) informs that Meghs were regarded higher in status than the Chamars. The sustenance of hierarchy among the dalits was an outcome of caste endogamy and hereditary occupations. This hierarchical differentiation that put Churhas, Sansis and Dums at the lowest rungs divided the dalits disabling them to organise into any political force when the impact of British colonialism initiated movements revolving around identity, equality and rights. In such a scenario, only those castes that were numerically preponderant could make an impact in the political sphere. Predictably two castes qualified for such a role in Punjab, namely, Chamars and Churhas.

It was not only the hierarchical differentiation among the dalits, but also the religious divisions among them that prevented any chance of their getting organised against the oppression of the upper caste landlords. Punjab consisted of three religious communities in the 19th century, namely, Hindus, Muslims and the Sikhs. The proselytising activities of the Christian missionaries contributed to the emergence of the fourth religious community of Christians. Interestingly, the dalits were also divided along religious lines. Notably, the caste nomenclature changed with the change in religion. To illustrate this aspect, we may give the instances of Chamars and Churhas. As Hindus, they were known by these names, but later on took over the caste name of Ravidasia and Balmiki from their respective gurus, namely, Guru Ravidas and Rishi Balmiki. As Muslims they were known as Mochis (Ibbetson, 1974) and Mussalis (Judge, 1997) respectively. As Sikhs, Chamars came to be known as Ramdasia and Churhas as Mazabis. Since the large-scale conversion of the Churhas occurred to Christianity, another name was added to this plurality of names, that is, Massih. The Aryasamajis started Shudhi movement in the beginning of the 20th century to bring back the converted Muslims into the fold of Hinduism. Some of the Chamars acquired another name of 'Chaudhary' and 'Mahashas' after becoming Aryasamajis. Still another name was added to it when in 1931 a new community of Ad-dharmis was recognised by the Government of India. In spite of all this plurality in nomenclature going to the extent of causing confusion did not bring about much change in the identification of the dalit castes for the upper castes. They continued to use Chamars and Churhas for the two major castes. Mirassi became an independent caste name and got distinguished from the actual caste of Dum. The reason was that in Amritsar and Lahore districts virtually all of them had converted to Islam. Over a period of time, Mazabi also acquired an independent identity and is now identified as a distinct caste from the Churhas/Bhangis.

The relationship between caste and religion was ambivalent in the sense that it was the basis of both unity and division. Religion became the idiom through which castes expressed their identity – a process through which they attained solidarity that enabled them to get organised to launch protest. Religion united them by separating them from other caste groups, which proved important for the organisation of protest. In this regard, the Ad-dharmi movement could be cited as an example. The issue of religion needs a serious analysis that must transcend the common sense perception of the significance of religion. Durkheim (1976) is of the view that the major function of religion was to create social order. Marx in his characteristic view thought that religion is the opium of the masses. When we peep into the experience of Indian nationalism, we essentially find that it was religious in nature (Chatterjee, 1993; Judge, 2005). Religion thus became a force that mobilised people and in the case of the dalits, it was the major avenue against the oppression of the upper castes. The final distinctive feature of the dalits of Punjab that facilitated the process of their mobilisation was that there was caste-based concentration in the various regions. For example, the Chamars were concentrated mainly in the Doaba region, whereas the Churhas in the Malwa and Majha regions. At the sub-regional level the Chamars were also concentrated in Gurdaspur and Faridkot districts. In the post-independent Punjab, Meghs, who migrated from Sialkot district, settled predominantly in Amritsar and Jalandhar. Dums were/are concentrated in Gurdaspur district.

Colonial Context of Dalit Assertion

It is obvious that the dalits peasants did not lead the struggle for equality. The leaders largely came from sections, which were relatively independent of the local economic system of interdependence of the castes. In the case of the Ad-dharma movement, the Chamars were the main actors as both leaders and participants. In the end, the Ad-dharma movement proved to be the identity assertion, but it influenced and shaped the future of the Ad-dharmis. It raised their consciousness that also gave them the reasons for getting organised. Ronki Ram (2004b: 900) is of the opinion that the Ad-dharma movement sought to construct and being recognised as a distinct religious identity separate from both the Hindus and the Sikhs thus: "Its central motif was that untouchables constituted a *quam* (community), a distinct religious grouping similar to that of Muslims, Hindus and Sikhs, which had existed since time immemorial." Ronki Ram (2004a) elsewhere remarks that the Ad-dharma movement had deep political implications in the system marked by inequality and hierarchy. In a way, it was a movement for equality.

The success of the Ad-dharma movement could be gauged in terms of the fact that there was political recognition to the new religious community in 1931. However, it may not be assumed that there was a widespread liberation of a section of the dalits. The period that followed the success of the Ad-dharma movement also involved the rising dalit consciousness all over India, largely due to the activities of Ambedkar. In Punjab, particularly in the princely states, there began the Praja Mandal movement in which the tenants spearheaded the struggle. The Praja Mandal was essentially an important occurrence in the sense that all the political parties were involved in it, and it finally culminated into the struggle of peasantry immediately after some of the political issues were resolved. The leadership of the communists gave it a turn towards mass mobilisation. Despite the fact that in the post-independence period some of the communists directed the movement towards militancy, the Praja Mandal movement remained the most important occurrence of the transitional period. The enactment of the tenancy reform laws in Punjab created two situations. First, most of the occupancy tenants who mainly belonged to the Jat caste in the PEPSU[4] region got the ownership rights. The same rights were not conferred upon the non-occupancy tenants. Second, a large-scale ejection of the tenants-at-will took place under the pretext of self-cultivation. Most of the dalits constituted the class of tenants-at-will. Thus, a class of cultivators turned into the class of agricultural workers – a process of downward social mobility. Bhalla and Chadha (1979) have noted how after the tenancy legislation in the tenant movement areas large-scale evictions of the tenants-at-will occurred.

Dalit Assertion in the Post-colonial Punjab

Despite the fact that the tenancy reforms in Punjab marginalised the dalit peasantry, the dalit movements of the 1950s ignored or did not pay heed to this entire process. In other words, the class dimension of dalits remained ignored. The faulty implementation of the land reform enactments in Punjab deprived the dalits from becoming the landowners (Harchand Singh Committee, 2001). An examination of this process little more thoroughly would make it obvious that the caste-class factors were inseparable. The land reforms were successful in those areas of Punjab where peasant movement had been strong, but it is hardly mentioned that once the peasantry got the benefits the movement collapsed, as it never took up the cause of the ejected tenants-at-will – predominantly belonging to dalit castes.[5] On the contrary, the dalit movement under the leadership of Amedkar remained oriented towards the caste issues and the struggle for equality remained confined to the caste hierarchy and was then moved to the formal political space through the organisation of the Republican Party of India. The religious issue became important for Ambedkar when he decided to convert to Buddhism along with his comrades.

The first decade of post-independence period was marked by trajectories of developments that did not converge to improve the condition of the dalits. The subsequent developments in the agrarian conditions led to the reinforcement of the subjugation and dependence of the dalits in Punjab. However, there was a distinct feature of this development, that is, there also emerged a class of dalit elites who appropriated the benefits that accrued to them. This class found the issue of the dalit oppression and discrimination highly functional for the perpetuation of their privileged positions. The communists in India in general did not take up the caste issue, which for them did not have much significance in their framework of class-based activism. Various struggles of the communists in Punjab in particular invariably mention the class status of the participants, as is the case of the agricultural workers movements. It may be noted that the most important struggle of the communists was the anti-betterment levy struggle in which the landed peasantry was involved (Talib, 1986). In Punjab, the dalits have remained on the margins of the communist movement as a result of which most of the struggles of the dalits remained localised and rarely drew the attention of the media and leaders.

The dalits might have waged what is called everyday form of resistance. The term coined by Marc Bloch and developed by James Scott (1985) at empirical level is of great help in understanding the forms of resistance of the oppressed sections of the society could offer in different circumstances. Unfortunately, we do not have any such study that could map the dalit resistance at the local level. However, in the early fifties when the dalits in large numbers recorded Hindi as their mother tongue, it was a kind of a protest against the domination of the Sikh landowners (Nayar, 1966). Before the Green Revolution the dependence of the dalit agricultural workers on the landowners was strong enough to dissuade them from struggling for better conditions. There are certain informal accounts available in various regions of Punjab where the dalit boys were forcibly prevented from going to schools. However, such a use of force was not all-pervading due to many political reasons. One of the important aspects that evoked localised protests was related with the sexual offences against dalit women. The sexual exploitation of dalit women was also a consequence of the declining caste rigidity and the economic dependence of the dalits on the landlords, which had made their women the most vulnerable social group. In the 1960s, the protests against the sexual abuse of dalit women took place though at the local levels and the information is available in the oral accounts of the people.

The Green Revolution phenomenon in Punjab unleashed forces of change in the conditions of the dalits. The emergence of educated dalit middle class coincided with the beginning of the Green Revolution – a phenomenon of high agricultural productivity. It is difficult to pinpoint the dalit mobilisation in a proper perspective, but in the beginning of the 1970s, the struggle for higher wages began to occur quite frequently in the villages of Doaba region. Invariably, this struggle would take the form of refusal to work in the fields of the landowners unless the wages were not increased. Most of the times the landowners retaliated by banning their entry into their fields. The landlessness among the dalits worked against their ability to hold on to their strike for longer periods. Generally, the confrontation would end as a result of the intervention of the authorities.

The influx of the migrant labour depressed the wages in Punjab and also put the dalits in a disadvantageous position with regard to their ability to negotiate for higher wages with the landowners. The arrival of the migrant labour coincided with the period when the Punjabi dalits started moving out of agriculture. Over a period of time, the alternative avenues of employment reduced their dependence on the landowners. The social mobility of those dalits who got education combined with their relative independence from the landowners became the basis for the emergence of a new kind of orientation. However, one form of contestation that remained consistent from the 1970s onwards may be discussed before describing the emergence of new form of dalit assertion.

The conflict over formal power began to occur in the Green Revolution period, but it remained confined to the village level. At the aggregate level we may find such a conflict in many villages, but it never turned into societal conflict. There are many villages in the Doaba region that have dalit majority and such villages became the centres of conflict during the panchayat elections. With the exception of the period of the Sikh militancy when the dalits were oppressed democratic processes at all levels were discontinued by the state, panchayat elections have continued to create conflicts. During the Sikh militancy, as some surveys show, the dalits were marginalised.[6]

It is interesting to note that despite the suppression of dalits at the village level owing to the threat of the Sikh militant violence, there was an emergence of a new kind of dalit assertion in the urban areas of Punjab.[7] The major development in 1980s that culminated into the full-fledged dalit assertion in 1990s was the formation of the BSP (Bahujan Samaj Party) under the leadership of Kanshi Ram. The BSP played power politics at the formal level, and it was and has remained the party of dalits with the objective of capturing formal power at the state and national levels. The BSP, in contrast to the RPI (Republican Party of India), brought a paradigmatic shift in the orientation of dalit assertion. Whereas the former approached the issue in terms of social equality for the dalits, the latter has been playing the game of power similar to that of other political parties. The ideological position of the BSP is a logical culmination of the dalit movements though the oppression and exploitation on the caste-class basis has not yet disappeared in India. The sustainability of the dalit assertion has become a possibility largely due to the emergence of a sizeable middle class among the dalits, which find it difficult to be assimilated in the caste society as equals. The BSP has radically altered the nature of collective self-assertion of the dalits. In the earlier period, the assimilation model of social development entailed the lofty idea of casteless society. The discourse of castelessness led the dalits to hide their identity and we find that in the earlier period the middle class dalits used upper caste surnames to hide their identity. However, it may be mentioned that there are some common surnames among the dalits and the upper castes in Punjab too. For example, surnames such as Sandhu, Gill, Bal, etc. are known to be the Jat surnames, but dalits also have these surnames. Similarly, 'Bhardwaj' is known to be the surname of Brahmins, but the Meghs (a dalit caste) also have it. The Jats are of the view that the dalits have adopted these surnames, whereas the dalits claim that it has not been the case. Whatever is the case, the BSP has certainly infused a sense of caste identity. It helped them to have confidence in their dalit identity and it has now become a part of the dalit collective self-perception in which is located the secret of the success of this party. An illustration of this change could be given of the surname 'Birdi'. Birdi or Virdi is the surname that is found among the Ramgarhias as well as the Ad-dharmis. Till recently, both the castes used to spell it as 'Virdi'. Now, some of the Ad-dharmis have begun to insist on writing Birdi so as to distinguish their caste identity from the Ramgarhias. Interestingly, still another fact came to the notice during the fieldwork in Boota Mandi in Jalandhar. It was found that a young dalit's scooter carried graffiti "Chamar Power", showing an assertion of one's caste identity.

A new form of dalit assertion and its contestation, which caught the social scientists unawares, has recently emerged. Mention may be made of the Ad-dharmi-Jat clash in village Talhan in Jalandhar district in June 2003. The root cause of this clash was the struggle for the control over the Gurdwara Baba Nihal Singh in the village. The dalits wanted to be partners in the management of the gurdwara (Judge, 2005). It may be pointed out that the clash over religious places is a new form of conflict between the castes that has started emerging in Punjab. The entry of religion into social conflicts is not new even with regard to the dalit issue. We all know that Ambedkar began his movement from the issue of entry into Hindu temples meant for high castes. His subsequent conversion to Buddhism and rejection of Hinduism was a form of protest, which was based on the assumption that in Hinduism the caste is immutable. The dalits of Punjab did not follow Ambedkar as no mass conversions to Buddhism took place. A few cases of conversion to Buddhism in recent years indicate the changing orientation of the Punjabi dalits to Buddhism though it is largely confined to the intelligentsia.

The middle class among the dalits has changed its orientation from assimilation to participation. This class wants to be equal partners in the conduct of the affairs of the village, city and state. Such an orientation may redirect the issue of castelessness in a somewhat different manner. The upper castes have been consistently coming out with social boycott as a weapon against the dalit assertion. Earlier, social boycott was regarded as the weapon of the strong, because the entire life conditions of the dalits depended on the landowners. In the changed socio-economic circumstances when the dalits are no more dependent on the landowners the way they were before, social boycott cannot be used as way of suppression. It is now used as a weapon to deprive the dalits from being equal partners in the affairs of the society. It is the means to remind them that despite their improved conditions, they continue to be low caste. The Talhan clash followed after all negotiations to end the social boycott failed at the informal level. The dalits of Talhan were not dependent on the Jat landowners because of their better economic conditions (Judge, ibid.). Why have the conflicts over religious places emerged in recent times? It is particularly important in the light of the fact that in many other villages, the possibility of such conflicts had existed in recent past. It may be reminded that in the past the religious places invariably depended on the patronage of the landed classes. The Jats of Punjab began to turn to Sikhism in a serious manner towards the end of the 19th century and then began the process of a shift to the religious places.

The construction of gurdwaras in Punjab began in great earnest due to the impact of the Singh Sabha movement, which also coincided with the entry of the landowning castes, particularly the Jats, into Sikhism. During this phase, the Sikhs did not only get the control over the gurdwaras, but also initiated the process of building the same in the villages. The Jat landowners were resourceful enough to construct the gurdwaras. The second phase of the construction of the gurdwaras, as mentioned earlier, began as a result of the Green Revolution in Punjab, which led to economic improvement of the people. Two kinds of gurdwaras came into existence in the villages. First, each locality of the village sought to construct its own place of worship in which the diaspora Punjabis in the Doaba region made significant contribution. As a result of overall improvement in the life of the people of Punjab, the lower and the dalit castes also started building their own places of worship. Among the dalits the Ad-dharmis were the first to improve their conditions and also the first to claim for equal participation in the collective religious life of the village. The discourse of the shared religious place changed into the contestations at different levels. Each caste community now tends to construct its religious past – a tendency that is more common among the lower castes than others. The Jats, who as landowners patronised and later on, appropriated the sacred spaces, are now being challenged by the others through the construction of past.

There is a reasonable basis to argue that since all these caste groups had a Hindu past, they also had a common religious place with the exception of the dalit castes, as they were not allowed to enter the temples. The life of the religious place depended on the patronage of the landowning castes. It was not a simple patronage; it also entailed the landowners as a part of the community of believers in a single faith. Since the religious boundaries remained porous, the domination of the landowners did not remain confined to economic relations only. When the Jat landowners turned to Sikhism under the impact of the Singh Sabha movement, they also appropriated the religious spaces and owing to their domination, this appropriation remained uncontested till recently when economic changes in the Indian economy has made the social mobility of the lower castes possible, conflicts over religious spaces have also started coming to the surface. The emergence of conflict over religious space is a new addition to the dalit assertion in Punjab and it has all likelihood to sharpen further in future. The Talhan clash got a wide coverage and attention, but there are many such conflicts and contestations that have remained unnoticed.

Two recent illustrations among many, besides the explosive case of Talhan, may be succinctly stated here. The conflict between the Jats and the dalits in village Mahem in Nakodar tehsil of Jalandhar district has come to the fore. The Jat Sikhs of the village forcibly occupied the Baba Khazan Singh Udasi Dera in 2003. It was looked after by the Ad-dharmis of the village. According to Kali (2003b), the major reason for this occupation should be located in the rising cost of land as well as the prosperity of the people of Doaba due to emigration to foreign countries. The donations and offerings have increased manifold. The Jat Sikhs removed all the symbols of Udasis and installed the Nishan Sahib and Guru Granth Sahib in the Dera's building. With the help of the Pendu Mazdoor Union, the Ad-dharmis were able to file FIR and stall the further designs of the Jats. The village Mahem has total population of 1,967 out of which 893, that is more than half, belong to the scheduled castes. Most of the scheduled castes belong to the Balmiki caste, whereas the Ad-Dharmis are about 20 per cent of the total population. Though the Jats are also about 20 per cent of the total population, there are two gurdwaras that have been constructed and controlled by them. There is one each Balmiki Temple and Ravidas Temple. The Udasi Dera is the fifth religious place in the village. Besides the above religious places, there are two *mazaars* (graves) that are places of veneration. The dispute over the Udasi Dera is now in the court and it will take some time to resolve it. The Ad-dharmis claim that for the last 60 years the Dera has been under their control. The Jats, on the contrary, claim that it is a gurdwara. The counter-argument offered by the Ad-dharmis is that there are graves in the precincts of the Dera and it cannot be a gurdwara.[8] As a matter of fact, collections at the Dera are huge and the Jats have taken it under their control due to the economic interests.

The story of Mahem is not an isolated phenomenon. It is spreading not as an aftermath of Talhan clash, but as a statewide phenomenon, particularly in those areas where the dalits have been organising themselves and have become conscious of their rights. Still another example is that of Nurmahal, where the dalits are again trying to reclaim the Dargah of Hazarat Shah Fateh Ali. Kali (2003a) warned that this religious place might lead to the Talhan-like situation. In 1994 the Sikhs tried to convert this place into a gurdwara and tried to demolish all graveyards. However, the people got organised and tried to prevent this demolition. Who these Sikhs were has not been clearly stated in Kali's report, but it was clear that the administration was hand in glove with these armed gangs. However, by this time, both samadhi (grave) and gurdwara are in existence. The *Hindustan Times* (2005) provides the latest detail of this conflict thus: "The weekly prayers at the Fateh Ali Shah Samadh here were held under tight security today following tensions over the erasing of writings from the façade of the samadh."[9] The Deputy Commissioner of Jalandhar district has announced that a partition wall would be constructed separating the two religious places.[10]

Impediments and Predicaments

The dalit assertion is progressively becoming visible with the passage of time. At the same time, however, this visibility is bringing to the fore various problems being faced by them. There are various factors that have been acting against the dalit assertion and these factors have emerged from within the dalit dynamism. The most important problem is the lack of unity among the dalits, that is, they are divided along various lines. It implies that there is a great degree of heterogeneity among the dalits, which can be identified along two lines, namely, class and caste lines. Let us discuss these in terms of how it is happening.

Class Heterogeneity

Indian sociology has been grappling with caste-class correspondence for long without any conclusive observation. Despite the fact that everybody mentions the formation of dalit elites, not much attention has been paid to the understanding of emerging classes among the dalits. Caste is treated as a social category whereas class denotes economic divisions at the descriptive level. The economic changes within the caste system have taken place over a period of time, but its pace has increased after independence. The industrialisation, expansions of the service sector, educational changes, all have broken the correspondence between caste and occupation. Various occupations have become available to people irrespective of their caste background where skill and education have become central in the employment of a person. Obviously, very few dalits have been able to acquire those skills to get employment independent of their caste. In certain cases the expansion of the caste occupation has become a source of social mobility. For example, leather work was the occupation of the Chamars. Dealing with raw hides was stigmatic in the traditional caste system. When the demand for leather increased during the First World War, some families among them began to trade in raw hides at the wholesale level. Boota Mandi, located on the road to Nakodar from Jalandhar, is now not only identified as the centre of dalit political activities, but also with the rich traders among the Ad-dharmis.

Mangoo Ram, the leader of the Ad-dharma movement of the 1920s was one of the pioneers among the dalit diaspora. The emigration of the dalits began in a noticeable way after independence. It is generally held that emigration results into the economic improvement of the migrants, but it should be reminded that migration to the foreign countries requires money. After migration further economic improvement takes place. The dalits who migrated to foreign countries – to England in the beginning and to Canada later – belonged to the better off sections among the dalits. Such dalits sent remittances to their families in Punjab. This phenomenon also created class variations among the dalits. Finally, education was another factor responsible for the emergence of classes among the scheduled castes. Education led to better employment in the public sector that improved the life of some families. Interestingly, all these changes took place in certain regions and among limited castes in Punjab. The Doaba region, consisting of Hoshiarpur, Jalandhar, Nawan Shahar and Kapurthala districts, witnessed these changes in a much prominent manner. Furthermore, the Chamarrs/Ad-dharmis, Julahas and Meghs did better than the other castes among the dalits.

The class heterogeneity among the dalits has both the individual and corporate character. Classes have emerged among the dalits across castes as well as within castes. Secondly, certain castes among the dalits have prospered and have entered into the middle class status positions. All these middle classes have different orientation towards the issues relating to mobilisation and identity.

Caste Heterogeneity

Success of dalit assertions depends upon the degree to which various castes combine to make a common front. There are 39 castes among the dalits. Chamars/Ad-dharmis and Balmikis/Mazabis are the most numerous among them (about 41% each). The overwhelming proportion of these two castes transforms the dalit issue into caste issue. The history of dalit protest amply demonstrates that the issue remains caste-specific. At the time of the Talhan clash between the Jats and the Ad-dharmis, the protest was localised in the social space and remained confined to the Ad-dharmis. Boota Mandi in Jalandhar was affected, whereas no disturbance could be observed in the Bhargo Camp populated by Meghs as well as Ali Mohalla consisting of Balmikis. In recent fieldwork done in Amritsar and Jalandhar districts in both the urban and rural areas, it has been found that the caste divide among the dalits is powerful and strong sense of hierarchy among these castes is mind-boggling. The possibility of any common front among them seems remote. This is in spite of the fact that Ambedkar is being recognised as the main dalit leader. The numerically small dalit castes are resentful of the Ad-dharmis for having taken the lion's share in power and distribution of resources, whereas the Ad-dharmis perceive that they can succeed without the small castes.

Divided Objectives

The change in the objective conditions of the dalits of Punjab has also transformed their subjective conditions. The times of Ambedkar have given way to those of Kanshi Ram. It is not a simple movement of time from one to another point. From the twin objectives of social equality and castelessness through education, organised efforts and agitation, the dalit movement has shifted to identity assertion and acquisition of formal power. It has been made possible by both the economic developments that have occurred and the state intervention through various affirmative programmes. The critics of reservation policy, to refer only one example, forget that it has been able to help a section of the dalits to attain social mobility, irrespective of whether it has failed to fulfil its objective of ending caste-based limitations.

Owing to all changes mentioned above, we are witnessing growing heterogeneity within and between dalit castes. The caste and class differentiation among them has given rise to the third predicament that acts as an important impediment against collective mobilisation of all dalits. For a section of dalit castes the issue has remained unchanged, which is true also of the lower classes present in every dalit caste. The issues of livelihood, caste-based oppression, discrimination in the labour market, and political marginality have not changed. On the other hand, for another section of the dalits, the above issues have become irrelevant and the question of equal social participation through the process of inclusion has become crucial. These dalits are asserting their identity to capture formal political power by appealing to all sections of the dalits, but its interest in the issues concerning caste equality and discrimination is constantly declining.

Concluding Remarks

Starting from the early 20th century to the present times, the nature of dalit protest has been constantly changing and evolving. The change in the issues and the objectives of the protest has remained a notable dimension of the entire period. However, there has been an underlying commonality among them. All these castes belonged to the lowest rungs of the caste hierarchy. Dalit assertions through collective mobilisation provide a paradoxical scenario emerging from the caste and class heterogeneities that have emerged visibly after independence. In the discourse of caste equality the context of class conditions of the dalits have been more or less marginalised and vice versa. The only rallying ground for the dalits to have a united front through mobilisation by cutting across caste-class lines is the political construction of an abstract dalit identity. To what extent, the politics of dalit identity would be helpful in ameliorating the conditions of the dalits is difficult to predict at this moment, but one thing can be certainly stated with a degree of certainty: it is going to empower the dalit elites further in their ability to negotiate with the other political parties to share power at the formal level.

Notes

1. The Arya Samaj movement struck its roots in Punjab in the late 19th century. Swami Dayanand Saraswati – the founder of the Arya Samaj – emphasised the need for going to the Vedas. More importantly, the Samaj initiated Shudhi movement to bring back people to Hindu faith from Islam and other non-Hindu religions by reconverting them (see Sharma, 2000).

2. The Singh Sabha movement also began in the second half of the 19th century in Punjab. It emphasised the distinct identity of the Sikh from the Hindus. It declared that there was no caste among he Sikhs (Barrier, 2000).
3. It refers to the conflict between Ambedkar and Gandhi on the issue of separate electorate for the untouchables in the second Round Table Conference for which the former had put the demand before the British. When it seemed imminent that Ambedkar's demand would be accepted, Gandhi went on fast as a result of which Ambedkar was coerced into withdrawing the demand in Poona Pact in 1932 (Mendelsohn and Vicziany, 2000). Moon (2002) has narrated the resentment of the Mahars in Nagpur against the Poona Pact and their subsequent hostility towards Gandhi as well as the clashed between the dalit organisations and the Congress workers in 1946 elections.
4. Patiala and Eastern Punjab States' Union.
5. Bhalla and Chadha (1979) have observed that the peasant movement areas witnessed a successful implementation of land reform legislation, but hey are silent on the issue of tenants-at-will, who, as they concede, suffered from land reforms. Most of them were dalits.
6. See Puri, Judge and Sekhon, 1999. It was found that dalits (both Sikhs and Hindus) were largely marginalised by the threat of violence. Militancy discouraged any dalit mobilisation. Some villages (Ghasitpur in Gurdaspur district is one such instance) witnessed militant attacks on the dalits. However, more significant was the alignment of the militants with the landowning castes against the dalit landless workers.
7. Reference has been made to the Khalistan movement; see Puri, Judge and Sekhon, ibid.
8. It may be pointed out that even in Talhan clash the issue of graves cropped up too. The Sikh position with regard to the worship of graves has remained quite clear in theory, that is, it is prohibited. At the level of practice the worship of graves is quite common. It should not be takes as a kind of non-Sikh religious place. The Sikh establishment in conflict situations involving graves has remained silent.
9. "Gurdwara-Samadh Row Re-ignited", *Hindustan Times*, August 26, 2005, p. 2.
10. Ibid.

References

Barrier, N. Gerald. 2000. "The Singh Sabha Movement in Punjab 1875–1925", in Harish K. Puri and Paramjit S. Judge (eds.), *Social and Political Movements: Readings on Punjab*. Jaipur: Rawat Publications, pp. 57–92.

Berreman, Gerald D. 1979: *Caste and Other Inequities: Essays on Inequality*. Meerut: Folklore Institute.

Bhalla, G.S. and Talib, B.D. 1979. *Agarian Structure and Peasant Movement in Punjab* (mimeographed). New Delhi: Jawaharlal Nehru University.

Briggs, G.W. 1975. *The Chamars*. New Delhi: B.R. Publishing Corporation (first Published in 1920).

Bloch, Marc. 1966. *French Rural History: An Essay on its Basic Structure*. London: Routledge & Kegan Paul.

Chatterjee, Partha. 1993. *The Nation and its Fragments: Colonial and Postcolonial Histories*. New Delhi: Oxford University Press.

Dirks, Nicholas B. 2002. *Castes of Mind: Colonialism and the Making of Modern India*. New Delhi: Permanent Black.

Durkheim, Emile. 1976. *The Elementary Forms of the Religious Life*. London: George Allen & Unwin Ltd. (First Edition, 1915).

Harchand Singh Committee. 2001. "Land and Corruption: A Report", in Sucha Singh Gill (ed.), *Land Reforms in India Volume 6: Intervention for Agrarian Capitalist Transformation in Punjab and Haryana*. New Delhi: Sage, pp. 152–168.

Ibbetson, Denzil.1974. *Punjab Castes*. New Delhi: B.R. Publishing Corporation (first published in 1916).

Judge, Paramjit S. 1997. "Green Revolution and the Bahujan Samaj Party in Punjab", in Paramjit S. Judge and Satish K. Sharma (eds.), *Dimensions of Social Change: Essays in Honour of Prof. P.N. Pimpley*. Jaipur: Rawat Publications.

—. 2002. 'Religion, Caste and Communalism in Punjab', *Sociological Bulletin*, 51 (2), pp. 175–94.

—. 2005. "Caste Conflicts in Punjab: An Examination of Recent Jat-Dalit Clash in a Village", *Man & Development*, XXVII (3), September, pp. 151–68.

—. 2005. *Religion, Identity and Nationhood: The Sikh Militant Movement*. Jaipur: Rawat Publications.

Kali, Des Raj. 2003a. "Nurmahal Vich vi Talhan banan di Udeek kar riha Parshashan?" *Nawan Zamana*, August 29 (Punjabi).

—. 2003b. Mahem Vich Udasi Dere te Kabaze nu Nathia Dalitan ne", *Nawan Zamana*, September 2 (Punjabi).

Mendelsohn, Oliver and Vicziany, Marika. 2000. *The Untouchables: Subordination, Poverty and the State in Modern India*. New Delhi: Cambridge University Press.

Moon, Vasant. 2002. *Growing Up Untouchable in India: A Dalit Autobiography*. New Delhi: Vistaar Publications.

Nayar, Baldev Raj. 1966. *Minority Politics in the Punjab.* New Jersey: Princeton University Press.

Puri, Harish K., Paramjit S. Judge and Jagrup S. Sekhon. 1999. *Terrorism in Punjab: Understanding Grassroots' Reality.* New Delhi: Har-Anand.

Ronki Ram. 2004a. "Untouchability, Dalit Consciousness and the Ad Dharm Movement in Punjab", *Contributions to Indian Sociology*, 38 (3), pp. 323–49.

——. 2004b. "Untouchability in India with a Difference: Ad Dharam, Dalit Assertion, and Caste Conflicts in Punjab", *Asian Survey*, XLIV (6), pp. 895–912.

Reddy, T. Nagi. 1978. *India Mortgaged: A Marxist-Leninist Appraisal.* Anantapuram: Tarimela Nagi Reddy Memorial Trust.

Scott, James C. 1985. *Weapons of the Weak: Everyday Forms of Peasants' Resistance.* New haven: Yale University Press.

Sharma, Satish K. 2000. "Arya Samaj Movement in Punjab", in Harish K. Puri and Paramjit S. Judge (eds.), *Social and Political Movements: Readings on Punjab.* Jaipur: Rawa Publications, pp. 93–110.

Talib, B.D. 1986. "Agrarian Tensions and Peasant Movements in Punjab", in A.R. Desai (ed.), *Agrarian Struggles in India After Independence.* Delhi: Oxford University Press.

Index